VINTAGE

KATHMANDU CHRONICLE

K.V. Rajan is a former member of the Indian Foreign Service who retired as secretary, Ministry of External Affairs, Government of India. During nearly forty years of diplomatic service, he was entrusted with diverse responsibilities that covered political, economic, cultural, academic, media-related and multilateral work and developed intimate knowledge about most countries and major international institutions across the world. His diplomatic service spanned several countries around the globe as well as special assignments, including adviser to the external affairs minister; prime minister's special envoy to the African Union; co-chair, Iran–Pakistan–India Gas Pipeline project; special adviser to the foreign secretary of India; head of Coordination Division, Ministry of External Affairs; and head of Europe Division, Ministry of External Affairs.

As India's longest-serving ambassador to Nepal to date (1995–2000), and subsequently in various other capacities, Rajan has unmatched personal experience of Nepal and understanding of various aspects of India–Nepal relations.

Rajan is a frequent speaker in India and abroad on international issues. He has authored several articles on foreign policy issues for leading publications and is the editor of an anthology of essays by distinguished senior former ambassadors, *The Ambassador's Club: The Indian Diplomat at Large* (HarperCollins, 2012).

Atul K. Thakur is a policy professional, columnist and writer with specialization in the interface of economics and politics. His interest in writing and research is quite diverse and encompasses the areas of public policy and affairs, macroeconomic policies, international affairs and sustainability, with a special focus on South Asia. He is an alumnus, inter alia, of Banaras Hindu University and Pondicherry University and has worked across sectors, spanning public policy and affairs, management consultancy, think tanks, journalism, publishing and media. As an author/editor, *India Now and in Transition* (Niyogi Books, 2017) is his second and widely acclaimed book. In 2013, he edited *India since 1947: Looking Back at a Modern Nation* (Niyogi Books), a major non-fiction book on modern India. In 2021, he curated and edited (with Nepal's former finance minister Madhukar S.J.B. Rana) *An Alternative Development Paradigm for Nepal.*

Among others, Thakur has extensively written for the *Kathmandu Post, The Hindu,* Firstpost, News18, the *Indian Express,* the *Financial Express,* the *Economic Times,* DailyO, *Mail Today,* the *Pioneer, Tehelka, Outlook, Mainstream, Daily Star, Daily Times, Republica, Record Nepal, India Quarterly, Strategic Analysis, Observer Research Foundation* and *Gateway House.* As a public intellectual and industry insider, he plays an important role in shaping India–Nepal economic cooperation.

ADVANCE PRAISE FOR THE BOOK

'*Kathmandu Chronicle* promises to be a bestseller. Ambassador K.V. Rajan, the principal author, is one of India's ablest diplomats, writing from his vantage point as our ambassador to Nepal from 1995 to 2000. It provides invaluable insights into many of the critical developments in Nepal such as the IC 814 hijacking, the Palace massacre, the Maoist insurgency and its mainstreaming, and the highly complex interplay of internal and external political forces. In the process, it also draws pointed attention to Pakistan's machinations working through the drugs and arms mafia and a calibrated disinformation campaign to undermine India and damage its ties with Nepal'—Satish Chandra, former deputy national security adviser of India and former high commissioner to Pakistan

'The security of Nepal demands internal cohesion and a clear aim of contesting political parties to improve national comity and diplomacy besides strengthening military forces to face the growing national threat. Instead, there are continual serious internal strifes, chronic instability and serious questions about the quality of democracy, governance and political leadership. India plays a vital role in assisting Nepal with its various problems and has done so since India's independence. Yet, on some occasions, Indian diplomacy has created problems between the two nations. Nepal has gone through several upheavals. This book will be of abiding interest not only to stakeholders of diplomacy and international relations but also to the lay public who will find the "international great game" fascinating'—General (Retd) Vishwa Nath Sharma, PVSM, AVSM, ADC, former Indian Army chief

'Ambassador K.V. Rajan, one of India's most successful diplomats who had a stint in Nepal is, together with a key voice on Nepal, Atul K. Thakur, most suited to write *Kathmandu Chronicle*. Nepal and India, two close neighbours, have had one too many ups and down in their relationship. Citizens of Nepal are working all over India. The Indian economy is on a major growth path, which opens many opportunities for both. Will that happen even as India wishes its neighbours to prosper? Notwithstanding these ups and downs, *Kathmandu Chronicle* gives the reader an insight on a country that is far more than Everest and high mountains. Wishing the book every success'—Prem Prakash, chairman, Asian News International, and author

'Nepal is India's closest and most intimate neighbour. Eight million of its thirty million people live and work in India. Nepal lives and thrives on

their earnings. The Nepalese State is the guardian of a major part of the Himalayas, which not only guard us from the harsh extremes of Central Asia's climate but also provide us with the life-giving water on which our agriculture and the livelihoods of two-thirds of our people depend. Yet, from the first days of our Independence, we have tended to treat our neighbour as a vassal state. Rajan and Thakur's book examines this uneven relationship and the way it has evolved towards greater equality and mutual respect in the past three decades. It also suggests how India should fine-tune and deepen this relationship in the turbulent years that lie ahead'
—Prem Shankar Jha, veteran journalist and author

'India–Nepal relations are perennially dynamic without losing the substance of the compulsions of geopolitics. *Kathmandu Chronicle* is based on the objectivity and intimacy of competent authors (Rajan as India's former ambassador to Nepal and Atul as a scholar on Nepal), which through capturing their endeavours made in Nepal for developmental purposes will be of immense benefit for a comprehensive understanding of India–Nepal bilateral relations'—Lok Raj Baral, former ambassador of Nepal to India and author

'The book should be useful to those looking to understand Nepal–India ties in a larger context'—Akhilesh Upadhyay, former chief editor, *Kathmandu Post*, and senior fellow, Institute for Integrated Development Studies, Kathmandu

Kathmandu
CHRONICLE
RECLAIMING INDIA–NEPAL RELATIONS

K.V. RAJAN
ATUL K. THAKUR

VINTAGE

An imprint of Penguin Random House

VINTAGE

Vintage is an imprint of the Penguin Random House group of companies
whose addresses can be found at global.penguinrandomhouse.com

Published by Penguin Random House India Pvt. Ltd
4th Floor, Capital Tower 1, MG Road,
Gurugram 122 002, Haryana, India

First published in Vintage by Penguin Random House India 2024

10 9 8 7 6 5 4 3 2 1

The views and opinions expressed in this book are the authors' own and the
facts are as reported by them which have been verified to the extent possible,
and the publishers are not in any way liable for the same.

ISBN 9780143463375

Typeset in Adobe Garamond Pro by Manipal Technologies Limited, Manipal

www.penguin.co.in

To our spouses, Gita Rajan and Chitralekha Thakur, who have been steadfast 'better halves' in every sense of the word in the unending task of building ever-stronger India–Nepal ties

Contents

Introduction

K.V. RAJAN AND ATUL K. THAKUR

Nepal's history in recent decades has been marked by tumultuous events and transformations, and its relations with India by sharp fluctuations. Many books on both subjects have been written by scholars and foreign policy practitioners, Nepalese as well as Indian. Yet too many unanswered questions remain, about the hows and whys of the past, the depth and challenges of present trends, and prospects for the future, in an increasingly uncertain post-Covid-19 world.

Hence this book.

We felt that a joint work—by one intimately involved with Nepal for several years during his diplomatic service as well as after retirement, together with a long-time Nepal scholar—could help address this gap by combining first-hand field experience, assessments and interactions with independent and objective research. In that sense, this is not only a new book but a new approach to an important and complicated subject.

Nepal registered several significant turning points in a relatively short span of time. Among them is the achievement, at last, of a full-fledged multiparty democracy after two popular upheavals and with little help from across the southern border; a

peaceful negotiated end to ten years of violent Maoist insurgency
and the mainstreaming of Maoists into the democratic polity;
adoption of a Constitution (albeit somewhat imperfect and hastily
rushed through); a peaceful and in the end dignified exit of the
institution of monarchy; and the assertion of a new identity as a
secular federal democratic republic.

High expectations were aroused of a 'new Nepal'.

Alas, these have not been fulfilled.

Nepal now seems stuck in an unending transition. Thoughtful
Nepalese commentators who were at the forefront of those
demanding changes are the first to voice their acute sense of
disappointment at how things are turning out—the poor quality of
democracy, rampant corruption and malgovernance, institutional
failures, economic mismanagement and chronic instability
punctuated with revolving-door governments and little pretence
of ideological consistency or adherence to political commitments.

Nepal's internal institutional shortcomings are a cruel reality.
Also cruel is the realization that for democracy to be meaningful,
it is not enough to have regular and reasonably credible elections
or even a free press and the right to dissent, which undoubtedly
exist to a laudable degree in Nepal today. Unless there are
independent institutions which cannot be remote-controlled by
the government of the day, there is a real danger of democracy
becoming a caricature of itself.

Nevertheless, there is hope within and among friends outside
Nepal, especially India, that it is on the right track, and that
with patience, perseverance, experience and support, the kind of
leadership and direction it desperately needs will emerge, and Nepal
will experience a speedier and smoother transition to a minimum
desirable level of governance and inclusive development.

There is also undoubtedly space for India and Nepal to jointly
create a sustainable positive trajectory for bilateral ties which

would do more justice to their exceptionally rich and unique civilizational links and economic complementarities and make a more meaningful contribution to a stronger subregion.

In this book, we have attempted to analyse how the situation unfolded in the way it did, and as to whether the principal actors (including India) might help shape a better future in keeping with the expectations and needs of the people on both sides of the border.

Both countries owe it to themselves to revisit the past and introspect, even if it means asking uncomfortable questions. It is more necessary than ever before to draw lessons from the past, for it has repeated itself far too often. We do need to reimagine, perhaps to 'repurpose', an age-old relationship, such that it can fulfil its real potential in a geopolitical and geo-economic landscape so completely different from the one it inherited when the British left India in 1947, and yet it is the latter which has somehow continued to shape mindsets and policies on both sides for so many decades.

One understanding that hopefully will flow out of this study is that *realpolitik*, bargaining-style diplomacy of the transactional kind and knee-jerk responses, need not and cannot be the basis for relations between two countries such as India and Nepal, with such unique and deep historical, familial, religious, cultural, geographical and economic ties.

Irritants, potential or real (including long-standing ones like the 1950 India–Nepal Treaty of Peace and Friendship) and differences (for example on the border, which appear to be devoid of chances of a political or diplomatic solution given the resolution passed by Nepal's Parliament) can and should be sought to be sorted out in the way hiccups within a family are tackled, keeping the basis as well as continuing need of unshakeable bonds always in mind.

Sporadic attempts through normal diplomatic exchanges on such issues have been going on for some time, with no signs of progress. A Track 2 initiative (High-Level Expert Group) blessed by both prime ministers was set up a few years ago and managed to prepare a confidential joint report with recommendations, but the report has yet to be presented because of the controversy that would result from non-implementation.

If such issues are discussed keeping the larger picture of an unbreakable age-old relationship and a vision of long-term interests always in mind, they will hopefully be subsumed by the latter, just as the major irritant of the Tanakpur Barrage constructed by India was subsumed by the larger vision of the Mahakali Treaty of 1996 which, unlike the former, was negotiated in a spirit of equality and respect for mutual interests, needs and sensitivities.

In that sense, Defence Minister Rajnath Singh's relaxed and friendly response to Nepal's strong objections to his inauguration of roads in border areas now claimed by Nepal, recommends itself over exchanging maps dating back to East India Company or British India days (*Our History, Their History, Whose History?*, to borrow the title of Romila Thapar's book), or issuing stern official statements and presenting counterclaims, which would be a standard official reaction.

Similarly, ambassador of Nepal to India Shankar P. Sharma's attendance of a New Delhi function to celebrate the consecration of the Ram Mandir at Ayodhya, and his reflection that Nepal's parallel claim to Ram's birthplace being in Nepal (former PM K.P. Sharma Oli had, in fact, earlier protested that India was 'manipulating history' to deny Nepal its rightful claims) should be taken simply as a confirmation of the rich shared cultural links between the two countries, commends itself over the strident condemnation of Oli's claim in India.

We realize that some of our assessments and assertions will be contested. We are confident, however, that on many issues, some facts which are not yet in the public domain will get known in due course, and bear these out.

One area of special sensitivity has been Nepalese resentment of alleged Indian involvement in its internal affairs. Indian writers tend to lay a major portion of the blame on sections of the Nepalese elite who indulge in ultra-nationalism for short-term gains. We have tried to examine the facts as objectively as possible. It has been wisely said that 'the essence of strategy is choosing what not to do'. This seems to have relevance for some actions of Nepal as well as of India, in the seven-and-a-half decades since India's independence.

Indian diplomats will argue that India's actions were well-intentioned and often in response to a felt need in Nepal. The fact, however, is that in hindsight, they might have best been avoided, for they have left a lasting impact on its perceptions of India.

We suggest this not as a *mea culpa* acknowledgement but rather in the spirit of External Affairs Minister S. Jaishankar's reflections in December 2023 (made in a wider context) of the importance of looking back and introspecting in order to keep correcting ourselves to set the foreign policy right: 'It is very important for us, after 75 years of Independence, to introspect about . . . because often, we tend to think that the decisions which were taken, were the only decisions that could have been taken, which may not be entirely true.'

As for Nepal, its political leaders will hopefully realize sooner rather than later that it is entirely in that country's long-term interests to consolidate its position as South Asia's dependable partner in India's quest to sit at the global high table.

At the time of writing, while India is led by a strong prime minister in Narendra Modi, Nepal is headed by the shrewd Maoist leader Prachanda leading a coalition, his Maoist party being the third largest, in a climate of political instability. There is a welcome trend towards pragmatic national self-interest in bilateral ties with India. Major agreements have been reached on bilateral and subregional energy cooperation, with welcome new emphasis on delivery and follow-up. One must keep one's fingers crossed that this trend continues. However, unfortunately, there seems to be a certain fatigue in expending political energy on self-destructive anti-India posturing, which cannot but pose new challenges to the continuance of a positive trajectory in bilateral ties. There are already ominous signs that the appetite for power at any cost may again lead to opportunistic political rearrangements with new uncertainties.

The relevance of the China factor in India's foreign policy has only increased in recent years. Tibet is not the only reason for Chinese activism in Nepal. But Nepal's traditional penchant for playing the China card to maximize benefits to itself from India has had to adjust to new factors. At the geopolitical level, the major Western powers are now much more alert to Chinese attempts to expand its influence and much more proactive in countering them as evidenced through mechanisms like the Quad and Indo-Pacific mechanisms. The Indian government itself under PM Modi is much more confident about dealing with China and much less vulnerable to blackmail tactics.

The Chinese have exposed themselves to Nepal's political elite through fairly clumsy attempts at intervention in internal politics which have backfired on them. Even on the economic side, they are not finding it as easy as before to impress Nepalese businessmen, bureaucrats or politicians. Significantly, even seven years after the Belt and Road Initiative (BRI) was launched and Nepal subscribed to it, not a single project has been negotiated by successive Kathmandu governments, each of which has found reasons to postpone decisions on Chinese terms.

Yet there is no reason for complacency. Neutralizing India's natural influence in its neighbourhood is clearly a high Chinese priority, and its actions in every neighbouring nation (most recently the Maldives) are confirmation, if confirmation was needed, that the *String of Pearls* concern is not in the realm of fanciful imagery but a strategic challenge to the India growth story.

Watching the frequent fluctuations in the graphs of India's relations with its neighbours, South Asian scholars often pose the question: 'Is India losing South Asia?' On the other hand, Indian diplomats with deep knowledge of India's repeated efforts to improve relations with its neighbours usually pose the question the other way around: 'Is South Asia losing India?' China's increasing footprint in the region, and the penchant for India's neighbours to frequently encourage it, is a subject of continuing debate. There is only one way to address this reality, and that is for India to get its act together, adjust its diplomatic functioning style, policies and priorities, create an ambiance of mutual trust, expand the thrust of Atmanirbharta to include at least selected close neighbours including Nepal, and give them their rightful place as co-passengers on the journey towards speedy inclusive development. Neighbourhood First needs to be perceived by our neighbours as a living day-to-day Indian foreign policy priority and not just a slogan.

But if there is one country with which India needs to make a fresh beginning, it is Nepal.

It is in that hope that this book has been written.

SECTION I

Diplomatic Gleanings:
A First-Person Account

K.V. RAJAN

Sunset Years of a Monarchy and Lessons for a Better Future

This is an account of personal experiences and interactions of an Indian diplomat in Nepal during an eventful period when the country appeared to be making notable progress as a constitutional monarchy and multiparty democracy, only to be overtaken by major upheavals including the Maoist insurgency launched in February 1996; the hijacking of IC 814 (Indian Airlines Flight 814: Kathmandu–New Delhi) shortly after take-off from Kathmandu on 24 December 1999; the Palace Massacre of 1 June 2001, which wiped out King Birendra and his entire family; the 1 February 2005 coup by King Gyanendra against democracy; the mainstreaming of the Maoists; the promulgation of a controversial constitution; and the apparently unending transition to a Federal Democratic Republic; with flashbacks and futuristic reflections on the fascinating story of India–Nepal relations. It is a story of repetitive patterns, avoidable misunderstandings, missed opportunities, mixed signals, poignant realities, deep mistrust and unlimited hope. A story

3

that deserves deep analysis and introspection as its lessons are so
relevant if there is to be a better future.

The Birendra Years: 1995–2000

I arrived in Kathmandu from London on a lovely sunny day in
early 1995, after barely a few hours of briefing in Delhi.
I was new to Nepal but knew enough about the country and its
deep but complicated relations with India to be excited about the
challenges ahead and also the unmatched opportunities it offered.
I also knew that Kathmandu was the assignment that could bring
the utmost professional satisfaction to Indian diplomats, but more
often than not, proved to be the burial ground of their reputations.

Four visionaries of great experience were in Delhi for
initial guidance and support, and within a matter of days, I felt
confidence and inspiration surging within me. They were Prime
Minister P.V. Narasimha Rao, External Affairs Minister Pranab
Mukherjee, Foreign Secretary Salman Haidar and Joint Secretary
Shivshankar Menon, who would go on to become foreign secretary
and national security adviser to the prime minister.

The last decade of the twentieth century had begun for
Nepal on a note of great hope, bordering on euphoria. The pro-
democracy agitation spearheaded by the Nepali Congress (NC)
and the communists (Communist Party of Nepal-Unified Marxist-
Leninist: CPN [UML]) had brought the monarchy to its knees
and succeeded, by 1990, in ushering in a constitutional monarchy
with full multiparty democracy. India's role in supporting the
democratic forces, including indirectly through a border blockade
(ostensibly precipitated by a trade and transit dispute) had earned
it considerable cross-party and public goodwill, even if it created
tensions with the monarchy. The first general election in 1990
resulted in a victory for Girija Prasad Koirala's NC. By 1994,

however, India's perceived proximity to Koirala and internal dissent within the Congress brought the Koirala government down in an atmosphere of nationalistic anti-Indianism. The new election led to the formation, in December 1994, of a minority government with veteran communist leader Manmohan Adhikari as prime minister. India's worries were on several counts. There was a clear prospect of political instability because of the hung parliament thrown up by the elections. It was necessary to swiftly normalize relations with the CPN (UML), a party which has manifested a certain hostility towards India in recent years. The controversy generated by the UML demand for abrogating the 1950 Treaty of Peace and Friendship needed to be defused.

In my very first call to Narasimha Rao, a man of few words, he gave me a two-minute briefing:

— *The King seems to have learnt his lessons. So have we. Let him know we take him seriously; we are not taking him for granted.*
— *Make all political leaders feel that they are equally important for us, whether they are supposed to be pro- or anti-India. I will not give an inch more to the pro-India prime minister, and not an inch less to the anti-India one.*

Good luck. You will need it.

The directive from him was clear: a new approach would be necessary to manage future relations with Nepal. King Birendra, who had come to power in 1976 and had never been considered a friend of India, was now a constitutional monarch but still wielded considerable influence among political parties as well as at the popular level. He also had full control of the Nepali Army. Rao was emphatic that improving relations with the King would have to be a major priority while attempting to forge good relations with all political parties, whether considered pro- or anti-India. A 'twin pillar' approach of building trust with the Palace, with which there was a huge legacy of tension and misunderstandings from the past, and impartial but close ties with the whole political spectrum, should henceforth be pursued. A stabilizing force in an evolving democracy could not be underestimated.

Rao clearly felt that the King could make a major contribution to a more mature relationship with India just as the King of Bhutan had. He was not very optimistic about our being able to achieve these goals because of the prospect of acute instability and misgovernance in the months ahead but wished me luck anyway.

Pranab Mukherjee had some golden words of advice. 'Your problem is not so much Nepal,' he said, 'but the pettiness of the Indian bureaucratic mindset.' He had been commerce minister earlier and had tried to push through a Trade Treaty that would offer duty-free access to the vast Indian market for all goods manufactured in Nepal irrespective of domestic content. 'It will have negligible adverse implications for the Indian economy but make a huge difference to Nepal and to India–Nepal relations.' But his bureaucrats in that ministry had ensured that the idea never got off the ground. 'Find a way of getting this done,' he advised, 'and you will see the difference.'

Salman Haidar for his part felt that the key lay in exploiting Nepal's huge untapped hydropower potential. 'It will transform the relationship into one of equality and interdependence,' he said.

Shivshankar had a simple formula. 'This is the best opportunity to restructure our relationship with Nepal,' he said, outlining a few possibilities in confidence.

I hit the ground running soon after landing in Kathmandu.

My efforts to build bridges with all political leaders met with immediate positive responses—including from Adhikari and his Communist Party colleagues. But attempts to communicate with the Palace got off to an inauspicious beginning. Letters to the King were returned unopened by the Palace Secretariat. Rather, as my alert secretary discovered, someone had opened the envelope, seen the contents, carefully resealed the covers and returned them to the embassy.

My embassy colleagues suggested that this could be because I had commenced each letter with 'Your Majesty' instead of 'May It Please Your Majesty' as prescribed by local Foreign Office protocol.

I thought this requirement to be distinctly anachronistic and unnecessary, all the more so as King Birendra was now a constitutional monarch, and Nepal supposedly a parliamentary democracy. But keeping PM Rao's directive in mind, I decided to persevere. I sent fresh letters with that grand ceremonial beginning, 'May It Please Your Majesty,' requesting an early appointment.

Still no luck.

No indication either of when I would be able to present credentials. And India was supposed to have a 'special relationship' with Nepal!

I complained to Foreign Secretary Salman Haidar.

The mystery began to clear up. Pranab Mukherjee had just returned from London where he and King Birendra were representing their respective countries, at a ceremonial international gathering in honour of Queen Elizabeth II. There he had made a courtesy call on King Birendra.

Mukherjee was about to leave when the King asked him an astonishing question: 'Excellency, you have sent a new ambassador to Nepal. Can I trust him?' The foreign minister inquired as to why His Majesty should have any doubts. 'Ambassador Rajan has been personally selected for this important assignment by the prime minister of India,' he told the King. 'He enjoys our utmost confidence.'

It appeared that in the gap between my predecessor departing from Kathmandu and my arrival there, a message had been conveyed to the King by a colleague in the embassy (not a career diplomat) through one of the Palace staff that the new ambassador need not be the channel of communication after he arrived, as there were many sensitive matters the King would want to convey in the coming months, and Government of India might have other channels in mind!

Of course, Mukherjee firmly disabused the King of such a notion.

Shortly after the King's return to Kathmandu from London, I was given a date to present my credentials and another immediately thereafter, for a private audience.

A few days later, I was in Delhi on consultations, and met the foreign minister, who confirmed the bizarre conversation that had taken place with the King and said he had asked the foreign secretary to look into it. Then he looked up at the ceiling with a quizzical smile and said, 'Something is worrying the King. Find out what it is. If we can help, we should.'

I found King Birendra to be affable, mild-mannered, soft-spoken and relaxed. He regretted that there had been so many misunderstandings with India, especially with the Nehru–Gandhi family, for whom he and his family had so much respect. He was confident that with Narasimha Rao (whose intellect and moderation he held in high esteem and with whom he had a good personal rapport), a new era of friendship and cooperation was possible. He was not unduly worried that communists had become such a strong political force—Manmohan Adhikari was a responsible leader who respected institutions, not a radical who was impatient for ideological change at any cost. However, democracy would take time to settle, and there might be turbulent times ahead—India's role would be crucial. We agreed to remain in touch through designated intermediaries or directly, as the occasion demanded.

An immediate outcome of the first audience was King Birendra's decision to give a public signal of normal relations with India by agreeing to spend an evening at India House with his immediate family—after decades of a freeze on such social-level contacts. The royal family, along with the entire political and civil society elite of Nepal, attended a concert on the lawns of India House by Ustad Amjad Ali Khan and his sons Amaan and Ayaan. It was quite an ambience: the setting sun, the tall pine trees, the birds singing as if on cue with the soul-stirring strumming of the sarod. Over dinner, the royal family really opened up. The conversation was a mix of banter and serious politics, anecdotes and personal reflections. It was a very relaxed evening that went on until the early hours of the morning, full of jokes, laughter and conviviality, a deliberate and substantive icebreaker exercise.

There were a few serious moments, for example when the King said, 'Your Excellency, what we discuss has to be confidential. I leave it to you to decide what you want to share with your prime minister. But please, no telegrams or messages to bureaucrats, here or in Delhi. I don't trust files!'

King Birendra said more than once that Nepal's democracy was here to stay; he would not turn the clock back. However, he was mildly sceptical about the capacity of political parties to deliver on the people's expectations. At another point in the evening, he leant over to say in a low voice almost as though he did not wish to be heard, even by Queen Aishwarya or Crown Prince Dipendra: 'Excellency, I can help you achieve India's objectives, but they must be in Nepal's long term interests.'

The King also suggested that very often it is the bureaucrats and diplomats on both sides who create complications, leaving their leaders in the dark. With a guffaw, he said that there was an Indian embassy official right now who was going around telling political leaders that he had the power to make or unmake prime ministers! (I kept quiet, almost certain that it must be the same official who had tried to ensure that there should be a misunderstanding between me and the Palace prior to my arrival).

We did notice that in the otherwise friendly and relaxed atmosphere, the Queen was keeping a watchful eye on Dipendra, who for his part seemed less relaxed in her immediate presence. When Dipendra and his brother excused themselves for a longish time, Queen Aishwarya grew restless. King Birendra's comment that they were only trying to smoke a cigarette on the sly was hardly a tactful reassurance from her point of view. The King said with a smile, 'My wife worries too much about Dipendra. He is a very peaceful young man. He wouldn't hurt a fly.'

Months later, when Dipendra and I were applauding Kapil Dev's magnificent sixers in an exhibition cricket match and I asked him whether he himself played cricket, Dipendra said that the only time he had done so at Eton, he had given his teacher a bloody nose with a particularly hard sweep to mid-on which had hit the poor master in his face. He had decided there and then never to touch a cricket bat again. The young man who would one day allegedly gun down his parents, brother and sister in a fit of inebriated rage, explained matter-of-factly: 'Excellency, I can't stand the sight of blood.'

There was only one awkward moment that evening. We were settling down in the drawing room after the concert, along with the royal family, leaving it to my deputy and embassy staff to see off the other guests who had been invited for the concert, including Prince Gyanendra and his wife, the prime minister and other dignitaries. A worried colleague suddenly appeared. Prince Gyanendra and his wife were waiting outside, he said, wanting to formally bid me farewell. I apologized to the King and went out. Prince Gyanendra had a peculiar expression on his face, as though he had been expecting to be invited to my dinner as well. He got the message that he was not when I said goodbye and thanked him for having attended the concert.

In the early hours of the following morning, after a fair amount of liquid refreshments, the royal family got up to leave. The King was in the driver's seat of the Palace car with the Queen beside him, while Prince Dipendra and the rest of the family went in the second car. His driver and bodyguard were in the back seat.

As he drove off, the King said, 'Excellency, democracy is fine, I am all for democracy, but political parties come and go. I may be gone soon, but while I am here, I have to think about the country's future for the next hundred years.'

As my wife and I switched off the lights, we could not help congratulating ourselves for having achieved a breakthrough for India by ending the cold spell of unfriendliness between India House and the Palace.

Some weeks later, Prabhakar Rana, a prominent business leader; chairman of the Soaltee Hotel, which was partly owned by Prince Gyanendra; and also a close friend of ours, rang to invite me for a dinner with the prince as he said the latter wanted to talk to me alone.

The prince and I met at the hotel. After some pleasantries, he asked me bluntly, 'Excellency, why did you decide to leave me out of the dinner?' I replied that it had not been my decision. I had inquired with the King's staff as to who else from the Palace should be invited and was advised that the King would prefer the two families to be alone together. Gyanendra looked at me in disbelief and said, 'I don't understand this. You know, people say all kinds of things, but he is my brother after all.' He blamed the Palace staff for not checking with the King and deciding on their own and muttered something about taking action against them. After that, it was back to a pleasant and casual conversation. Gyanendra, however, repeatedly said that he was not anti-India as he was made out to be.

Once the ice had been broken, King Birendra and, indeed, the entire family warmed up to us. Even Gyanendra softened his demeanour and began to have more frank exchanges in private conversations. He was seriously interested in the environment, classical music, and issues of development and governance. He was also very dismissive about prospects of democracy taking root in Nepal, and clear about the need for a stronger monarchy to ensure Nepal's stability and sustainable good relations with India.

Queen Aishwarya dropped her traditional reserve. She came across as a relaxed, informal person interested in charitable activities and the arts. She insisted on accepting an invitation from my wife to inaugurate an Indian women's charity event even when it meant walking in a heavy rainstorm that suddenly burst over Kathmandu.

I had the opportunity in the following months to accompany the King on a series of visits to several of India's holy sites, at his request, the Government of India being happy to invite him as a State guest. The hours spent in airport transit lounges, long road trips when air travel was not possible due to weather or logistical reasons, with few official meetings and engagements, enabled me to get to know the King and build an informal rapport which would have been impossible in protocol-bound Kathmandu. I found him to be a very different person as compared to his public persona.

Political dispensations changed in both capitals, but leaders on both sides seemed eager to ensure stable bilateral relations and there was an unprecedented regularity of high-level visits and important milestones achieved on various aspects of cooperation, from Bollywood to trade, security and hydropower.

The Mahakali Treaty providing for major hydropower stations on the two banks of the Mahakali River at Pancheshwar, on the India–Nepal border, was negotiated with a CPN (UML) government, signed by a successor coalition government headed by Sher Bahadur Deuba of the NC, ratified by cross-party consensus by over two-thirds majority of the Nepalese Parliament, and instruments of ratification were exchanged between Inder Kumar Gujral and yet another prime minister, Lokendra Bahadur Chand, who had been an opponent of the Treaty.

This was a historic milestone since there was such a backlog of resentment in Nepal about previous experiments in water resources cooperation, dating back to the Koshi Barrage during King Tribhuvan's time in the 1950s (which was considered to be solely for India's benefit), to the Tanakpur Barrage built on Indian soil but utilizing a small bit of Nepal territory without legal authorization, which became such an anti-India issue that it led to the fall of the Koirala government in 1994.

The longer-term question was whether any cooperation on water would ever be possible with Nepal. Tanakpur seemed to be a pointer that such treaties would inevitably be hopelessly politicized and were therefore doomed to fail. Moreover, the constitution required that important treaties involving the use of Nepal's natural resources must be ratified by more than a two-thirds majority in Parliament—a remote prospect in this age of coalition politics and minority governments. In short, the bleak reality seemed to be that India and democratic Nepal might never be able to have a major treaty on water, even if the people of both countries desperately needed it for their future well-being.

Negotiations on the Mahakali Treaty were first commenced
with the Adhikari government, which fell in a matter of months
and resumed with the successor coalition government headed
by Sher Bahadur Deuba. This was one of those rare transitions
when there was a change of government without India being
dragged into Nepal's domestic politics. The new government
was enthusiastic about taking India–Nepal relations to new
heights, and the Opposition was not inclined to object. With
a talented and competent Minister for Water Resources like
Pashupathi Rana, Foreign Minister Prakash Chandra Lohani,
and Deuba himself willing to be proactive, the Mahakali
Treaty was revived in a novel way. Even as government-level
negotiations proceeded, Rana and Lohani, with firm support
from Deuba, tried to get the backing of other parties for a
treaty based on the original draft discussed between India
and the Adhikari government. There were countless informal
interactions between the different players, including Salman
Haidar and myself. These included walks in the woods with
Rana, unpublicized visits to Delhi, and departures from
protocol as meetings took place with increasing frequency at
private homes, hotels, India House, on Kathmandu–Delhi
flights, in transit lounges, even the Pashupatinath Temple.

Soon there was a critical mass of Nepal's younger political
leaders cutting across party lines who had taken the trouble to
understand the basic elements of the Mahakali Treaty and realized
that its provisions regarding power and water were very much in
Nepal's interest. Nepal's political elders including Adhikari and
Koirala were not quite in the loop, nor were they very interested
in understanding the complexities of an agreement on water of
this magnitude; they mildly grumbled at the speed at which they
were being asked to approve a decision of this importance but
were not actively opposed to it.

The result of all this was that when Pranab Mukerjee arrived in Kathmandu on Republic Day, 1996, there was not only a cross-party consensus on the main elements to guide the Nepal government in its final negotiations on the treaty, there was also a sense of Nepali ownership about the treaty itself, as something which was in Nepal's interest—a big difference from the past, when India used to propose treaties to harness Nepal's water resources mainly to satisfy India's irrigation and power requirements. After several hiccups and moments of high drama, the treaty was finalized and signed in the presence of Deuba.

The next morning, Nepal's newspaper headlines announced: 'Equality at last!' The accompanying euphoria and self-congratulatory mood in Nepal were particularly satisfying to those of us from the Indian side who had laboured hard to prove a point: that transparency, consensus, equal partnership and prime consideration to Nepal's needs were foundations on which water agreements with a democratic Nepal were possible.

An Agreement on Trade along the lines Mukherjee had desired, basically permitting duty-free access to the Indian market for all goods manufactured in Nepal, without any restrictions as to minimum local labour or material content, was reached by first negotiating an understanding between leading Commerce Chambers of both governments before seeking an official stamp.

Interestingly, during the Deuba visit to India in February 1996, Deuba formally suggested this when Minister of Commerce P. Chidambaram called on him at the Rashtrapati Bhavan; Chidambaram conveyed his regret at India's inability to accept this demand, since 'Indian industry would never agree, as it would hurt their interests.' That evening, however, at the signature ceremony in the presence of the two PMs, the two business delegations presented their joint report containing precisely the same recommendation. With his characteristic grace,

Chidambaram walked up to Deuba and said that he would like to withdraw his objections, conveyed the same morning, to the Nepali proposal. 'Who am I to turn your request down, Mr Prime Minister, when my own industry have said in my prime minister's presence that they want Nepal to get these facilities!' he said.

When Inder Kumar Gujral became PM the following year, a transit route through the sensitive Phulbari Route on the Chicken's Neck corridor in the North-East was achieved thanks to Gujral's personal intervention and innovative arrangements for ensuring security. Equality and consensus formed the basis of every negotiation. There was unprecedented goodwill towards India throughout Nepal.

Of course, irritants like the 1950 Treaty, considered unequal in the eyes of most Nepalese, were raised as usual. Gujral did not dampen Nepalese hopes that India would go the extra mile in meeting their expectations, in line with his famous doctrine. In fact, at the joint press conference addressed by the two prime ministers, Gujral and Lokendra Bahadur Chand, the former went to the extent of saying that he was willing to sign a 'blank cheque' for Nepal. The result was a visit to Delhi within a few weeks, by Foreign Minister Kamal Thapa, who took with him a draft of a new Friendship Treaty based on consultations with Nepalese experts.

The 1950 Treaty had been signed between the Indian ambassador and a discredited Rana prime minister who was on his last legs. It was basically an updated version of an earlier treaty between British India and Nepal, which gave Nepal significant economic concessions in exchange for a virtual Indian veto in Nepal's dealings with third countries on defence and security matters. Nepal had always been sensitive to the suggestion implicit in the treaty that its sovereignty was negotiable; what it was looking for, but was usually hesitant to suggest, was a new or amended treaty which would ensure respect for India's legitimate security concerns, continue to offer the economic opportunities available to Nepalese nationals in India, but remove constraints on Nepal's freedom to have defence arrangements with other countries as long as they did not have security implications for India. India had traditionally considered any such suggestion emanating from Nepal as an unfriendly act.

Nepal's foreign minister Kamal Thapa's India visit was an eye-opener for those who might have assumed that Gujral was soft with neighbours on all issues. In the discussions with Thapa, he was emphatically negative to any suggestion for amending the treaty. Thapa returned empty-handed, and probably not a little shocked at Gujral's robust defence of the treaty. However, the Nepalese did not allow this diplomatic misadventure to sour the positive atmosphere of bilateral ties, underlining the importance of style over substance. I recall sharing with Foreign Secretary K. Raghunath my foreboding that all hell would break loose on my return to Kathmandu since in my view, 'the Gujral Doctrine had just been strangled with the entrails of the 1950 Treaty during the visit of Kamal Thapa to India.' Well, I was wrong.

The basic approach that paid off was to involve and consult the Opposition to the maximum extent possible on every major issue being discussed with the government, usually with the knowledge and support of the latter, and let all parties bask in the credit of an agreement reached or issue resolved.

Another conscious approach was consideration and courtesy towards political leaders of all parties whether in government or Opposition, even when we were not expecting cooperation on any specific issue. An early example of this was when Narasimha Rao departed from protocol to send a message to Adhikari after the latter had to step down as prime minister and was hospitalized. I went to Bir Hospital to deliver the letter. Adhikari was in bed in a dark and depressing ward, quite alone, without political aides or family, apart from being without political power. But his sense of humour was intact. He wanted to thank Rao for his gesture and also to promise him that his party would work constructively on strengthening bilateral ties. 'I am going down,' he wheezed, 'but that does not mean that India–Nepal relations have to go down with me!'

As it happened, a few days later, in an exciting photo finish, the UML politburo approved the treaty by a single vote (Adhikari was brought in on a stretcher from the hospital on his insistence to ensure this).

My consultations with Nepalese political elders—Ganesh Man Singh, Manmohan Adhikari, Girija Prasad Koirala, Krishna Prasad Bhattarai and Surya Bahadur Thapa—yielded new insights into Nepal's turbulent politics as well as its relations with India. They spoke with a historical perspective stretching back over several decades, and despite their political and individual differences, it was clear that they converged on the importance of strong India–Nepal relations for Nepal's well-being.

Ganesh Man Singh, possibly Nepal's tallest political figure, revered for his courageous leadership against the monarchy during the pro-democracy agitation, and his refusal to accept the prime ministership in the first democratic government that came into being in 1990, felt that Nepal's democracy could be consolidated provided India resisted the temptation to run Nepal's internal affairs. This was a fairly explicit reference to the damage done by (in the Nepalese perception) the blatantly intrusive role of some Indian ambassadors since C.P.N Singh; he also referred to India's propensity to play favourites with Nepalese political actors (an implicit reference to the perceived partisanship shown to Koirala in recent years). He was by now in very poor health, speaking in barely audible whispers. I could make out that despite his reservations about some aberrations in India's past policies, he wanted India to be actively engaged in strengthening and protecting Nepal's fragile democracy.

Manmohan Adhikari, the firebrand CPN (UML) prime minister, was surprisingly relaxed and positive about India even in my first meeting with him. He praised my predecessor as a good man who had been unfairly criticized (by him!) for favouring Koirala, suggested that India should not read too much into his anti-India election rhetoric; and emphasized his party's commitment to building stronger ties with India even if it would not agree to their being described as 'special relations'. He specifically discounted worries about his opposition to the 1950 Treaty of Peace and Friendship: 'Excellency, friendship treaties are not to be abrogated.' He wanted the treaty to be 'reviewed', and suggested that in the end, both countries would be happy with a 'few full stops and commas being changed'. This, of course, was music to Delhi's ears.

Contrary to my expectation, Communist Party of India (Marxist) (CPI[M] or CPM) leaders in India did not seem very sure as to how the rise of the CPN (UML) should be viewed in India. West Bengal Chief Minister Jyoti Basu, for example, felt that while we could strike a good understanding with a veteran like Adhikari, we should make our own assessments regarding the CPN (UML) as a whole, especially about the extent of influence of 'Naxalite-type elements'. When Adhikari visited Kolkata during his first official visit, the media commented on the lukewarm nature of the welcome he was accorded by the state government despite their shared ideological affiliation.

Girija Prasad Koirala, deeply sincere about ties with India, was not a man for details. He was a democrat to the core as far as Nepal was concerned but had his own ideas about running his party. As a supreme tactician, he was dismissive of Nepalese politicians who made anti-India noises because of domestic compulsions.

The anti-Indian rhetoric in Nepal was at that time limited to the Kathmandu Valley urban elite and India did not need to worry about its security implications. He mentioned a sampling of Nepalese attitudes towards India that he had personally conducted when India–Nepal relations were going through a particularly difficult phase in 1989: an absolute majority of opinion found a serious confrontation with India to be 'unacceptable'; as for the 1,30,000 ex-servicemen who had been in the Indian Army and were now islands of prosperity in rural Nepal, they would be prepared to actively resist any sinister attempt to undermine the relationship at the cost of the interests of the Nepalese people. He was perhaps the only leader who had the style and stature to scold his peers, chide them in public, bully them, or indeed engage in brinkmanship, if his political instinct led him to do so. The day would come when these qualities would enable him to carve out his place in the history books—for ending the Maoist insurgency and bringing them into the mainstream of Nepal's multiparty democracy.

Nepal's prime minister Krishna Prasad Bhattarai struck me as being a philosopher-politician with a deceptively frivolous attitude to life and a wicked sense of humour. He felt that decades of brainwashing by Rana and royal regimes, with the active guidance of the British, had created an aggressively nationalistic Nepalese mindset vis-à-vis India which would take decades more of patient and transparent diplomacy and people-to-people contact to change. He once narrated a hilarious story of a winter day he had spent on the lawns of India House during the Rana period, when the Indian ambassador and he had an animated discussion on the political situation, while finishing off an entire bottle of brandy.

The ambassador's spouse, irritated that several messages sent through the support staff had not succeeded in ending their session, finally appeared in person and lambasted His Excellency in Marathi, assuming that Bhattarai would not understand. The ambassador (again in Marathi) pleaded not guilty, blaming Bhattarai for the unending conversation as well as the high beverage consumption. When Bhattarai, after passively witnessing the husband–wife exchanges, innocently inquired of the ambassador as to what had upset Madam so much, the ambassador dismissed it as a problem she was having with the cook. Finally, Bhattarai got up and took leave of his host in impeccable Marathi, before riding off on his bicycle, chuckling at the look of stunned embarrassment on the faces of the ambassadorial couple as they saw him off!

Surya Bahadur Thapa was possibly the most articulate of leaders when it came to discussions on strategic approaches to various issues of concern, domestic or bilateral. One could not but respect his intellect and capacity for lucid analysis. Alas, he belonged to the wrong party, and his excellent administrative skills could not assist the country despite his frequent prime ministerial stints in subsequent years.

Key leaders like Girija Prasad Koirala, Surya Bahadur Thapa and the Madheshi leader of the Nepal Sadbhavana Party, Gajendra Narayan Singh, seemed to feel that the real danger to Nepal came not from the Palace but from the strengthening of radical forces on the Left. Their hope was that India would not take the minority CPN (UML) government too seriously since it was likely to be short-lived, apart from not being either 'democratic' or 'genuinely friendly' towards India.

On 15 August 1997, I hosted a massive Independence Day anniversary reception at India House. The royal family, entire cabinet, former prime ministers and Nepal's civil society elites turned up. The mood was one of genuine celebration of India–Nepal friendship. On the spur of the moment, I thought of requesting all the former and present Nepalese leaders, along with the King and Queen, my wife and myself, to assemble for a

photo opportunity which would also be an assertion of bilateral
relations built on Indian support for constitutional monarchy
and multiparty democracy. King Birendra readily agreed but
whispered that I should sound the Queen out separately, since
her sari would get wet in the drizzle that had commenced. But
the Queen enthusiastically agreed, too, as did all the other leaders.
The photograph taken outside the royal tent on India House
lawns was front-page stuff in every newspaper and the subject of
much positive public comment the following day.

India's twin-pillar strategy of supporting multiparty
democracy and constitutional monarchy was working well—or
so it seemed!

* * *

Political instability, erosion of governance and democratic
indiscretions now began to take centre stage. A small, extreme-
Left group, calling themselves Maoists, issued a forty-point
declaration calling for the end of royal privileges, abrogation of
the 1950 Treaty with India and the Mahakali Treaty. They also
demanded wide-ranging social, economic and political reforms,
and an inclusive power structure, with a deadline of a few weeks for
implementation, failing which an insurgency would be launched.

As prime ministers and governments changed with alarming
frequency and parties joined hands and broke alliances with
the sole aim of being in power, the Maoist influence expanded
rapidly, even as the institution of monarchy, and King Birendra
personally, continued to attract increasing respect.

Generally, King Birendra enhanced his credibility by seeming
to be above the political games that were being played. Privately,
he expressed his distress to me more than once at the deteriorating
political and security environment. I started gently probing him

about any personal concerns, recalling Pranab Mukherjee's words some months ago.

I knew King Birendra was not popular with the hardliners in his entourage for having given up his absolute powers and becoming a constitutional monarch in 1990 so easily. The Queen and Prince Gyanendra were openly against the compromise. The Maoists were unhappy at the spectacular improvement in India–Nepal relations. So were the Pakistanis and the Chinese. The Pakistan-based drug and arms smuggling mafia (D&Co. for short) was worried at the increasing discreet cooperation between the Nepalese Army (then directly under Palace control) and India, as it was aimed against their activities in Nepal and their exploitation of the open border between the two countries.

However, all that King Birendra would say was, 'Excellency, I have many enemies. I am in their way for what they want to achieve.'

But he was grateful for my concern and promised to let me know if he needed India's help.

The King's unwillingness to deploy the army against the escalating Maoist insurgency, despite the demonstrated inability of the police to counter the threat, was in the meantime being increasingly interpreted as a deliberate Palace ploy to expose and discredit democracy in the eyes of the people.

King Birendra was worried that if D&Co. and Nepalese Maoists got together, they could become a much greater direct threat to Nepal, its identity and international reputation, and to the institution of monarchy. The convergence in terms of enemies was clear. The monarchy and India were already declared targets. So was Nepal's Hindu identity. The Maoist leadership and cadres were declared fervent opponents of Hindu rituals and traditions and were committed to Nepal turning into a secular republic. Some years later, Maoist leader Prachanda would openly admit that the Inter-Services Intelligence (ISI) had indeed reached out to the Maoists in their Indian jungle hideouts, suggesting that they work together against their common enemies.

It was fairly well known among a small group of Western diplomats that, under pressure from some hardline rightist advisers to take advantage of the deteriorating situation and demonstrate royal proactivism, King Birendra sent emissaries out to London, Washington DC, New Delhi and Beijing to seek the concurrence of these capitals to interventionism of some kind with the democratic process, in order to curb the growing Maoist threat. All the capitals except Beijing strongly discouraged adventurism of the kind contemplated; the Chinese, cautious and inscrutable as ever, said they would leave the decision to the King, in whom they had complete faith.

King Birendra, by nature somewhat timid, gave up the idea, went into a retreat and actually had a heart attack from which he recovered quickly.

* * *

President K.R. Narayanan paid a State visit to Nepal from 28 to 30 May 1998.

On the evening of his arrival, which was just a few days after India had carried out five explosions as a declared nuclear power, news came in of Pakistan having carried out five explosions of its own. The mood at the State banquet was sombre. I could see Narayanan and King Birendra having a long and serious chat during and after dinner.

Narayanan was generally pleased with his interactions with leaders across the political spectrum, and especially the King.

After I had escorted him to his Palace suite on his last day and was preparing to return home after a long and tiring presidential visit, his secretary came up to me and said that Narayanan wanted me to join him alone.

I found him sitting in his tiny ante room. There were two chairs, two glasses, a bucket of ice cubes, and a bottle of whisky. There we were, the President of India and I, sipping whisky and soda in silence. 'This is a different Birendra,' he said, adding that he was happy I was keeping the King well informed on issues like Pakistan's misuse of the open border. 'This is going to be a particularly difficult and dangerous time for our region,' he said.

He raised his glass. I raised mine.

Mentally, I crossed my fingers.

Within a few days I had a call from Foreign Secretary Krishnan Raghunath to say that the president had suggested on his return to Delhi that King Birendra should be invited as chief guest for India's Republic Day in 1999. How would this be received by the political leaders? Would King Birendra accept if a formal invitation was extended to him?

I told him that I had no doubt the King would be delighted to accept, but in the context of the turbulent political situation and against the background of the events of 1989–90, I would consult the political leaders and revert. All the political leaders without exception seemed to be pleased at the idea, partly because by now, King Birendra had won respect as a comparatively 'democratic' monarch, but mainly because they saw this as a gesture of friendship and goodwill towards the country as a whole, without any political overtones.

I called on King Birendra to inform him about the Government of India's invitation, and as expected, he accepted, expressing deep appreciation for the gesture—something most people would have considered as inconceivable a few years ago. When asked about the kind of programme he would like to have after the Republic Day function, he said simply: 'Excellency, I want only to have one visit outside Delhi—to Puttaparthi. I would like to have a meeting with Sri Sathya Sai Baba.'

Sai Baba's following in many countries was considerable, and in Nepal, huge. I was not entirely surprised by this royal request. In recent days, a number of Sai Baba's Nepalese devotees had come back with the same message: Sai Baba was very concerned about Nepal and wanted to meet the King. In fact, only a few days earlier, the King's aunt, Princess Helen Shah, had met me and requested for a darshan of Baba, which I was able to arrange, thanks coincidentally to a chance meeting with Ashok Singhal, the Vishwa Hindu Parishad (VHP) leader, a Baba devotee who happened to be in Kathmandu at the time and was on his way to Puttaparthi.

When Princess Helen returned from Puttaparthi, she reported to me that she had clearly conveyed a very specific message from the Swami to the King, and he was now anxious to have his own personal darshan of the Baba without any further delay.

I recalled Pranab Mukherjee's words to me in 1995: 'Something was clearly worrying Birendra.'

Thus, it was that the King, accompanied by his wife, son Nirajan and daughter Shruti, visited Puttaparthi immediately after a high-profile presence in New Delhi as chief guest on Republic Day. Nepal's highly effective and respected ambassador, Bhekh Bahadur Thapa, and I, along with our spouses, accompanied them. Sai Baba spent a fair amount of time alone with the King.

Afterwards, King Birendra invited us for a quiet dinner and seemed to be in a happy but quietly introspective mood. At one point he referred to his one-to-one meeting with Sai Baba and said, 'Excellency, it is important that I come here to see Sai Baba once every year, not as King of Nepal but as a private citizen. This is what he wants. Can you arrange that for me?'

I told him that when the time came, I was sure something could be worked out.

I had no idea how it was going to be possible to enable the Head of State of a neighbouring country to visit India incognito, but by diplomatic training, my response to difficult high-level requests was usually to accept the challenge and then examine ways of addressing it.

I was posted back to Delhi as Secretary in the Ministry in mid-2000, after some five-and-a-half years in Nepal. My farewell calls on all the political leaders were charged with emotion, since all the political leaders and parties had worked so closely with the embassy to keep ties on a positive growth path, irrespective of whether they were in power or not. I had a particularly significant and long one-to-one with King Birendra, at the end of which he again reminded me that he would need to visit India quietly for personal reasons.

The tenure in Nepal had been full of professional challenges, and there had been many rewarding and satisfying moments. Despite changes of government both in India as well as in Nepal, political leaders on both sides had risen to the challenge of providing some continuity in direction, creating a basis for cooperation in water resources and hydropower, expanding trade and economic exchanges on a long-term basis, defusing old irritants like the 1950 Treaty, and developing people-centred rather than security-dominated cooperation.

Had this indeed been the best of times, or would it be remembered as the worst of times, the beginning of the end of Nepal's promise as a successful democracy? On the horizon was the gathering storm caused by the explosive cocktail of deteriorating governance and expanding Maoist violence. The monarchy was neither down nor out—democracy would take years to stabilize—and the Maoists were coming . . .

My last thought as my Air India flight took off at Tribhuvan International Airport was: A three-way confrontation between the

Maoists, political parties and the Palace seemed to be on the cards; the twin-pillar strategy favoured by Narasimha Rao might soon well be a thing of the past.

King Birendra did not visit India again.

* * *

In the Ministry, as Secretary, I was no longer dealing with Nepal, but External Affairs Minister Jaswant Singh, National Security Adviser Brajesh Mishra and Prime Minister Atal Bihari Vajpayee would call me from time to time regarding the situation in Nepal. Leaders in Nepal, including the King, also kept in touch, purely because I was considered a friend and well-wisher in a personal capacity.

In early 2001, just a few weeks before I was due to retire from service, Jaswant Singh called me and Meera Shankar, the Joint Secretary dealing with Nepal, to his office in Parliament House. The ambassador-designate to Washington, outgoing Foreign Secretary Lalit Mansingh and his successor, Chokila Iyer, were also there. Singh gave instructions that since there was an administrative matter of importance requiring me to go to Kathmandu on a short visit, I should avail of the opportunity to call on the King, PM Deuba, and other leaders and give a detailed assessment of the disturbing trends in Nepal on my return. Shankar was asked to send necessary instructions to the embassy in Kathmandu.

On my return, I reported my impressions after meeting King Birendra and all the top leaders in writing and verbally to the PM, Singh and Brajesh Mishra. (Incidentally, King Birendra's parting words to me after my call on him were: 'Excellency, please don't forget. You have to arrange my private visit to Baba's ashram in Puttaparthi quickly.')

Vajpayee's immediate response to my detailed report, as informally conveyed to me by his Joint Secretary P.S. Raghavan, was: 'Jaswant must go to Kathmandu immediately.' Unfortunately, due to the minister's various other commitments, this was not possible, but various back-channel contacts did take place.

* * *

Around 10 March 2001, I accompanied President Narayanan on a State visit to Mauritius. On the flight back to Delhi on 12 March, Narayanan came up to me in a very kind gesture. He had come to know from his Additional Secretary Shamsher Sharif.

We had a brief chat about Nepal. 'King Birendra seems to want India to switch from a twin-pillar to a three-pillar policy, to include the Maoists also,' he said with his standard philosophical smile. He added: 'That's not going to be easy!'

A day before I was due to retire (31 March 2001), Jaswant Singh requested me to continue in the ministry as an adviser. He said I would deal with the same charge as I was handling as secretary but would be available on call for informal consultations on Nepal, as he was extremely worried about the situation there, and since I enjoyed the trust and confidence of key leaders there, including the King. I asked him if this wouldn't be an awkward arrangement as it might entail crossing of wires and treading on toes with those still in service handling Nepal, especially in our Kathmandu embassy. His terse reply was that he would look after that aspect, I should simply do my job.

Shortly after that, in April (now wearing a new hat as adviser to the foreign minister), when I was accompanying Prime Minister Vajpayee on a historic visit to Iran, I received a number of alarming telephone calls from Kathmandu, some on behalf of the King. Something was clearly terribly wrong, and the King wished to convey a message to the PM urgently. I conveyed this to Jaswant Singh, who decided that we must brief the prime minister without delay. Singh and I met Vajpayee in his hotel room well past midnight, as soon as he had finished an interview with Saeed Naqvi, just a few hours before we all boarded the return flight to Delhi.

Vajpayee heard me out attentively and looked inquiringly at Singh as if to invite his suggestion on how we should respond. Jaswant said, 'Atalji, I think we should ask Rajan to go immediately to Kathmandu, meet the King and come back with a detailed report.'

Vajpayee closed his eyes and seemed lost in thought for some time. Then he said, 'It might be better for us to invite a special emissary of the King.'

I was instructed to send a suitable message to the King and get a date for his envoy's visit to Delhi.

Next day, on the return flight from Tehran to Delhi aboard the PM's special plane, I briefed Brajesh Mishra about this development. Mishra called the Joint Secretary to the PM, Shakti Sinha, who was in a nearby seat, and asked him, 'Did---- call on PM last week?' The joint secretary nodded. Mishra sighed and said, 'I would have handled things differently. I hope it is not too late.'

On the night of 1 June 2001, in the midst of a get-together of the royal family at Narayanhiti Palace in Kathmandu, a heavily drugged and drunk Crown Prince Dipendra allegedly killed both his parents, King Birendra and Queen Aishwarya, his younger brother Prince Nirajan, sister Princess Shruti, King Birendra's brother Dhirendra who had renounced his title, other members of the family including Princess Jayanti, Birendra's cousin Princess Shanti, sister Sharada and her husband Kumar Khadga. Prince Gyanendra's wife was also shot and wounded but survived. Their son Paras was spared. Crown Prince Dipendra who allegedly shot himself, went into a coma, was crowned King and died without ever gaining consciousness. Prince Gyanendra himself happened to be visiting Pokhara when the killings took place. Princess Helen Shah, the King's aunt, had left the room for a few minutes to be with the Queen Mother when the bloodbath took place. One eyewitness report claimed that when she came to King Birendra's blood-splattered body, there was one shining object around the neck which stood out: the chain and locket that had been presented by Sai Baba to the King when he visited Puttaparthi in January 1999. He was wearing that as an auspicious and protective omen, when he was allegedly gunned down by his son.

* * *

Palace Tragedy: An Untold Story

The second half of the 1990s was a period of much warmth and positive movement in India–Nepal relations. India's 'twin-pillar' policy initiated by P.V. Narasimha Rao, supporting both the monarchy as well as multiparty democracy, was yielding real dividends, and his successors, especially I.K. Gujral and Atal Bihari Vajpayee, continued with this policy. As a result, despite political instability in both countries, important agreements with India were reached on a variety of subjects including water resources, trade and transit. There was also a procession of high-level visits from Nepal to India and vice versa.

A prominent component in this improvement was very rapid, striking warmth in informal contacts between King Birendra and India. The King seemed keen to signal to India that the decades of frosty ties between the monarchy and India now belonged to the past that he had adjusted to his role as a constitutional monarch—a role he had been pushed into accepting thanks to the mass agitation supported by India. In fact, a new phase was initiated between the Palace and India, in which the former discreetly used its influence to ensure cooperation with India on important issues, including security.

New security concerns began to surface for the Palace by the late 1990s, which made an impact on him and increased his felt need for even closer coordination with India.

He was aghast at the conversion activities of Western missionaries as well as foreign Islamist fundamentalist groups among poorer sections of the population, and even more so of misuse of the open border by the powerful smuggling/terrorist/ criminal (D&Co.) underworld supported fairly blatantly by official Pakistani agencies, to which many tragic incidents in India were traced. NGOs with foreign funding had been allowed by a succession of permissive elected governments to operate freely. The Pakistani ambassador had written open letters seeking funds for certain jihadi front outfits targeting India but also targeting the monarchy as it was perceived as supporting Indian intelligence through the Royal Nepal Army (RNA). Unfortunately, on the Indian side of the border, as I discovered on my first tour of the Tarai soon after arrival, controls were even more lax. In fact, the police chief in one of our border towns actually advised me not to travel in the car bearing the flag on the Indian side in the evenings as they could not guarantee my safety!

I duly reported this to Indian Deputy PM, L.K. Advani, and strengthening the entire system of cross-border checks began. Until then, it had basically been left to the people on both sides to look into this aspect. US ambassador in Delhi, Frank Wisner, whom I had known well when we were both in Zambia years earlier, had detailed information regarding terror-related activities across the open border indulged in by Pakistan-based outfits backed by the ISI, and his counterpart in Kathmandu was able to brief me from time to time. Later, much of the information came out through Wikileaks.

There were situations when King Birendra personally intervened to ensure that India's concerns were taken seriously, when the elected political leaders seemed too distracted to do so. Thus, when a feared mafia don much wanted in India was believed to be staying at a particular place, it was the King who arranged with the army to close in on the premises, since the normal law-and-order machinery was not up to the job. The action by the army was not shared with the government or police, but to which my Defence Attaché, Colonel Muthanna, and I from the embassy, were privy. We later learnt that the secret operation was leaked by someone in the Palace to an influential political leader across the border—one of the latter's staffers actually rang me up to say that as an Indian ambassador, I should concentrate on the welfare of the Indian community and prompt passport and visa services instead of harassing God-fearing Pakistani businessmen visiting Nepal on bona fide business activities! The exercise in the event was unsuccessful. But the message to D&Co. was loud and clear.

Of direct concern to the royal family was a systematic parallel exercise by imported fundamentalist elements aimed at undermining the identity of Nepal as a Hindu nation, and discreet but sustained propaganda against the monarchy.

Although a constitutional monarch, King Birendra was far from being powerless. He had the army with its intelligence apparatus very much under his control. Moreover, he also had a good chunk of membership of each political party including the communists, who were loyal to the Palace. And then there were the people, with whom his popularity increased in direct proportion to public disenchantment with political parties, thanks to instability and poor governance.

Occasionally, last mile delivery on an important issue concerning Indian security was held up because of divergent views within the government of the day. In such situations, more often than not, it took little more than a nod, a wink or a telephone call from the Palace to swing things in favour of timely decisive action, of the preventive or punitive kind. D&Co. and its ISI support with fake diplomatic passports were repeatedly exposed, often thanks to very discreet Palace intervention when even the usually efficient and reliable local intelligence felt constrained by the embassy's insistence on diplomatic immunity. India's twin-pillar policy enabled the monarchy and politicians to work together and was becoming increasingly effective against the activities of D&Co.

Almost routinely, members of the underworld and even Pakistan embassy personnel were caught red-handed in illegal criminal activity. In one case, the Pakistani ambassador of the day, a lady, was present at the residence of a colleague who had locked himself in a room and was busy burning crores of counterfeit Indian rupee notes while police surrounding the house were hesitant to raid it because the ambassador was waving the diplomatic immunity flag. The Palace helped in ensuring that the police stormed in, overriding the ambassadorial objections. Foreign Minister Ram Sharan Mahat himself rang me up to report that the diplomat was picked up, given the typical police treatment such activities deserved, had confessed, and was being deported in somewhat poor physical condition.

Although the King's support in exposing and humiliating D&Co. and ISI involvement was very discreet, never publicized or even put on paper for obvious reasons, the Pakistan embassy got wind of it, apparently via a Palace leak with a lot of exaggeration regarding King Birendra's personal role. The motive for the latter was not very clear, but in retrospect it would seem that it may not have been well-intentioned. One day, the Pakistani ambassador called on me and said, cheekily, '*Achha, toh aap aur Raja Saheb mil kar ISI-Vy-si khatam karne wale hain?* [So, you and the Palace are going to finish the ISI here?]'

As national security adviser and foreign minister, Brajesh Mishra and Jaswant Singh, respectively, were kept informed about occasional Palace support in selected cases, but others within the bureaucracy were not in the loop, in deference to King Birendra's wishes.

Singh made a statement in the Lok Sabha on 1 March 2000:

> The Government of India has discussed from time to time with the Government of Nepal our concerns about the ISI misusing the Nepali territory and the open India Nepal border for activities inimical to India's. Reports received by the government indicate increasing evidence of ISI using Nepal as a staging post for terrorist activities directed against India. The Nepalese Government has been sensitized on this issue. The Government of Nepal has assured us that their territory would not be used for activities inimical to India's interest.

What he did not mention, for obvious reasons, was that the government was taking the discreet help of the Palace to supplement and complement the cooperation from the government.

What worried King Birendra was that with governments falling every few weeks, institutions getting politicized afresh with each such event, intra-party and inter-party feuds, coalitions being formed with no pretence of ideological affinity or principle, criminalization of politics and the cancer of corruption would invite the international underworld and terrorist nexus to spread their wings, especially near the open border where it already had a strong presence.

During President K.R. Narayanan's State visit to Nepal in May 1998, they had informally talked about the Maoist phenomenon. Narayanan shared the thought that very often Maoist ideology was more dangerous than Maoist weapons—especially in developing countries, where their ideas could quickly take root and become a threat to existing institutions and to democracy itself. Mainstreaming far Left movements by giving them ownership and credit for inclusive development offered the possibility of their becoming more moderate, more tolerant of diversity and accepting competitive politics instead of going in for radical transformation which often turned out to be a recipe for national self-destruction. He gave the example of his home state, Kerala, and of West Bengal.

The second thing Narayanan said was that since using the nuclear weapons option was for all practical purposes a non-starter for a country like Pakistan, it was likely to intensify informal methods of warfare, including proxy war, smuggling and terrorism to hurt India.

King Birendra was worried that if D&Co. and Nepalese Maoists got together, they could become a much greater threat to the monarchy. (Years later, the fact that such contacts had indeed taken place was confirmed. The months immediately following his Republic Day visit to India turned out to be particularly stressful for King Birendra. D&Co. escalated their activities. The Palace, in turn, very discreetly, became increasingly helpful in trying to check them through increased cooperation with India.

Pakistani 'diplomats' were caught red-handed in activities relating to smuggling of counterfeit currency and terror-related activities, their homes raided, at times in the presence of their ambassador and over his/her objections claiming diplomatic immunity. The Pakistan embassy's involvement was repeatedly exposed as well.

* * *

The Hijacking of IC 814

24 December 1999 proved to be a turning point for Nepal and for India–Nepal relations, in more ways than one. That evening, I was chief guest at a function to announce a collaboration between Binod Chaudhary's Chaudhary Group and the Norvic Hospital Group in India. Chaudhary had just finished speaking and I rose from my chair to deliver my address when my deputy came up to the stage and handed me a small note. I glanced at it. The words scrawled on it were barely decipherable but unmistakable in their significance: *Sir, the Indian Airlines flight to Delhi has been hijacked.*

I mumbled a few words on the mike and rushed back to India House.

The phone rang. It was Foreign Minister Jaswant Singh.

'Rajan, you know the news?'

'Sir. IC 184.'

'It's now in Amritsar. How could the Nepalese let this happen?'

'Sir, spoken to everyone concerned, will have detailed information very soon.'

'Get them involved too,' he said, meaning the Palace. 'We need to get to the bottom of this before public opinion goes out of control.'

'Sir, have already contacted them. Will have the inside story very soon.'

What I did not tell him, since we were speaking on an open line, was that two embassy colleagues with special responsibilities were also on board.

The hijacking was a stunning blow to Nepal's image and self-esteem, as well as to the goodwill it had always enjoyed in the eyes of the people of India. New Delhi, for its part, demonstrated a certain recklessness in encouraging the demonization of Nepal through the statements and insinuations of Indian leaders, clearly to divert attention from the government's own mismanagement of the episode. I found this to be particularly regrettable at a time when the Nepalese authorities at operational levels and indeed at the highest level were providing excellent cooperation to their Indian counterparts in identifying the hijackers (none of whom were Nepali, although in his initial statements to the media, Jaswant Singh let it be known that this was the case) and unravelling the details of the entire episode. When I pointed out to New Delhi that there was growing resentment in Kathmandu about the disproportionate blame being placed at Nepal's door, the response was that India had to counter Pakistani propaganda that the Research and Analysis Wing (R&AW) had cooked up the entire hijacking in order to malign Pakistan!

Later, there was more evidence of fairly crude attempts to discredit Nepal as much as possible. I was asked by New Delhi to facilitate access inside all areas of Kathmandu airport for one of our well-known media channels, ostensibly to project Nepal in a good light after the damage done by earlier official statements and media reports. I requested Prime Minister K.P. Bhattarai's intervention to get the necessary permissions; the Indian TV reporters spent a couple of days interviewing airport personnel and taking shots of various restricted areas. To everyone's astonishment, the 'breaking news' story that came out a few days later was that even several days after the hijacking, security arrangements were so poor that reporters from the TV channel had succeeded in moving around undetected even in the most sensitive areas! My protests to the ministry and the channel did not cut much ice—the atmosphere was too charged. But the longer-term cost of the breakdown of trust and goodwill at the people-to-people level, which has always been the foundation of the much-vaunted special relationship with Nepal, was possibly ignored.

In the event, the hijacked plane ended up in Kandahar in Afghanistan via Dubai, and the Government of India chose to negotiate with the hijackers to secure the release of the passengers. Jaswant Singh went to Kandahar accompanied by the three terrorists whose release from Indian prisons was part of the bargain, and came back to India with the passengers, one of whom had been killed by the hijackers at Dubai to show that they meant business. The three notorious terrorists released by India were: Maulana Masood Azhar, founder of Jaish-e-Muhammad, which had a role in the attack on the Indian Parliament in 2000, the Mumbai attacks of 2008 and others; Ahmed Omar Saeed Sheikh, involved in the murder of Daniel Pearl and 9/11 attacks in the US; and Mushtaq Ahmed Zargar.

There was relief at the end of the long ordeal for the passengers and their families in India and elsewhere, but also much criticism of the manner in which India had handled the crisis, especially in permitting the plane to take off from Amritsar when special troops were ready to storm it. Even before the drama ended on 30 December, an Indian investigating team in Kathmandu with excellent cooperation from their Nepalese counterparts (with some discreet higher-level help at our request) had unearthed the full details of the identity of the hijackers, the support that they received from D&Co. from beginning to end, direct local involvement of the Pakistan embassy and ISI, and accomplices in India.

The hijacking was carefully timed to seriously damage India–Nepal relations in addition to other objectives. In speedy joint investigations on which King Birendra's confidants helped behind the scenes, the involvement of Pakistan was again exposed. All four hijackers—Sunny Ahmad Qazi, Shahid Saeed Akhtar, Zahoor Ibrahim Mistry and Farooa Abdul Aziz Siddiqui—were Pakistani nationals and members of the terrorist outfit Harkat-ul-Mujahideen (HuM). The hijackers were given weapons by Pakistani diplomats who had access to the departure lounge just before the flight took off. Eventually the ISI station chief in Nepal working under diplomatic cover, who was directly implicated, was arrested and deported. And, the terrorists exchanged for the release of the passengers were taken off the plane at Kandahar and driven off to Pakistan instead of being arrested.

The degree of India–Nepal cooperation, multiple arrests of Pakistani nationals and deportation and exposure of Pakistani diplomats within a five-year period shook D&Co. out of its conviction that it could violate Nepalese territory with impunity. The brashness and confidence with which it had conducted its anti-India activities from Nepal until then disappeared. ISI operatives became more circumspect and cautious in the knowledge that retribution from Nepalese authorities for any illegal activity they were caught undertaking would be forthcoming. The Nepalese response, under pressure from India on one hand and full cooperation from it on the other, had sent a clear message to the ISI—it would not tolerate another hijacking or other terror-related activities on its soil.

But the Hrithik Roshan riots of December 2000* were a clear signal that D&Co. was not about to give up. They were still bent

---

* ABC News, 'Indian Film Star Sparks Riots in Nepal', ABC News, January 6, 2006, https://abcnews.go.com/International/story?id=81838&page=1.

on creating tensions in India–Nepal relations and major concerns for India. The informal signals conveyed by the Palace were that political parties were not able or willing to take serious action in time to prevent such incidents or at least contain the damage once they had taken place. My successor in Kathmandu, Deb Mukharji, wrote that he had shared his assessment with Prime Minister Vajpayee that Nepalese prime minister Girija Prasad Koirala and his government could have managed the situation better to prevent it from going out of control, that this disappointment was conveyed by Vajpayee to his Nepalese counterpart, and Koirala expressed his unhappiness to the ambassador for having shared such an assessment with Delhi!

Unfortunately, the communication style even of leaders friendly towards India tended to confirm this impression. For example, I recall being present when PM Bhattarai was surrounded by Indian press members who wanted to have his take on the IC 814 hijacking. In his bantering style Bhattarai laughed and said, '*Aare bhai, hijacking kaunsi badi baat hai? Sab jagah hijacking hota hai* [What's the big deal about hijacking? It happens everywhere].' This obviously went down very badly with the Indian public, who had been shaken to the core by the incident. I recall Deputy National Security Adviser Satish Chandra calling me up from Delhi to convey his shock and dismay at such an insensitive remark by a Nepal PM.

The Pakistan-based group had cultivated a number of Nepalese leaders by providing them with funds and various other forms of assistance. Rumours—not always without substance—began to surface about secret but separate contacts between political leaders of the major parties as well as the Palace with Maoist leaders in India, which were in the know of if not encouraged by, India, with the objective of persuading the Maoists to give up violence and their radicalism and join mainstream politics for a win-win scenario in Nepal.

Maoist leaders now reached out to the Palace to suggest, inter alia, a working arrangement in which the monarchy could continue 'in some form' and the Maoists could come into the power structure. King Birendra's idea seemed to be to try a step-by-step approach: get the Maoists to give up force, accept monarchy, and then get them to give up their radical demands vis-à-vis India, and then finally to moderate their stance on multiparty democracy. Once again, some governments were consulted informally. The 'idea that was not yet a proposal' was never put down on paper.

King Birendra was convinced that there was a direct threat to the institution of monarchy from the rise of Islamic fundamentalist-terrorist related activities along the border which he was determined to curb, and on which he was collaborating with India directly but discreetly. He had also given me ample hints that he saw a threat to him personally. Both threats seemed to increase manifold once the Maoists began to assert themselves successfully against the Nepal police. He was willing to be proactive and take control of the situation but wanted India to be on board. India's advice was clear: the multiparty system should not be touched. Subject to that, India had no views on the Palace responding to Maoist overtures.

It was indeed a strange situation in which each concerned party—Nepal's prime minister, the King, other mainstream political parties like the CPN (UML), India and the Maoists—was keeping a close watch on the others, somewhat distrustfully, was keen to strike a deal where possible and seek advantages where possible over the others. For D&Co., it was important that New Delhi, the Maoists and the King did not reach an understanding. They would have known that the formal dialogue between the King and Maoists was set to begin towards the end of April 2001 in Kathmandu, and that Delhi was in the picture. This would certainly be a major setback for their strategic game plan.

Positive noises began to be publicly made on behalf of the Palace and Maoists about one another. Prince Dipendra was said to be on board initially about such a dialogue. Journalist Sudheer Sharma's book *The Nepal Nexus* gives one excellent 'inside account'—paraphrased below. It gives a flavour of the strange goings-on of the time.*

King Birendra felt that Maoists were likely to intensify attacks against the police but realized that they could not achieve their objectives as long as the army was under Palace control.

In October 2000, Prince Dhirendra had described the Maoists as 'nationalists, even if they are Republicans'.

On 29 April 2001, a secret meeting was held in a private house in Kathmandu between Prince Dhirendra and the Maoist representative.

At the meeting, the latter presented views that were in accordance with his party's approach. He talked about the 'need for the monarchy to take initiatives to end oppression and tyranny in rural villages'—something that was sure to bring the two forces together. He also spoke about their socio-economic programmes. Prince Dhirendra was not opposed to the Maoists' checklist of transformational land reforms or to their left-leaning socio-economic policies. He said that the Maoist negotiators had given ample indication that they would not be opposed to some form of monarchy if there was an understanding on cooperation among nationalists.

---

* Sudheer Sharma, *The Nepal Nexus: An Inside Account of the Maoists, the Durbar and New Delhi* (Penguin Viking, 2019).

Prince Dhirendra's last words before they left the meeting venue: 'Thuldai (King Birendra), Maldai (then Prince Gyanendra) and myself, we all agree that the Maoists are a nationalist force and should be utilized for bringing about national prosperity. Through you, we want to assure Prachanda that the military will not be mobilized at any cost.'

A conclusion on whether a power alliance between the Palace and the Maoists was possible may perhaps have been reached through one-on-one talks between King Birendra and Prachanda. Preparations were underway for such a meeting. Prachanda was already putting together the points he would present before the King.

And Prince Dhirendra was telling them to come up with their replies within a fortnight. Crown Prince Dipendra and Prince Gyanendra were on board. But in the middle of preparations for this summit meeting, calamity struck—and it took the lives of the King who wanted to meet Prachanda, a prince who was arranging such a meeting, and the crown prince who was in the loop. That happened just a month after the Maoist emissary and Dhirendra met; just a week after the Palace had sent a nine-point letter to the Maoist chief. The royal massacre left only the Maldai (Gyanendra) unharmed. And he became the new King.

Prachanda was asked in an interview by journalist Sudheer Sharma in 2006: 'So, what was your relationship with King Birendra like?' The answer was: 'Whether because he felt that army mobilization would result in more bloodshed, or whether he felt the time was still not ripe for such action, he (Birendra) was surely not in favour of bringing the army into the picture. We also did not want to confront the army just then. We felt that if the army mobilization could be stopped by approaching Birendra and Dhirendra, then so be it. Because we had not become strong. Our army was not very strong. We did not have good weapons. So we felt it would be a bad idea to fight the army. That is the point where our interests met. That's what we called "undeclared unity in action".'

When asked the reason for such unity in action with King Birendra and not others, Prachanda said, 'Birendra became a King in the natural course of events, so he had a natural tendency to be concerned about his country and countrymen. Though he belonged to the feudal class, he did not have any appetite to see people being killed. Take, for instance, the events of 1979 (when an anti-monarchy agitation was heightened). There had not been too many casualties, but he quickly declared a referendum. Similarly, had 1000 people been killed in 1990, the People's Movement would have been finished. But instead of taking that course, he restored the multiparty system. So it seems that he wanted options besides resorting to bloodshed. That is why we saw liberal feudal characteristics in him.' Prachanda added, 'Besides, he was also exploring a peaceful resolution of our movement. He sent Dhirendra. He also wanted to meet us himself. Maybe it was because of his own interests that he wanted to meet us, to take advantage of the situation. But I feel that was not the sole reason. I don't think he just wanted to squeeze us. Perhaps he thought that the country could be saved by some compromises.'

In the words of former Maoist leader Rabindra Shrestha, who was quite close to Prachanda back then: 'Prachanda-Baburam imagined convincing King Birendra to turn into a president, or, if that was not possible, to let him continue as a ceremonial monarch while taking over control of the army.' But would King Birendra have agreed to this? That is something that could not be confirmed by any source. But one thing is certain, though. King Birendra did not like the government policy of trying to control the Maoists through police action, and the ensuing bloodshed among his people, and he felt that there should be a peaceful resolution to Maoist insurgency. It was for this reason he was in talks with the Maoists through his brother Dhirendra.

Sharma also describes the progress that was being made by Prime Minister K.P. Bhattarai in his efforts to reach an understanding with the Maoists. This is revealing because it shows the level of distrust within each party on reaching out to the Maoists:

Prime Minister Bhattarai started exploring the possibility of holding talks with the rebels. Nepali Congress president Girija Prasad Koirala, also came to know about it from the Palace the same day. The following day (12 March 2000), at Koirala's instruction, sixty-nine Congress members of Parliament registered a no-trust motion against the prime minister. Facing certain defeat at the hands of his fellow Kangressis, Bhattarai resigned on 16 March. He was prevented from embarking on that tour. His visit had to be cancelled because he was planning to hold talks with Maoist leaders somewhere in Europe during the tour. Neither Koirala nor the Palace wanted the talks to take place under his leadership. Forced to resign, Bhattarai made an emotional farewell speech at Parliament on 16 March 2000. 'Since 1996, the so-called "people's war" of the Maoists has become everyone's concern. But just when they are preparing to resolve the problem through talks, and are assigning their negotiators, the plots begin to be hatched to derail the process. Why?' In a written statement, he further asked, 'When will we, Nepal, be free from the so-called curse on our patriots? Isn't democracy all about abandoning such political trickery and embracing transparency?' Bhattarai had been a victim of double design, by Koirala and by the royal Palace. The irony was that Koirala pulled the rug from under him on the pretext of his inability 'to control Maoist terror', whereas it was because of him that Bhattarai's efforts to end the 'terror' were being derailed.

Even as the terrorist-related border incidents escalated, members of D&Co. group began to contact members of the royal family, Crown Prince Dipendra in particular, and a sinister plan to damage the credibility of the monarchy and make it implode from within began to unfold. Dipendra fell into their trap by taking personality changing drugs and alcohol and started behaving strangely every now and then. He was also fed on fabricated stories of the King being ready to compromise with the Maoists and accept a ceremonial position like that of President.

The SOS from the Palace to me in Tehran in April 2001 during the Vajpayee visit was to convey a message to the prime minister regarding talks with the Maoists which were scheduled for the end of April and also to his rising concern about Prince Dipendra's increasingly strange behaviour. The latter seemed to be completely trapped by an ISI front company in Kathmandu.

The 1 June 2001 massacre was due to extreme frustration felt by a Crown Prince who thought that there was no future for him in Nepal, in addition to the problems he was already having in convincing his parents about marrying the girl of his choice.

D&Co. in Pakistan would have been celebrating. With the deaths of King Birendra, along with that of Crown Prince Dipendra and Prince Nirajan, the credibility of the institution of monarchy and its continuity was in great doubt. They would have assumed that with Gyanendra at the helm, the prospects of a deal between India, the Maoists and the Palace were now highly improbable—Gyanendra's poor equation with India was widely known, as was his determination to use force to crush the Maoists and his impatience to dismantle democracy. And the Maoists were sure to blame India for conspiring to kill the Royal Family—as they did. An unstable Nepal, a failed State, and disturbed India–Nepal relations were all very much in their interests.

But the future unfolded in a totally unexpected way.

King Birendra paid with his life for playing a part in exposing Pakistan's terror-related activities in Nepal and the humiliation of its diplomats and for cooperating against the large-scale cross-border smuggling and terrorism industry of D&Co.; for his tentative three-pillar idea, i.e., India supporting the Palace, Maoists and the mainstream parties; for the monarchy's new-found enthusiasm for forging friendly ties with India.

But the victory of D&Co. turned out to be a Pyrrhic one. Even though Nepal soon lost its identity as a Hindu Kingdom after the monarchy was abolished and it was transformed into a secular republic, the Maoists were repeatedly part of the power structure and Nepal went into a seemingly unending transition with chronic political instability and serious challenges to governance, it refused to be fertile ground for terrorism against India as Pakistan had devoutly hoped.

A day would soon come when a one-time fiery Maoist prime minister would visit sacred Hindu temples in India during an official visit and tacitly endorse Nepal's Hindu identity. And Nepal's ultra-nationalism which so many Indian governments railed against in the past, would energetically resist attempts by China and Pakistan to recruit it for the encirclement of India.

When I discussed all this with the one other person who knew the whole background, an Indian Administrative Service (IAS) official close to Vajpayee who had been privy to some of the back channel stuff between India and Nepal, I was pleased when he said, 'I totally agree with you, sir 100 per cent.'

But then he threw a spanner in the works by asking three simple questions:

— *How could all this have happened unless there was a Palace insider also involved?*

— *If there was an insider, didn't it stand to reason that he was someone who stood to gain from the whole operation—the final exit of King Birendra as well as Prince Dipendra and his siblings, the opportunity to implement his ideas on curbing democracy, suppressing the Maoists, opening up to China, asserting Nepal's sovereign space?*

— *Assuming that such an insider was highly intelligent and shrewd, might he not have 'used' the D Company just as the latter had 'used' Prince Dipendra to make the King Birendra line implode from within?*

'And don't forget,' my friend concluded with a sigh, 'no one saw him (Prince Dipendra) die . . . do you remember "Who Killed Cock Robin?"'

This was of course the nursery rhyme of everyone's schooldays, later to become a household phrase thanks to one of Agatha Christie's thrillers:

Who Killed Cock Robin?/I, said the sparrow/With my bow and arrow/I Killed Cock Robin/Who saw him die?/I, said the fly/With my little eye/I saw him die.

No one saw Pince Dipendra die, said my friend. No one saw him die.

I could barely gulp in response. I remember saying to myself, 'That's the difference between the IAS and Indian Foreign Service (IFS). Their minds can go ten fathoms deep.'

That was the last time I saw him.

* * *

I realize that there would be many questions on the reader's mind. While the headlines of the anniversary of the Palace tragedy each year almost always speak of the reasons being shrouded in mystery, most people have reluctantly accepted the version of the Crown Prince killing off the entire family and himself because he was not permitted to marry the girl he loved.

Was King Birendra that kind of person?

His public persona was that of an affable, mild-mannered leader given to compromise but not one who took his duties too seriously.

But does anyone really know anyone?

Recently there was a biography of Atal Bihari Vajpayee which showed a very different side of his personality when it came to his views on democracy and secularism, than what most people knew. In another work, Ambassador Chinmaya Gharekhan speaks of a warm, friendly, caring, human side of Indira Gandhi which many thought never existed.[*]

I had the opportunity of spending many hours with King Birendra on tours to religious places in India, travelling hundreds of kilometres by road, stuck in transit lounges because of flight delays or in small hotels in small towns, and can vouch for the fact that he was very different from his public image. He took the threats to his life and to the monarchy—whether they were real, imaginary or exaggerated—extremely seriously, although he opened up on these subjects with very few people.

Why did the possible involvement of D&Co. in the Palace tragedy not become a matter of public speculation earlier?

One reason was that so few knew that he was personally determined to expose and neutralize them. Even in our embassy,

---

[*] Chinmaya R. Gharekhan, *Centres of Power: My Years in the Prime Minister's Office and Security Council* (Rupa Publications, 2023).

where I had the good fortune of receiving support from some of the finest bureaucrats in India like Atish Sinha, P.K. Hormis Tharakan and Ashok Kantha, I had to deal with some sensitive matters with the King on my own or with my defence attache, since the RNA was involved.

In Delhi, in deference to King Birendra's personal request, apart from Vajpayee, Jaswant Singh and Brajesh Mishra, there may have been just two or three of their personal confidants who knew of Vajpayee's quiet encouragement to King Birendra to save the identity of Nepal as a Hindu Kingdom. In one conversation with Vajpayee, I timidly and tentatively suggested that Nepal's credentials as a Hindu State were of comparatively recent origin, its raison d'être being King Mahendra's determination to impose the hill culture of upper caste Hindus and uniformity of culture and dress in a bid to stamp out diversity and sources of challenge to royal monopoly on power. But I saw his expression of disagreement with this view, recalled his famous statement of the seventies as foreign minister which had endeared him to the Nepalese to this day (every pebble of Nepal has Shiva's name engraved on it), remembered the story narrated to me by K.P. Bhattarai that he had shown extraordinarily deep respect for King Birendra at their first meeting and overruled the latter's protest (Your Majesty, this Atal remains firmly unshaken in favour of someone pursuing *swadharma*, *rajdharma* and *satya*). I kept my counsel to myself.

In Nepal, a handful of people would have been in the know of the possible involvement of D&Co., but they were Palace loyalists, good at keeping secrets to themselves all the way to the crematorium. Another possible reason for non-leakage: too many skeletons in a few cupboards!

* * *

The Gyanendra Years

When Prince Gyanendra became King soon after the Palace tragedy of 1 June 2001, the main question for those in the know was whether the tentative initiative for secret talks between King Birendra and the Maoists would be revived. Prince Gyanendra's personal preference was to use the army and suppress the Maoists by military force. A few months earlier, when K.P. Bhattarai was prime minister (King Birendra was alive then), he had been making some progress with the King's knowledge in initiating a dialogue with the Maoists, but Koirala was privately against it, as was King Birendra, for different reasons. Koirala succeeded in forcing Bhattarai to resign as he was confident of being able to extinguish the Maoist threat by using force; he was prime minister at the time of the Palace tragedy and resigned as a matter of principle since the RNA was not deployed against the Maoists. Sher Bahadur Deuba, willing to go along with Prince Gyanendra, then became prime minister.

From July to November, there were ceasefire talks between the government led by Deuba and the Maoists. Knowing how the latter viewed Prince Gyanendra and vice versa, no one was optimistic that there would be a positive outcome.

Shortly after the Palace massacre, I informed both Jaswant Singh and Brajesh Mishra that I would like to be relieved of my duties on extension with the ministry. I told them frankly that I felt I was treading on too many toes both in Delhi as well as in Kathmandu and was keen to stay away from Nepal affairs as much as possible. Both respected my wishes but both felt that it would be a pity if I wasted my Nepal experience and suggested that I join think tanks and NGOs which were active in Nepal's search for peace.

I followed their advice and got myself involved with a few NGOs which took me to Nepal on visits and were meant to be private but could not possibly remain so. On each visit, I would end up meeting Nepalese politicians and occasionally even King Gyanendra, usually without seeking appointments and sometimes much to my embarrassment and surprise.

In one meeting with the King shortly after Gyanendra succeeded Birendra, I found him to be clear, self-confident and determined to show that he could succeed when the political leadership had failed. His parting words to me when I left him were, 'The political leaders are not competent enough to solve this problem. Anyway, what is democracy? Just a word. I only have to press "delete" and that will be the end of democracy.'

I rushed to India House straight from the Palace to inform Ambassador I.P. Singh about the exact words used by King Gyanendra, which could well be a signal of his intent. I felt that the Government of India needed to be alerted. The ambassador laughed and said, 'Impossible! He will never do this because he knows we will never accept it.'

No telegram was sent to Delhi.

The Nepali Congress witnessed a split. On 4 October 2002, King Gyanendra sacked Prime Minister Deuba for incompetence, assumed a more direct political role, and appointed a loyalist, Lokendra Bahadur Chand, as prime minister. Chand was replaced by Surya Bahadur Thapa in a few months, then Deuba was brought back again in the game of musical chairs.

In February 2003, the second ceasefire was signed between the Nepal government and the Maoists. But in August 2003, the RNA executed seventeen unarmed Maoists in Doramba. The civil war resumed. On 30 April 2005, the Parliament that Prince Gyanendra had dismissed earlier was reinstated and Sher Bahadur Deuba, the PM he had dismissed, was reappointed.

As the civil war resumed and intensified, King Gyanendra took the long-expected step of assuming direct executive power, arresting political leaders, stifling civil liberties and declaring a state of emergency.

The Maoists promptly declared that the party's immediate political objective was to make Nepal a 'democratic republic' and monarchy and feudalism were categorized as the principal enemies.

On 22 November, a twelve-point understanding was signed between the Seven Party Alliance and the Maoists in Delhi with proactive persuasive interaction with all concerned to fight 'autocratic monarchy'.

I recall taking some well-known figures from India with me to some peace conferences in Nepal with second-rung Maoist leaders attending but not participating or speaking. They would hear former Human Rights Commission Chairman Karthikeyan and Mahatma Gandhi's great grandson Tushar Gandhi and privately concede that a compromise which would end suffering and violence was a desirable objective. After some time, they started speaking in panel discussions and even endorsing general declarations on the restoration of peace.

In April 2006, a nineteen-day People's Movement, the second Jana Andolan, succeeded in forcing King Gyanendra to concede that sovereignty rested with the people. The Parliament, dissolved in 2002, was reinstated. A ceasefire was declared and Girija Prasad Koirala took oath as prime minister.

In May 2006, the Monarchy suffered the decisive blow by the restored Parliament with bringing RNA under direct civilian rule and declaring Nepal a secular state.

On 1 February 2005, the inevitable happened. King Gyanendra assumed direct executive power, arrested political leaders, stifled civil liberties and declared a state of emergency.

The institution of monarchy was now pitted against both Maoists and democratic forces and demands for a 'democratic republic' gathered momentum. Monarchy and feudalism were categorized as the principal enemies by Maoists and on 22 November 2005, a twelve-point understanding was signed between the Seven Party Alliance and the Maoists in Delhi to fight 'autocratic monarchy'. The Ministry of External Affairs' (MEA) senior bureaucracy played a discreet but proactive role in bringing the political parties and Maoists together against the monarchy, even as its official spokesman continued to swear by the twin-pillar approach initiated by P.V. Narasimha Rao. India also continued to exert pressure on the King to roll back his actions in other ways, refusing to participate in the South Asian Association for Regional Cooperation (SAARC) Summit in Dhaka, putting on hold its defence supplies to Nepal, rallying the international community to change its policies towards the Maoists, and even leaning on China to dilute its consistent solid support for the monarchy. Pakistan, based on its assessment that a reliable anti-India figure had replaced King Birendra, continued to support Gyanendra.

The Gyanendra coup could not survive in the face of international, particularly Indian, pressure.

His conviction that democracy was irrelevant to Nepal and his actions after becoming King to dismantle it to the ground after assuming absolute powers, along with the Indian establishment's traditional antipathy towards the monarchy after Tribhuvan, proved ultimately to be the undoing of the man as well as the institution a few years after the Palace tragedy.

I should mention that earlier, in July, I happened to be in Kathmandu at a peace conference, and ran into Lakhdar Brahimi, the United Nations Secretary General's Special Envoy, who was staying in the same hotel. Brahimi and I had worked closely together at Algiers when I was ambassador there, and he was President Chadli Benjadid's close adviser. We had an hour-long chat. He listened with rapt attention to my reading of the situation. He asked me to meet with him again when I was visiting New York in September, which I did. As I walked into his room at the UNHQ, I bumped into Gyanendra's Foreign Minister, Ramesh Nath Pandey, who was being seen off by Brahimi after their lengthy meeting. Once again, Brahimi and I exchanged thoughts on how sustainable peace and stability could be promoted in Nepal. As our meeting ended, he said, 'I hope your government is taking advantage of your Nepal experience, or words to that effect.' I assured him it was doing no such thing, as Delhi had too many experts on Nepal already. He smiled, 'I know what you mean, Ambassador.' He had gone through a similar experience in Algiers.

The fact of the matter is that retirees in MEA usually find that the ministry has no use for their advice. The reasons are understandable. Retirees can be a pain in the neck when serving foreign secretaries and senior officials who would like to have space to try out their own initiatives. And in a place like Kathmandu, overly prone to conspiracy theories, a retired ambassador can insist with all the force he can muster that he is a private citizen now and cannot speak for the government, but eager listeners will with equal determination over-interpret every word he is saying, resulting sometimes in embarrassment or controversy.

In the present case, I was (perhaps understandably) given some special treatment by my old ministry. Foreign Minister K. Natwar Singh had called a series of informal round table discussions with present and former senior officials with Nepal and UN experience, to discuss the present situation and options available for India. In the first meeting, Singh asked participants for their opinion on what kind of structure would be in Nepal's and India's interests. With the Maoists coming into government in the near future, what should India's stand on the monarchy be? I mildly suggested that maybe a monarchy without King Gyanendra, under a regency arrangement as a temporary measure, was the answer, since Nepal without even a temporary institutional underpinning could go into free fall and there would be no one to hold things together and stand up to the Maoists if they decided to come up with extreme demands. Since the Maoists had always been waiting to transform Nepal into a secular republic immediately, it could be game, set and match for them (and also incidentally for the ISI and their friends in the smuggling underworld). The clear impression through their statements, in public and private, was that even mainstream leaders from political parties including Girija Prasad Koirala were hesitant to see the monarchy disappear abruptly. They simply wanted it to be reined in more firmly to a ceremonial role.

The next meeting in Singh's office took place after a week without my knowledge, and I had a call from Ambassador Chinmaya Gharekhan, former permanent representative to the UN, who had also attended the earlier meeting as to why I was absent. I rang the minister's office to be informed that they had been 'instructed' by a senior MEA official that I need not be troubled for these consultations from now on. Similarly, my old friends from different political parties in Nepal who were now frequently visiting India for consultations with the MEA to which they were invited, told me cheerfully that 'a senior MEA official' had insisted that there should be no contact with me on the main subject being discussed with the ministry, which was that it was time for Nepal to get rid of the monarchy once and for all.

In the end, bureaucracy had its way. It was India that played a key role in the restoration of Nepal's monarchy in 1951, from its virtual imprisonment under the century-old feudal rule of successive Rana prime ministers. It is one of the many ironies in the India–Nepal story that it was India again that played a key role in the final collapse of the monarchy more than five decades later.

* * *

Flashbacks and Turning Points

Starting with Jawaharlal Nehru, Indian prime ministers had a clear idea about Nepal's importance in India's security perspective. Nehru genuinely wished to make a departure from Britain's historical policy of keeping a firm grip on Nepal's external as well as internal affairs while granting Nepal nominal independence. It was Nehru who enabled the escape of King Tribhuvan from the custody of the Ranas to India, and brokered the deal which enabled him to return as a constitutional monarch at the head of a multiparty democracy. Under him, India worked overtime for an end to Nepal's international isolation, its entry into the UN, opening the doors to its progress by giving Kathmandu its first post office, hospital, airport and connectivity to the outside world. But concerns about an increasingly assertive communist China were already casting their shadow. Nehru felt compelled to moderate his liberal urges.

The 1950 Peace and Friendship Treaty was a straightforward imitation of the 1814 Sugauli Treaty which traded off free access of people and goods from Nepal to India against constraints on Nepal's external and defence relations. It was signed in Kathmandu on 31 July 1950 between the last Rana prime minister and India's first ambassador to Nepal, Sir C.P.N. Singh.

Tribhuvan was understandably daunted by the range of challenges Nepal would be faced with, severely underdeveloped as it was even in comparison with India's poorest states. He reportedly even suggested to Nehru that Nepal merge with India and become an Indian state. It is well known in the Congress leadership circles that Sardar Vallabhbhai Patel favoured the accession of Nepal to India, while several other leaders preferred an independent Nepal as a buffer state. In fact, Nehru himself was more inclined towards a free but politically reliable dispensation in Nepal. Tribhuvan was more than receptive to this arrangement, which he saw as necessary to ensure the survival of the monarchy as well as of Nepal as a nation.

There may indeed have been some discussion with Tribhuvan on Nepal's possible accession to India as suggested by Patel. According to several Indian leaders including former foreign minister K. Natwar Singh and most recently former president Pranab Mukherjee in his posthumously published autobiography, Tribhuvan was in favour, but Nehru rejected the idea. Mukherjee adds: 'If Indira Gandhi had been prime minister, she may have reacted differently.'

Nepali analysts tend to either pooh-pooh this suggestion as a figment of India's imagination, or dismiss it as the ramblings of a drunken Tribhuvan.

When King Tribhuvan returned to Kathmandu, there was euphoria, high expectations, a sense of liberation at last, and (initially) appreciation of India's role. But the high-profile interventionist activities (real, exaggerated or imaginary) of India's ambassador Sir C.P.N. Singh, and Palace Adviser Govind Narain, suggested that Tribhuvan was permitting India to micromanage the political scene to have a pliable ruling structure.

India was soon perceived as playing favourites among political leaders, a pattern which would be repeated many times during democratic phases in Nepal's history—as for example when Nehru had to disappoint the trust that his old friend B.P. Koirala had in him by entrusting the prime ministership to his half-brother Matrika Prasad Koirala. As per a US diplomatic archives quote from a communication from India,

In BP's own words, Nehru had turned cold on him over two meetings that August. At both meetings when (Koirala)

endeavoured to point out to Nehru the errors which the
Indians were committing in Nepal in the implementation
of their policy, he was cut off and told that because of its
geographic location, Nepal was going to have to develop under
the aegis of the Government of India. BP tried to point out that
Nepalis were slowly but surely developing a nationalist spirit,
that this nationalist spirit could be channelled into agreeable
Indo–Nepal relations which could be mutually beneficial to
both countries.

B.P. Koirala claimed to have 'very drastically revised his opinion
of Nehru' and this made a big impact in politically aware sections
of the Valley.

Some Nepalese researchers have also suggested that King
Tribhuvan was not everything he was projected as being, and his
commitment to democracy was at best nuanced. In Sagar Rana's
words, he played ball with Nehru, partly because he himself felt
the need to expand the powers of the monarchy at the cost of
democracy and it suited him to expose the shortcomings of elected
politicians and allow India to take the blame for being excessively
interventionist.

But the fact was that Tribhuvan had great difficulty in
managing the situation he had inherited from the Ranas, to
which was now added the real threat from an assertive communist
regime in China. India was allowed to station its military mission,
maintain checkpoints along the Tibetan border, and harness the
Gandak and Koshi rivers for mutual benefits.

In April 1954, Nepal and India signed a controversial
agreement on the Saptakoshi High Dam Project. The dam, which
fell within Nepali territory, displaced a large number of Nepalis,
but the benefits, especially in case of the share of irrigation water,
were perceived as highly favoured by India. The deal was viewed

as a sell-out to India and had a long-term impact on future India–Nepal cooperation. There was an unprecedented public outcry against M.P. Koirala and the Indian government.

There were tales shared with Indian interlocutors by several Nepalese leaders, including Girija Prasad Koirala, Manmohan Adhikari and Ganesh Mansingh, that while the seeds of anti-Indianism had been well-laid by the British among the Kathmandu Valley elite, whom they repeatedly warned about India's sinister designs when it became independent, some of India's initial actions after Tribhuvan's return from exile came as a huge disappointment to expectations of a true independent democracy evolving in Nepal, and rapidly fuelled suspicions that British warnings about India's Nepal designs were for real.

The misperceptions about India during the Tribhuvan years—the 1950 Treaty with the Ranas, Sardar Patel's views about Nepal's merger with India, high profile participation in decision-making in the Palace and in cabinet meetings on Tribhuvan's return, preference of M.P. Koirala over B.P. Koirala as PM due to the latter's passionate commitment to Nepal sovereignty, the Koshi project perceived as giving disproportionate benefits to India over Nepal—would haunt India–Nepal relations for decades to come and influence the posturing of successive Nepalese regimes towards India as well as China to create suspicions, misunderstanding, delays on important cooperation projects at every turn of the road and result in a self-perpetuating trust deficit.

By the time Tribhuvan died, in 1955, there was a growing constituency in Kathmandu which resented India's perceived penchant for proactive intrusiveness, the passive acquiescence of Tribhuvan as well as pliability of elected politicians eager to be in India's good books and willing to make Nepal's sovereignty subject to India's core interests. India was seen as having killed

Nepal's innocence in its quest for a democracy like India and taking advantage of Nepal's weaknesses to impose its own security priorities.

An important lesson from the Tribhuvan years remained unlearnt by India for several decades thereafter, resulting in serious misunderstanding and tensions with Nepal as a nation apart from the Palace, and for which both countries would pay a heavy price. The lesson here was that with a small and vulnerable neighbour, the style of diplomacy matters as much as the substance; that even when Nepal appears to be seeking India's advice and support, it is not necessary to broadcast it so loudly that it echoes and re-echoes in this Mountain Kingdom, and can be magnified by a handful of people who are keen to fuel suspicion and misunderstanding about Indian intentions. From a high profile requested advisory role to a judgmental, prescriptive, intrusive one was a small invisible step for vested interests to achieve.

* * *

The Mahendra Years

Despite political instability, the whispering campaign against India and rising dissatisfaction among the Kathmandu Valley elite, the reality was that by 1954, Nepal's transformation from a backward, isolated, exploited population to a people aware of their rights had begun, and democratic aspirations were taking root. Disempowered but still powerful members of the Rana clan had the ear of King Mahendra, who was encouraged to affect a Palace coup in 1960, dismissing Prime Minister Koirala and arresting prominent leaders.

B.P. Koirala was sworn in as PM in May 1959. In a matter of months, King Mahendra dismissed him in November 1960, and imposed a party-less Panchayat system directly under himself. Nehru had not been comfortable with a bold and independent-minded B.P. Koirala, albeit friendly towards him and India as PM, but was shocked at the move against democracy. Yet such was his need for King Mahendra's cooperation with the Chinese threat looming larger than ever, that he had to restrain his natural urge to put full pressure on the King to reverse his steps. The King exploited the China opportunity to the full to counter India's overwhelming influence and presence and moderate Nehru's enthusiasm for democracy in Nepal. King Mahendra crossed several red lines on China, inviting it to build a road between Kathmandu and Kodari, and take on a security role in violation of the 1950 Treaty. India's support for democratic forces was in direct proportion to Mahendra's wooing of China, and vice versa.

India's tensions with China and the humiliation Nehru suffered in the 1962 conflict had a huge impact. On the one hand, it damaged India's image and encouraged Palace loyalists to advise the King to ignore Indian sensitivities on China. On the other hand, India felt obliged to disappoint old friends struggling for the restoration of some form of democracy with Indian support. Tactical U-turns and transactional compromises would leave lasting perception—in Kathmandu of Indian inconsistency, unreliability and insincerity—and in Delhi, of Nepal's ingratitude, deviousness, and how easily it could be led astray. King Mahendra quickly built up a reputation of being totally anti-India. Yet, several Nepalese political stalwarts told me that this was not true, that he was opposed to democracy and was sensitive to Indian interests. India's former Foreign Secretary and Ambassador to Nepal M.K. Rasgotra, who had served in the embassy during and after the Mahendra years, had, in fact, told me once that King

Mahendra would have been the most pro-India monarch in Nepal if only 'India had treated him better'.

It was also the assessment of many that King Mahendra, while unhesitatingly playing the China card, was sensitive to India's China concerns and willing to extend core cooperation to the extent possible. According to those who were part of King Mahendra's government, like Rishikesh Shah, the border dispute between India and Nepal in the Kalapani area owes much to King Mahendra's permissive attitude to India's need for a vantage checkpoint in an important area. India of course disputes this version. Interestingly, the Palace did not raise the Kalapani issue despite King Mahendra's anti-India reputation. The border problem will be discussed in a separate section of this book.

* * *

Birendra: The Tense Years (1972 to 1995)

When King Birendra succeeded his father Mahendra upon the latter's death in 1972, he was barely twenty-six years old. His exposure to India from early childhood was a bit unusual, to say the least.

As a toddler, he was among most of the family members of the royal family when his grandfather King Tribhuvan was wrist away in a cloak-and-dagger operation from an ostensible picnic outing to the Indian embassy and thence to Delhi. There, at Hyderabad House, Jawaharlal Nehru tried to teach him how to play cricket—a game he intensely disliked—at the urging of his grandfather. His father, then Crown Prince Mahendra, who loved Indian classical music, also tried very hard to get Birendra to appreciate it—Birendra hated to attend these performances, as he told me himself (although I must add that he made it a point to accept invitations I sent him for concerts by Pt Ravi Shankar, Dr L. Subramaniam, Ustad Amjad Ali Khan, Pt Jasraj and others). Thereafter, in his formative years, he saw the tensions between India and his father, now King Mahendra, the three-way tussle between the Palace, multiparty democracy and India, the rise of an assertive China, the humiliation of India in the Sino-Indian conflict of 1962. Then came the 1971 war between India and Pakistan in which Pakistan was defeated, partitioned and forced to surrender 90,000 of its troops. Indira Gandhi seemed to tower over the entire South Asian subcontinent.

The advice that young Birendra received from Palace loyalists when he became King was that he must stand up to India and, ignoring the reality of Nepal's needs from India and its Treaty obligations, assert Nepal's independence and obtain international support for non-interference in its internal affairs (the subtext being its right to import military supplies from China and end India's support for democracy.) There was a frosty first meeting between Birendra and Indira Gandhi at the Algiers Non-Aligned Summit in 1973 when there was apparently a protocol mix up because Gandhi was led to believe that King Birendra would call on her and then later informed by Nepalese protocol that this was not possible since the King was a Head of State and Mrs Gandhi a mere Head of Government. To add salt to the wound, Birendra chose the summit podium to float his first ideas on Nepal being declared internationally as a Zone of Peace.

As it happened, in neighbouring Sikkim, the Chogyal was having ideas about inching from the status of a protectorate of India to that of an independent nation like Bhutan with membership in the UN.

Unlike her father, Indira Gandhi had very clear ideas about dealing with challenges like these. She would take decisive steps as necessary to safeguard India's national interest and security. Rajiv

Gandhi, who succeeded her, was even more impatient in dealing with problems in neighbouring countries. These were the years that were packed with misunderstandings, tensions, reactions and overreactions, perceptions or misperceptions which would have a long life and which India for some reason could not address in time. One set related to the inability or unwillingness of senior bureaucrats to suggest alternative, more moderate options to their political bosses. This was at times when there was a strong centralized power structure in New Delhi, for example, during the Indira Gandhi or Rajiv Gandhi years.

King Birendra chose to invite the Chogyal of Sikkim to his coronation on 24 February 1975.

There were reports that at the coronation, the Chogyal had shared his concern that action to dislodge him by India was imminent and he had sought advice regarding his personal safety from the King as well as from the Chinese and Pakistani dignitaries attending. (Sikkim, after a mass agitation since 1973 against the Chogyal's feudal rule, had already opted to be an associate state of India). On 9 April 1975, the Sikkim Parliament announced that the Chogyal was no longer the King and that Sikkim would become part of India, and within a few days, on 16 May 1975 to be precise, the Indian Parliament officially accorded it the status of the twenty-second state of India.

In his coronation speech, King Birendra also formally launched his proposal that Nepal be declared a Zone of Peace with international support and guarantees.

This was received as a double provocation for Mrs Gandhi.

The Zone of Peace proposal was followed up with an all-out diplomatic offensive by Nepal around the world to harness support and isolate India, which was what actually happened.

The fact that India had in the meantime become an undeclared nuclear weapons power by exploding its first 'peaceful' nuclear device in 1974 did not hamper the King's efforts to 'stand up' to India.

When Sikkim decided to become part of India, there was an international outcry, and anti-India rioting in Kathmandu. Seeing Mrs Gandhi's mood, officials, including Foreign Secretary Kewal Singh and India's ambassador to Nepal, M.K. Rasgotra, who were otherwise inclined to calm the King's security fears and normalize relations with the Palace, decided to take a hardline approach, accuse the Palace of instigating the riots, threaten to review ties and bring King Birendra to his knees for daring to take on India. This had the desired effect of stern measures by the authorities to prevent disturbances, but at the same time fuelled fears in Kathmandu about Indian designs to 'Sikkimize' Nepal.

Interestingly, when Indira Gandhi lost the elections and Morarji Desai became PM, his Foreign Minister and future PM Atal Bihari Vajpayee visited Nepal and the atmosphere of bilateral ties suddenly turned cordial. Vajpayee even publicly refused to be dismissive about the Zone of Peace proposal, saying that it would be considered by the new government.

When Rajiv Gandhi took over as prime minister after Mrs Gandhi's assassination in 1984, relations between India and Nepal took a turn for the worse. According to the Indian version, the personal chemistry between Rajiv and King Birendra was awful, and the latter was repeatedly warned to respect Indian sensitivities, especially concerning China, 'or else . . .' King Birendra would appear to be momentarily responsive to these sledgehammer tactics, but they actually had the effect of strengthening and emboldening the anti-India interests among the elite, and mutual trust dwindled to rock bottom levels.

But both Birendra and Gyanendra scoffed at suggestions that relations at the personal level with the two leaders had anything to do with bilateral relations when they nosedived. King Birendra described Indira Gandhi as the one towering leader South Asia had produced, of the stature of General Charles de Gaulle. He had personally requested her to come to Nepal after she lost the post-Emergency elections. As for Rajiv, they had nothing but praise for his charisma and futuristic vision. Gyanendra said Rajiv would honour him by driving him around personally in his car when he visited Delhi. They blamed advisers on both sides for creating mistrust and misunderstandings and leaking mischievous false stories to the Press, such as the sensational one about Queen Aishwarya's secret plot to assassinate Rajiv Gandhi.

By 1985, it was clear to India that Nepal had no intention of respecting its security obligations vis-a-vis India either in letter or in spirit. During 1988–89, a number of agreements, including the crucial one on trade transit and purchase, had expired. Nepal demanded separate transit and trade treaties with India, which was not accepted.

Since 1979, King Birendra had been facing popular protests, particularly from students, on the absence of democracy and he finally called a referendum of sorts, obtaining a majority to support his party-less framework.

By 1989, the economic woes of the people, openly supported by prominent Indian leaders, had gathered strength. An opportunity to defang the monarchy emerged when relations of the Palace with India plummeted alongside the escalating agitation by a long-suffering, politically aware population.

In March 1989, the Indian government closed border entry points to Nepal creating acute shortages, including in Kathmandu.

Once the Transit and Trade Treaty expired, there were serious shortages including essential commodities like petroleum, and China came to Nepal's rescue.

G.S. Iyer writes in *Four Crises* that on 31 March 1990, at the height of the people's movement in Nepal, Foreign Secretary

S.K. Singh was in Kathmandu although the PM and his government had just resigned and there was no question of any substantive discussion. Singh was apparently armed with a proposal to help save the regime. According to Nepali versions, had King Birendra agreed to the proposal, not only would Nepal have to hand over all its hydro-resources to India, but it would also come under India's security apparatus. In effect, Nepal would have been reduced to the status of Bhutan. Singh's counterpart asked him to return the next morning. Although there was nothing to discuss except the weather, so that the press would not speculate too much on the poor state of India–Nepal relations because there was no second session!

Another bizarre instance narrated by Iyer relates to the briefing he received from the foreign secretary on the eve of his departure for Kathmandu as chargé d'affaires designate. Singh told him that the new ambassador (Gen. Sinha, recently retired from the Indian Army) appointed by Prime Minister V.P. Singh, who had just replaced Rajiv Gandhi after winning in the general elections, would be arriving soon in Kathmandu. The peculiar advice given to Iyer was that the new government would take time to understand the Nepal situation, and Iyer as the second-in-command in the embassy should take instructions only from the ministry and not from his ambassador acting on instructions from the new government! Thus there was a peculiar situation in which even as Iyer was boycotting the new government appointed by King Birendra, Ambassador Sinha was sending congratulations to the Nepali foreign minister, calling on him and even advising the leaders of the agitation against the King and his government to include Palace loyalists in any new democratic government coming into being after a successful agitation!

As Iyer rightly observed, this phenomenon of 'mixed signals' was a recurring pattern in previous crisis situations between India and Nepal also. In the years to come, during the Gyanendra period after he had imposed his direct rule by dismissing the elected government and arresting political leaders, the Ministry of External Affairs spokesman was still talking about India adhering to the twin-pillar policy of supporting the monarchy and multiparty democracy while the foreign secretary and the secretary of R&AW were trying to persuade a collection of political representatives from Nepal to come together with the Maoists and dislodge the institution of monarchy once and for all.

Many in Nepal believe that India has played a similar role in trying to extract strategic concessions from any Nepalese regime in trouble with its back to the wall.

In February 1990, the Nepali Congress led all political parties and masses of agitating civil society people in a peaceful peoples' revolution, a Jana Andolan. The non-radical communists united under the banner of the United Left Front (ULF) and joined the Jana Andolan under the leadership of Ganesh Man Singh. The mass agitation was launched. It was openly backed by Indian political parties across the spectrum, and the encouragement by visiting political leaders like Chandrashekhar had an electrifying impact. The support of several Western democracies also boosted the morale of protesters. China as usual was silent, continuing with its traditional backing of the monarchy.

The pressure was too much for King Birendra, who gave in despite pressure from his family, especially Queen Aishwarya and Prince Gyanendra, not to compromise on the core issue of absolute monarchy.

Nepal's identity as a Hindu Kingdom was retained. Fundamental rights were guaranteed. Only the radical Left forces rejected the Constitution. Some of its adherents would go underground and re-emerge as the Maoist movement.

Millions of dollars' worth of arms supplies were delivered through the Lhasa–Kathmandu highway in June 1989. China had now become a strategic partner, a relationship which would only grow stronger with time, and impossible to reverse, given Chinese capacity, resources and potential gains for the beneficiaries. On 16 April 1990, King Birendra, through a royal proclamation, dissolved the National Panchayat and its lower bodies. Later, he invited Ganesh Man Singh to form and lead a new government. Ganesh Man Singh declined ostensibly on grounds of poor health, but actually because he was getting increasingly disillusioned by the attitude of political leaders hungry for power at any cost. On his recommendation, Krishna Prasad Bhattarai or 'Kishunji' was appointed as PM, with a cabinet made up of representatives from across the political spectrum. Yet, a Constitution was finalized with speed, with help from the British government, limiting the monarchy's role to a constitutional one but with retention of control over RNA, a general election was conducted, and multiparty democracy fully restored.

Bhattarai, a veteran supporter of India's freedom struggle, paid an official visit to India soon after taking charge, assuring Indian leaders that all policies of King Birendra which were considered unfriendly to India would be reversed, and that delivery of the remaining arms supplies from China would be cancelled. However, G.S. Iyer writes in *Four Crises*, on returning to Nepal, no cancellation orders were issued and the arms supply contract was fully respected by the new government.

So much for pro- and anti-India figures on Nepal's political stage!

In the 1991 elections, the Nepali Congress won a majority and Girija Prasad Koirala, an old friend of India, was elected prime minister. But the Nepali Congress was not united, the main Opposition, CPN (UML), was alert to the government's proximity to Indian interests, and the Palace was sulking. Kishunji would share with me later that India was too complacent, ignored the divisions within the NC, did not consider the need to extend small courtesies to the King as though Birendra was no longer relevant as he was a ceremonial figure, and annoyed the UML by appearing to be so partial towards Koirala that during the 1994 election campaign, Adhikari actually asked for his recall. Once again, perceptions were not fair to reality, but they were there and forward trends resulting from some excellent initiatives taken by Koirala and Indian PM Narasimha Rao were temporarily reversed.

* * *

The Summing Up

Over the past seven decades, thanks largely due to Nepalese failings but in part also due to India's mismanagement of ties with Nepal, what the British initiated two centuries ago through their unequal treaty relationship and sly propaganda against India has over the years matured into ever deepening and widening mistrust between the two nations.

In the final years, mainstream political parties and their leaders, including Girija Prasad Koirala, Madhav Kumar Nepal and K.P. Oli, were hesitant to agree with India on conceding to core Maoist demands as a precondition for ending the insurgency. There was a certain haste with which a few bureaucrats pushed Nepal's political parties to end the monarchy, going to the extent of ignoring or marginalizing anyone who was counselling patience or a more balanced approach which could have temporarily maintained the institution under a Regency arrangement without Gyanendra—including Foreign Minister K. Natwar Singh and senior knowledgeable figures like Karan Singh, the Indian Army Chief and Intelligence Bureau.

India's tryst with the monarchy in Nepal ended not only with the institution of monarchy being abolished, but Nepal losing its identity as a Hindu nation as well. The abrupt transformation of Nepal to a federal secular republic without any credible institutional underpinning is turning out, at least in the medium term, to be something of a self-goal for all those who worked discreetly for ending the Maoist insurgency quickly and at any cost, including and in particular, India. Granted that the monarchy had more often than not been a thorn in India's side. But as one former foreign secretary who knows Nepal well said in an informal think tank discussion after Nepal had published its new map, even in the most trying times, you could at least send a (veteran Indian diplomat) Ronen Sen as Rajiv did, to warn King Birendra of the consequences of his China-linked adventures. Who do you talk to when there is a free-for-all democracy, obsessed with power and vote bank politics, riding on a frenzy of anti-Indianism, and there is no institution, including the Presidency, with even the pretence of being apolitical; and an entire Parliament ratifies a new map with Indian territories included inside Nepal?

As King Birendra's last few years showed, it was possible to transform relations from poor to cordial simply by showing a consistent attachment to non-intervention, impartiality and goodwill towards all political players and sensitivity to the interests of the people of Nepal. One must hope that this kind of option will be available as Nepal's democracy matures and gains strength. Recent trends in bilateral interactions would seem to encourage such hopes.

The decision to transform Nepal into a 'secular republic' was also one which clearly was a concession to the Maoists to end the stalemate after the Comprehensive Peace Agreement. The question that was asked in the street was: how could a 350-member Assembly decide on a question like this? Neither political leaders in the mainstream parties nor Indian leaders were in favour of this decision. There was popular agitation in the Tarai region and consternation among India's spiritual leaders, many of whom had a huge following in Nepal. Journalist Mark Tully's comment comes to mind about the decision at India's independence to become a 'secular nation', which he called the Congress Party's single biggest mistake. Secularism, according to him, connotes a denial of religion and hostility towards all religions, which is risky in the region's countries like India (and Nepal) since it opens up space for a backlash in terms of intolerant and extreme forms of religion. One would hope that the current trends in Nepal where there is conspicuous display of Hindu religiosity even among Maoist leaders, who used to condemn any form of religious worship earlier, will not end in intolerance and disharmony in a traditionally tolerant nation.

New Delhi framed the peace deal and acted as its de facto guarantor, pressing all parties to comply with its terms, exerting strong diplomatic pressure whenever it was in danger of getting stalled, persuading the international community not to treat the Maoists as pariahs to be kept out because of the violence they had been guilty of. But the moment the Maoists, to India's shock and dismay, emerged with a strong showing in the elections, formed the government, and sent out friendship signals to China, India had a change of heart and course. In the words of the Brussels-based International Crisis Group, India 'unbalanced the peace equation without offering any alternative'.

However, the subsequent evolution of Nepal's political environment has had its consoling features. The Maoists had a radical agenda for change which initially was not taken seriously. The political parties failed miserably in either improving governance or addressing the deep socio-economic fault lines resulting from years of self-serving feudal dispensations or even dealing with the Maoist phenomenon as a law-and-order problem. The Palace turned its back on the rapid Maoist expansion hoping it would provide the pretext for its own comeback to absolute rule. India's long-term obliviousness to the Maoist headquarters and presence of its top leaders in jungles on its soil, their comings and goings across the open border, was puzzling but probably an accurate reflection of the poor quality of intelligence concerning Nepal.

Over the years, the Maoists have had several opportunities to taste power through elections, and have become increasingly pragmatic. There is progressively less ideological posturing on issues relating to India, the economy, or in foreign policy matters. In the process, they have lost much of the credibility and appeal they used to enjoy, especially with the vast majority of Nepal's populace which is poor and marginalized from the power structure. There is disillusionment with all political parties including the Maoists, as voting patterns in successive elections have shown.

The India–Nepal relationship is routinely described as 'unique'. Not so long ago, it was described as 'special', a term occasionally still used by the Indian side, although almost never by the Nepalese.

In my very first meeting with Prime Minister Manmohan Adhikari at the beginning of my ambassadorial tenure in the spring of 1995, Adhikari wanted to assure me that he was not anti-India, was keen to work with me to expand cooperation in every field but admitted that he was allergic to the phrase 'special relationship' as it had certain connotations. I was bold enough to suggest that although I was new to Nepal, my impression was that the relationship was indeed 'special' for people on both sides of the border in a very real, human, familial sense, irrespective of how it was managed in the hands of politicians and diplomats.

Much has happened since that conversation. Nepal as a country has been transformed, and India has continued to grow to its present stature as a major player on the global stage. But the reality is that the special relationship between India and Nepal is very much intact. It has nothing to do with banquet speeches, joint declarations, the 1950 Treaty or the ups and downs of the political relationship. It is simply a living reality. It is also a great basis for building a bright future for people on both sides of the border, if only influential sections of Nepal's political and intellectual elite do not try to live in denial of it, and India realizes the importance of nurturing it on a daily basis.

Will people-to-people relations, cultural and familial links, now come under stress?

Anti-Indianism today has the potential to derail the bilateral relationship in a much more serious way than before. And there is a possibility of the cultural underpinning, the people-to-people factor which has been a silent pillar of strength whenever there were serious hiccups in the past, increasingly losing its effectiveness in curbing it.

BJP leader Ram Madhav suggests (by implication in an article) that Narendra Modi's 'neighbourhood first' policy and India's soft power—culture, religion, family linkages—carry diminishing appeal for neighbours who would rather strengthen their uniqueness than commonalities shared with India. 'We can grow together,' is a better plank to sell to neighbours, he suggests. This is a relevant thought if we are serious about repairing and restoring India–Nepal ties.

India has no choice but to deal with the situation in Nepal as it evolves, as best as it can. It cannot afford to live in the past, but can, indeed must, learn from it. The key lessons are that the style of diplomacy matters as much as the substance; that when Nepal is in difficulty, the best course is to empathize rather than take advantage of its weakness; that mixed signals, bureaucratic turf wars, and lack of transparency and consensus can be a serious brake to steady growth; that pragmatism and economic cooperation should be in the driving seat along with normal security concerns; that problems should not be allowed to fester until they become deadly irritants, and that perceptions that India does not believe in equality, respect and sensitivity in relations with its neighbours must be taken seriously and addressed in time.

Nepal, too, is in the same boat in that respect. It needs to pay attention to India's intentions; to its own advantages from agreements like the 1950 Treaty; to the fact that even before and well after I.K. Gujral invented his famous doctrine, India does not fashion its policies on the basis of reciprocity expectations but some reciprocity in terms of respect for vital interests is a necessary underpinning for sound relationships; that unless it addresses its serious internal challenges like criminalization of politics, corruption, politicization, lack of accountability, the chances of becoming a failed State are far from negligible; that playing the China card is a self-defeating long-term strategy; that it just has to ride on India's shoulders to reach unprecedented economic heights in a foreseeable time frame.

And both countries need to accept their special relationship as a real asset and sound foundation for model ties; recognize technology and hydropower as game changers for inclusive prosperity and jointly devise and speedily implement futuristic projects; prioritize human security over transactional politics; and fashion a new twin-pillar policy of strengthening democratic as well as civil society engagement for regional good.

SECTION II

Transitions of the Himalayan Kind

K.V. RAJAN AND ATUL K. THAKUR

Nepal's Search for Democracy

An objective understanding of contemporary Nepal's trials, tribulations and challenges requires that we shed oversimplification and romanticization, which only magnify the sense of shock and surprise at the twists and turns in its history and complicate the search for road maps to a better future.

Nepal always had a strict hierarchical structure before the first rumblings of democracy were felt. First it was the Shah dynasty, then the Ranas (who became the de facto rulers after 1846). They, along with a handful of upper-caste Hindu families, exercised total power. There was no question of giving space to the vast majority of people or to the many ethnic, linguistic, religious and cultural identities that constituted the Nepali nation. The Rana autocracy lasted for 104 years during which the monarchy existed only in name. Nepal was isolated from the rest of the world, knew no development, and the bulk of the population was completely marginalized until the Indian freedom struggle against the British began to make its impact felt. Nepal's leaders living in exile in India participated in that struggle and drew inspiration from it to light the fire of opposition against the Rana regime. Under Nehru's supervision and with an eye on the increasingly assertive communist regime in China, the Ranas were forced to give back power in 1951, but not before a Treaty of Peace and Friendship on the lines of the Sugauli Treaty was signed, giving Nepal economic concessions against overriding security powers for the government of independent India. From 1951 to 1960, Nepal basked in its first experience of multiparty democracy. It was also the time when the first tensions between the monarchy and democracy surfaced, as also between the monarchy and India, after the death of King Tribhuvan in 1955.

Nepal's search for democracy since then has been marked by undeniable progress towards credible democratic processes and awareness which are irreversible. It is also true that Nepal has shown remarkable resilience in recovering from serious setbacks and overcoming some major challenges. It is important that this is not overlooked when its young democracy's serious shortcomings and weaknesses are discussed.

These have a lot to do with leadership and institutional constraints, the circumstances in which the stirrings of democratic aspirations have taken place or sought to be suppressed—social, economic and political—the limitations on India's liberal urge to expedite democratic transitions in Nepal—because of the China factor, the style more often than substance of Indian diplomacy, and something in the psyche of Nepal's political elite which yearns for, but also deeply resents, India's involvement in Nepal's democracy story.

The latter is closely interwoven with the story of India's relations with successive Kings of Nepal, all of whom with the exception of Tribhuvan and Birendra during his last few years were considered to be anti-India. What tends to be overlooked is that each King's attitude towards India was a direct function of the degree to which India was willing to support democracy in Nepal, which all Kings including Tribhuvan considered to be in opposition to the monarchy's interests. Whenever India's relations with China were tense, India found it expedient to dilute its commitment to strengthen democratic forces, and its relations with the King of the day were consequently warm. The question which many Nepalese, and indeed many Indians including eminent thought leaders, like former foreign secretary Jagat Mehta, asked was: if India can take in its stride dictatorships in so many countries far and near, why did it find it necessary to take an intrusive interest in defanging Nepal's monarchy every now and then, knowing that this would only fuel anti-India sentiments and encourage the monarchy to play the China card? And was it surprising to see even so-called pro-India democratic leaders falter in their support for India if the latter could not be depended upon in times of need? To this there has never been a clear answer.

* * *

Bridging the Trust Deficit

It is an undeniable fact that even after seven decades since India gained independence, the two countries have still not succeeded in forging ties of mutual trust and understanding that people on both sides of the border deserve. A central reason being that despite the huge assets they enjoy by way of linkages of history, geography, religion and culture, and at people-to-people level, there is a certain absence of mutual empathy: India is unable to fully understand Nepal's yearning for equality and sovereign space, and Nepal, in turn, is unable to understand India's geopolitical compulsions.

There is a repetitive pattern in the story of avoidable mishaps, misunderstandings and downturns in relations; and why Nepal, in the recent words of a reputed Nepalese analyst, 'has evolved as a sullen neighbour when it should be the friendliest of all'. India has tried every trick in the diplomatic book, with the best of intentions and with a focus on Nepal's long-term interests even as it sought to promote its own. Every Indian prime minister—Jawaharlal Nehru, Indira Gandhi, Rajiv Gandhi, Chandra Shekhar, P.V. Narasimha Rao, I.K. Gujral, Atal Bihari Vajpayee, Manmohan Singh, right up to Narendra Modi—has paid special attention to Nepalese needs and expectations in the hope of steadying ties on a sustainable basis, but as the French would say, '*plus ca change, plus c'est la même chose* [the more that changes, the more it's the same thing].' The relationship continues to be marked by uncertainty and shortcomings.

A long-standing Kathmandu perception about India is that it is constantly engaging in macro and micro management of Nepal's internal affairs. India's response to this is that Nepalese tend to suspect the worst about India's intentions, and blame India when things go wrong. Ignoring India's generosity, the fact that India has Nepal's interests always at heart and that its advice or involvement, when it takes place, has almost always been in response to a felt and locally expressed need. The truth is that perceptions rather than hard reality have had a disproportionate influence on the evolution of India–Nepal relations. If India is to be faulted, it is for not addressing Nepal's misperceptions about its policies, actions or intentions seriously enough and in time.

Since 1947, successive Indian governments have generally followed well-intentioned and generous policies towards Nepal. Why then the outbursts of anti-Indian sentiment which are a regular feature of the India–Nepal landscape? Why does the 'roti–beti' relationship which Indian leaders love to extol (as Defence

Minister Rajnath Singh did only recently at the height of the controversy over Kalapani) seem to count for so little when there is any kind of a political problem? More importantly, is anti-Indianism taking new dimensions which should necessitate a review of the India–Nepal relationship itself?

Nepal's psyche of a small, landlocked nation—excessively dependent on India, and whose identity is so much in the shadow of India's cultural influence that it has the feeling that it is 'India-locked' and therefore has to constantly assert itself vis-à-vis India—has always offered fertile soil for provoking anti-Indian sentiment.

Part of the explanation for this sentiment also lies in the kind of unequal relationship which was sought to be fashioned during the East India and British Indian government years, with the small ruling elite of the day in Kathmandu basically ensuring that the core interests of the former were respected against protection from any domestic forces for democracy and development. This arrangement worked as long as Nepal was isolated from the world and ruled in autocratic fashion by a handful of influential elite families. It cannot possibly sit comfortably with the multiparty republican set-up of today's Nepal.

Incidentally, the British also constantly dinned into influential Nepalese ears in every way available to them that 'Indians were never to be trusted'. According to Nepalese political veterans, some of whom have passed on, several decades of brainwashing created a sense of insecurity about India, which continues to influence political attitudes to this day. Until recently, anti-Indianism in Nepal was limited in space and depth. It was to be found mainly in the Kathmandu Valley, where a pampered, over-politicized elite has for long specialized in anti-Indian activity whenever an opportunity arose. More often than not, such activity was born of frustration on the part of one or other political group in Nepal, because it expected India's support in order to come to power (or stay in government) in the usually unstable political environment in Kathmandu—and New Delhi's inability or unwillingness to extend such support.

In recent years, however, anti-Indianism has become more strident, more frequent, with a longer 'shelf life', and more effective in acting as a serious speed breaker in efforts to enable the relationship to achieve its true potential. A few factors have converged to make this happen. One was the fall of the monarchy which, despite its anti-India credentials, could act as an institutional moderating influence once New Delhi drew the red lines for any adventure contemplated. When India invited King Birendra to be chief guest on Republic Day in 1999, despite the many tensions in the past over issues like Nepal's Zone of Peace proposal, it was a recognition of this fact.

The rise of the radical Left and mainstreaming of the Maoists in the power structure was another factor. The third is the China factor, the assertion of interest by China in Nepal going far beyond a legitimate interest in promoting bilateral relations. The fourth is India's frequent misreading of Nepal's determination to do its own thing, its penchant for publicly advising Nepal in its internal affairs and thinly disguised expectation that that advice was to be heeded, or else . . .

The communication style has also changed over the years at the political-diplomatic level. In essence, earlier India was more accommodating when Nepali political leaders pleaded domestic compulsions when asserting nationalistic positions which were not in tune with Delhi's views as long as core interests were respected. In recent times, this has been replaced with a realpolitik, a no-nonsense approach, which basically says 'do as you please' but places a price tag for such aberrations. This policy evolution was probably overdue, but Nepal has not been able to digest it—the tendency in Kathmandu is to take reckless risks for short-term political gain in an '*après moi, le deluge* [after me, the deluge]' mode. The problem of perceptions on both sides is serious. For too many people in India, Nepal is unappreciative, anti-India and pro-China, ever a foreign policy migraine. For too many in Nepal, India comes across as insincere, inconsistent, insensitive and usually dismissive of Nepal's point of view; over seven decades, every government in India has been responsible for creating serious misunderstandings and suspicions about its true intentions.

Conclusion? Over the past seven decades, thanks largely due to Nepalese failings but in part also due to India's mismanagement of ties with Nepal, what the British initiated two centuries ago through their unequal treaty relationship and sly propaganda against India has over the years matured into ever deepening and widening mistrust between the two nations. The then prime minister of Nepal K.P. Sharma Oli's success in challenging India's territorial boundary through the 'new official Nepal map' and rushing through a constitutional amendment to give parliamentary approval to this, immensely complicated the atmosphere at the political level. But there are other irritants, too, waiting to come alive when the time comes.

As India prepares for anti-Indianism 2.0, it will eventually have to also address the deeper Nepalese yearning—for a sense of equality and mutual respect. Showing willingness to restructure the bilateral relationship so that British Indian legacies are buried forever, would be the surest way to restore and sustain a positive direction in bilateral ties. The hope has to be that a critical mass of Nepal's political establishment will realize that ultra-nationalism cannot be a substitute for better governance—before it is too late.

* * *

Power Struggles of the Past

As per the Government of Nepal's official record, an ambitious Gorkha King named Prithvi Narayan Shah embarked on a conquering mission that led to the defeat of all the kingdoms in the Valley (including Kirtipur which was an independent state) by 1769. Instead of annexing the newly acquired states to his kingdom of Gorkha, Prithvi Narayan decided to move his capital to Kathmandu, establishing the Shah dynasty which ruled unified Nepal from 1769 to 2008. A well-known and important fact is that history of the Gorkha State goes back to 1559 when Dravya Shah established a kingdom in an area chiefly inhabited by Magars. During the seventeenth and early eighteenth centuries, Gorkha continued a slow expansion, conquering various states while forging alliances with others. Prithvi Narayan Shah dedicated himself at an early age to the conquest of the Kathmandu Valley. Recognizing the threat of the British Raj in India, he dismissed European missionaries from the country and for more than a century, Nepal remained in isolation.

Baburam Acharya's book *The Blood-Stained Throne* is a translation of *Aba Yasto Kahilyai Nahos*, a compilation of historical essays that recount some of the bloody battles for power in tumultuous period—a phase that spanned more than one hundred years. Acharya writes: 'Nepal, the land of Buddhism and misty mountains, is not a nation whose history one would expect to be filled with blood. And yet, the struggle to gain and keep control over the mountain kingdom is one marked by a long history of violence and murder.'*

---

* Baburam Acharya (author) and Madhav Acharya (translator), *The Blood-Stained Throne: Struggle for Power in Nepal* (1775–1916) (Penguin India, 2013).

During the mid-nineteenth-century, Jung Bahadur Rana became Nepal's first prime minister to wield absolute power relegating the Shah King to mere figureheads. He started a hereditary reign of the Rana prime ministers that lasted for 104 years. The Ranas were overthrown in a pro-democracy movement of the early 1950s with support from the-then monarch of Nepal, King Tribhuvan Shah. Soon after the overthrow of the Ranas, King Tribhuvan was reinstated as Head of the State. In early 1959, Tribhuvan's son and successor King Mahendra Shah promulgated a new Constitution, and the first democratic elections for a national assembly were held. The Nepali Congress Party was victorious and their leader, Bishweshwar Prasad Koirala formed a government and served as prime minister. But by 1960, King Mahendra had changed his mind and dissolved Parliament, dismissing the first democratic government.

The quest for democracy was suppressed but not over. After many years of struggle, when the political parties were banned, they finally mustered enough courage to start a people's movement in 1990. Paving the way for democracy, the-then King Birendra Shah accepted constitutional reforms and established a multiparty Parliament with the King as the Head of State and an executive prime minister. In May 1991, Nepal held its first parliamentary elections and before that an interim government was formed under the leadership of Nepali Congress leader and Prime Minister Krishna Prasad Bhattarai.

While the democratic upheavals were on, in February 1996, the Maoist parties declared a People's War against the monarchy and the elected government. Nepal entered a very difficult situation with a fledgling democracy, challenged monarchy and unprecedented challenges coming with insurgency.

Then on 1 June 2001, a horrific tragedy wiped out the entire royal family including King Birendra and Queen

Aishwarya with many of their closest relatives. With only King Birendra's brother, Gyanendra, and his family surviving, he was crowned the King. King Gyanendra Shah abided by the elected government for some time and then dismissed the elected Parliament to wield absolute power. In April 2006, another people's movement was launched jointly by the democratic parties focusing on Kathmandu which led to a nineteen-day curfew. Eventually, King Gyanendra relinquished his power and reinstated Parliament. On 21 November 2006, Prime Minister Girija Prasad Koirala and Maoist chairman Prachanda signed the Comprehensive Peace Agreement 2006, committing to democracy and peace for the progress of the country and its people.

A Constituent Assembly (CA) election was held on 10 April 2008. On 28 May 2008, the newly elected CA declared Nepal a Federal Democratic Republic, abolishing the 240-year-old monarchy and status as the lone 'Hindu nation' in the world. Henceforth, a president as Head of State and a prime minister as Head of the Government constitute the top two power centres in Nepal.

The CA made some progress to accomplish the mandate of writing a new democratic Constitution of Nepal during its first four-year term with carrying an exercise in that direction, including collection of public inputs on the contents of the new and intense deliberations in the Assembly. However, due to political disagreements on some contentious issues like federal provinces and form of government, the first CA could not accomplish the historic task and there was the natural termination of its mandate in 2012. The election of CA-II was held in November 2013 and in its first meeting, leaders of political parties set the timeline of one year to complete the task of writing the new Constitution.

In April 2015, a devastating earthquake of 7.8 magnitude hit Nepal, followed by several powerful aftershocks, causing loss of life, infrastructure and property on an unimaginable scale. Most mid-hill districts of Nepal including Kathmandu Valley saw massive devastation. This terrible experience created a sense of urgency among political parties to expedite the Constitution writing so that a political process would come to a meaningful conclusion and the country could divert all its focus on post-disaster reconstruction. After weeks of zeroing in on the most contentious issues, political parties sorted them out paving the way to finalize the Constitution. The new Constitution of Nepal was promulgated through an overwhelming majority of the votes of CA members on 20 September 2015. Of late, a Constitution made through an elected representative body had been realized. As per the provisions of the new Constitution, elections of the new President, prime ministers and some other State positions have been successfully held. Among the key achievements of the Constitution, they deserve a prominent mention.

* * *

Chronology of the Democratic Transition

The year 1951 marked the end of the 104-year-old autocratic Rana oligarchy. King Tribhuvan Shah, the Nepali Congress and Rana rulers made the consensus for a compromise in Delhi, mediated by India's first prime minister, Jawaharlal Nehru. With the result of it, it was agreed to hold elections for a Constituent Assembly. It took time, and in 1959, the parliamentary elections were held in Nepal under a Constitution granted by King Mahendra Shah. The Nepali Congress fought and won two-third majority and B.P.

Koirala became the first prime minister of a democratically elected government in Nepal. However, on 15 December 1960, King Mahendra dismissed the government.

The move was aimed to create the bedrock of an alternative with royal supremacy and that was known as the 'Panchayat System'. In 1962, King Mahendra promulgated a Constitution that institutionalized a party-less framework and centralized power in the Royal Palace. For sure, the party-less framework was a big jolt to the emerging prospects of a multiparty system. At the crossroads, a natural course of democratic transition was altered. In 1972, King Mahendra died at the young age of fifty-two and his elder son and Crown Prince Birendra Shah took over as the new King of Nepal. Around 1979–80, much influenced by the student protests across the world against the old school of governance, the student protests in Nepal had forced King Birendra to call for a referendum on the nature of the polity.

The simmering protests finally turned into a people's movement in 1990, popularly known as the Jana Andolan, and led to the restoration of multiparty democracy. While the new Constitution limited the monarchy's role, it retained Nepal as a Hindu Kingdom, paved the way for a parliamentary system, and granted fundamental rights on the line of the movement's key demands. Radical Left forces including the CPN (UML) and Maoists rejected the Constitution and called for continuance of struggle against the monarchy as a feudal institution and for a democracy based on socialistic foundation.

In 1991, elections were held and the Nepali Congress secured the majority and Girija Prasad Koirala became the second elected Prime Minister of Nepal after his elder brother B.P. Koirala. By 1994, an internal rift surfaced in the Nepali Congress that led to mid-term polls; the CPN (UML) emerged as the single-largest party and a veteran Left leader Manmohan Adhikari became the first elected communist prime minister of Nepal. In South Asia, there was no such example earlier. With twists and turns, the democracy in Nepal went to maturity. In 1995, a seasoned Nepali Congress leader Sher Bahadur Deuba became prime minister with the support of a pro-monarchy political group, the Rastriya Prajatantra Party (RPP).

The year 1996 marked the launch of the people's war by the Communist Party of Nepal (Maoist) that aimed to overthrow the existing system with a mix of monarchy and parliamentary democracy. It soon turned into a civil war, and between 1996 and 1999, Nepal entered a new unprecedented phase of instability, with three different prime ministers in as many years. In 1999, the third parliamentary elections resulted in a victory for the Nepali Congress and Krishna Prasad Bhattarai became the elected prime minister. In 2000, Bhattarai initiated back-channel talks with the Maoists, but was replaced by Girija Prasad Koirala, who advocated a more pugnacious approach.

In June 2001, King Birendra and his immediate family were massacred at Narayanhiti Palace in Kathmandu. The official investigation indicted Crown Prince Dipendra, amid widespread perception of a deep conspiracy. King Birendra's younger brother, Gyanendra, took over as the new King. Between July-September, ceasefire talks were held between the government, now led by Sher Bahadur Deuba, and the Maoists. In May 2002, as the president of the Nepali Congress G.P. Koirala opposed the extension of the emergency, the then Prime Minister Deuba dissolved Parliament with the support of the Palace and the Royal Nepal Army. The Nepali Congress witnessed a split. On 4 October 2002, King Gyanendra sacked the government and dismissed Prime Minister Deuba labeling a charge of 'incompetence', assumed a more direct political role, and appointed a loyalist, Lokendra Bahadur Chand, as prime minister.

In February 2003, the second ceasefire was signed between the Nepal government and the Maoists. But by August 2003, the Royal Nepal Army executed seventeen unarmed Maoists in Doramba. The civil war resumed. On 1 February 2005, King Gyanendra assumed direct executive power, arrested political leaders, stifled civil liberties and declared a state of emergency. The institution of monarchy had a tough time ahead with the Maoists' and other democratic forces' renewed resolve for a 'democratic republic'. Monarchy and feudalism were categorized as the principal enemies by Maoists and on 22 November 2005, a twelve-point understanding was signed between the Seven Party Alliance and the Maoists in Delhi to fight 'autocratic monarchy'.

Prakash A. Raj sums it up in his book *The Dancing Democracy*:

Monarchy, as an institution, suffered erosion in its support base after the Royal takeover in 2005. Even parties such as Nepali Congress and Nepali Congress (Democratic)—both of which had previously supported 'Constitutional Monarchy' in their party manifesto—have now declared that they are neutral as far as this institution is concerned.

The word for democracy in Nepali is *Prajatantra*, *Praja* means 'subject'. There was a slogan during the time of the Jana Andolan that said 'Praja Hoina Nagrik Banaun' meaning 'let's be citizens and not subjects'. Some puritans felt that the use of this word in Nepal's context was relevant only if Nepal were to remain a kingdom. Many politicians started using another Sanskrit-based word 'Loktantra'; 'Lok' meaning 'people'. This is also the Hindi word used for democracy in India. Some Maoists in Nepal use the word 'Jantantra' to signify the People's Republic. The Maoists had supported the removal of 'His Majesty ("Shree Paanch" in Nepal)' from 'His Majesty's

Government' in offices in Dang and Piushan in Rapti Zone-insurgency-affected areas.*

In April 2006, a nineteen-day people's movement, the second Jana Andolan, succeeded wherein King Gyanendra conceded that sovereignty rests with the people. Parliament, dissolved in 2002, was reinstated. A ceasefire was declared and Girija Prasad Koirala took oath as the prime minister once again. In May 2006, Parliament cut royal privileges, brought the Royal Nepal Army under direct civilian rule, declared Nepal a secular State and abolished untouchability. In a single stroke, the monarchy was forced on to a weak turf. In the next big development, on 16 June 2006, the Maoist chairman Pushpa Kamal Dahal 'Prachanda' appeared overground, escorted by Nepal's home minister, Krishna Prasad Sitaula, and the peace talks began at Prime Minister Koirala's residence. On 21 November 2006, the Comprehensive Peace Agreement declared the end of the civil war and created a road map for elections to a Constituent Assembly.

On 15 January 2007, an interim Parliament was constituted with participation of the Maoists and an interim Constitution was also promulgated that replaced the Constitution of 1990. On 16 January 2007, Upendra Yadav of the Madheshi Janadhikar Forum was arrested in Kathmandu after he set fire to a copy of the interim Constitution. On 17 January, a young protestor, Ramesh Mahto, was killed in Lahan. Subsequently, the Madhesh movement erupted across Nepal's southern plains. Sensing the decisive nature of the movement, on 7 February 2007, Prime Minister Girija Prasad Koirala promised federalism and an equitable electoral system. On 1 April 2007, an interim government, with ministers

---

* Prakash A. Raj, *The Dancing Democracy: The Power of the Third Eye* (Rupa Publications, 2006).

from the Maoist party, was formed. In December 2007, parties agreed to institutionalize a mixed electoral system and to abolish the monarchy by the time the Constituent Assembly held its first meeting. In February 2008, the second Madhesh movement broke out. An eight-point agreement failed between the government and Madheshi parties, committed to a Madhesh province, the group entry of Madheshis into the Nepali Army, and to ensuring the proportionate and inclusive representation of Madheshis in different organs of the State. In March 2008, the 'Free Tibet' protests started in Kathmandu, and China asked the Nepal government to crack down on the protesters. On 10 April 2008, elections were held, and in an unanticipated result, the Maoists emerged as the single-largest party. On 28 May 2008, the Constituent Assembly convened its first meeting. The monarchy was abolished, and it was decided that Nepal will have a Federal Democratic Republican Constitution. In July 2008, the Nepali Congress General Secretary, Ram Baran Yadav, was elected Nepal's first-ever president. In August 2008, the Maoist Chairman Prachanda was elected the first prime minister of the new republic. Prachanda opted for a China visit first on the pretext of attending the concluding ceremonies of the Olympics—and thus signaling the priority of his government as far as the neighbourhood was concerned. In September 2008, Prime Minister Prachanda visited Delhi. In November 2008, the Maoist party organized a conclave in Kharipati; the party's ideology took a radical, confrontational turn against India and the Nepali Congress.

The Nepali writer in English Manjushree Thapa's *The Lives We Have Lost* brings out a comprehensive account on the sets of contradictions of radical movements pursued by the Maoists and the fallout of a decade in violent transition:

For Nepalis there is an alternative to trying to understand all that has happened—and all that has not. Nepali society is not large enough, or atomized enough, for people to insulate themselves against national events. Everything affects everything here; everything is interdependent. This can feel like a curse, for who would rather not shut out the prevailing disorder and get on with their lives? Yet interdependent is life—anywhere. Buddhist philosophy points out that all phenomena, physical or mental, come to bring in relation to all others is (directly or indirectly) a causal link between them. The conditions of one affect the conditions of the other . . . Interdependence is particularly apparent in small societies like Nepal's. An example, I firmly believe that the majority of Nepalis want to bring about reform and revolution through nonviolent means. But when some Nepalis decide that their interests are better served by violent means, everyone is obliged to live with violence. The individual is not powerless; but his or her arena of action is modest. We cannot escape others, even when other people are, in Jean-Paul Sartre's words, hell. We may try, within our range, to intervene and make things better, but mostly we, however down in survival mode and wait for a better day.*

On 3 May 2009, the Maoist-led government dismissed the Army Chief General Rookmangud Katawal. President Ram Baran Yadav asked him to stay on. On 4 May, Prime Minister Prachanda resigned from office, terming the President's move 'unconstitutional', and blamed 'foreign forces' for conspiring against the Maoists. On 25 May, CPN (UML) leader Madhav Kumar Nepal was elected the new prime minister. Following the bizarre developments, another round of instability was around the corner. On 1–7 May 2010,

---

* Manjushree Thapa, *The Lives We Have Lost* (Aleph Book Company, 2013).

the Maoists called for an indefinite, nationwide strike, demanding Prime Minister Madhav Kumar Nepal's resignation. The strike failed and middle-class defiance forced the Maoists to withdraw. On 28 May 2010, the Constituent Assembly's two-year term was extended by another year. Prime Minister Madhav Kumar Nepal agreed to resign and make way for a national unity government. The deadlock continued as a prime minister couldn't be elected even after repeated rounds of voting in Parliament. In February 2011, Jhalanath Khanal was elected prime minister on the basis of a confidential seven-point pact between the Maoists and the CPN (UML).

In May 2011, as the Constituent Assembly's term lapsed for the second time, parties agreed on a three-month extension. Prime Minister Khanal agreed to resign to make way for a unity government. In June 2011, a tactical alliance between Maoist leaders Mohan Vaidya 'Kiran' and Baburam Bhattarai made Chairman Prachanda nominate Bhattarai as the prime ministerial candidate. On 28 August 2011, Bhattarai was elected Nepal's thirty-fifth prime minister, with the support of Madheshi parties, and on the basis of a four-point agreement. On 1 November 2011, a seven-point agreement was signed. Parties agreed to integrate a maximum of 6500 former combatants into the specially created Nepali Army directorate. Combatants started to ponder their options for the future.

Known by his pen name Ajay Sharma, a CPN (Maoist) ideologue Yogendra Dhakal writes in his book *Revolution, Yes! Right Liquidationism, No!* about the changes in priorities of Maoists representing the majoritarian views of party cadres:

> The essence of the development of democracy in the twenty-first century presented by our party seeks to establish a multiparty competition system, in both a new democratic and socialist

state, as a safeguard against the danger of counter-revolution. It states that a multiparty competitive state system is an adequate procedure and an institutionalized process to stop the danger of counter-revolution. Federal restructuring of the state, on the basis of race, caste, ethnicity and language in Nepal is in contradiction to the development of modern human society. Differences and malice between the different race, caste, ethnic communities are gradually lessening because of the development of capitalism and the intensity and broadness of class struggle in the country.

The Nepali Maoists fought a ten-year people's war and claimed at one time to control 80 per cent of the territory of Nepal; however, about a decade since the end of the Peace Process, they have lost all the gained—their moment has liquidated itself. The blame for this cannot ultimately be placed on their enemies, but on the leadership itself and the political like adopted by them.*

On 10 April 2012, a dissent broke out in the People's Liberation Army (PLA) ranks. The Maoist-led government sent the Nepali Army to take over People's Liberation Army cantonments. The peace process was now declared to be 'irreversible.' On 15 May 2012, the parties reached a pact on constitutional issues, including a mixed form of government and eleven federal provinces. On 16 May 2012, the Mohan Vaidya 'Kiran' faction of the Maoists, the Upendra Yadav-led Madhesi alliance, MPs belonging to ethnic minority groups, and second-rung leaders of the Madhesi front opposed the pact. On 17 May 2012, the Maoists and the

---

* Yogendra Dhakal, *Revolution, Yes! Right Liquidationism, No!: Series of Letters sent to the headquarters of the Communist Party of Nepal (Maoist)* (Aakar Books, 2016).

Madhesi parties sought a revision of the earlier agreement. The Nepali Congress and CPN (UML) rejected it. On 18–20 May 2012, a three-day strike called by an umbrella ethnic organization paralysed the country.

On 22 May 2012, Law Minister and Nepali Congress leader Krishna Prasad Sitaula registered an amendment bill in Parliament to extend the Constituent Assembly's term by three months. However, Nepali Congress President Sushil Koirala opposed the extension. On 24 May 2012, Nepali Congress ministers resigned from the government, bowing to pressure from within the party to disallow further extensions to the Constituent Assembly's term of operation. On 25 May 2012, the Supreme Court forbade any further extensions to the Constituent Assembly's term. On 27 May 2012 (10.45 p.m.), negotiations failed and the cabinet called for elections to a new Constituent Assembly to be held on 21 November. On 27 May 2012 at midnight, the term of Nepal's first elected Constituent Assembly ran out without a Constitution having been written. On 29 May 2012, President Ram Baran Yadav termed the Prime Minister Baburam Bhattarai-led government a 'caretaker' government and restricted its role. In June 2012, the Unified Communist Party of Nepal (Maoist) split. Mohan Vaidya 'Kiran' splintered off to form the Communist Party of Nepal-Maoist and accused Prachanda of 'Right-wing revisionism'. Between June and November 2012, the Nepali Congress and the CPN (UML) refused to participate in elections under a government led by the Maoists. Prime Minister Bhattarai failed to hold polls on 21 November.

In February 2013, the Maoists, led by Prachanda, organized a party convention and reiterated their commitment to peaceful political change, a new Constitution, a moderate stance on India as well as to formally drop the protracted people's war line. In March 2013, an interim election government was formed under the Chief Justice Khil Raj Regmi to hold polls to elect a second Constituent Assembly. Members of the Council of Ministers included former bureaucrats. On 19 November 2013, elections for a second Constituent Assembly were held and the Nepali Congress emerged as the single-largest party while the Maoists and the Madheshi parties faced a severe electoral rout.

On 25 February 2014, Nepali Congress President Sushil Koirala was elected prime minister with the support of the CPM (UML). Amidst the protests against the new Constitution for various discriminatory provisions, on 20 September 2015, President Ram Baran Yadav promulgated the Constitution of Nepal (2015) replacing the interim Constitution of 2007. On 26 September 2015, former Prime Minister Baburam Bhattarai of CPN (Maoist Centre) resigned from the Parliament and quit the party. On 10 October 2015, Prime Minister Sushil Koirala resigned honouring a pledge to step down once the Constitution is promulgated. On 11 October 2015, the CPM (UML) leader K.P. Sharma Oli was elected as the prime minister by Parliament with the backing from CPN (Maoist Centre). Former Prime Minister Sushil Koirala lost the election. Considered politically close to Sharma Oli, on 29 October 2015, Bidya Devi Bhandari became the second president of Nepal.

On 12 June 2016, in a significant development, the former prime minister and once a key Maoist leader Baburam Bhattarai established a new party under his leadership called the Naya Shakti. On 24 July 2016, Prime Minister Oli resigned after CPN (Maoist Centre) withdrew its support from the government, making it short of a majority mark in Parliament. On 3 August 2016, Prachanda became the prime minister for the second time after a power sharing agreement with the Nepali Congress. On 26 April 2017, the Madhesh region saw an important move with six Madheshi political parties united to form Rastriya Janata Party

Nepal. On 24 May 2017, Prime Minister Prachanda resigned honouring a power sharing agreement with the Nepali Congress. On 7 June 2017, Sher Bahadur Deuba became the prime minister for the fourth time with the support of CPN (Maoist Centre), Rastriya Prajatantra Party and other small outfits.

Nepal's general elections of 2017 were held in two phases. CPN (UML) led by K.P. Sharma Oli emerged as the single-largest party with 121 seats; the Nepali Congress secured sixty-three seats while the CPN (Maoist Centre) got fifty-three seats. On 15 February 2015, K.P. Sharma Oli became prime minister after his party CPN (UML) and CPN (Maoist Centre) entered into a coalition. On 17 May 2015, in a bid for institutionalizing the Left unity, the ruling parties CPN (UML) and CPN (Maoist Centre) merged to form Nepal Communist Party (NCP) with Oli and Prachanda as chairmen. The next noticeable political alignment took place on 6 May 2019 when Naya Shakti Party, Nepal, led by Baburam Bhattarai and Federal Socialist Forum, Nepal, led by Upendra Yadav merged to form the Samajbadi Party, Nepal. In a further development, on 23 April 2020, Samajbadi Party, Nepal, and Rastriya Janata Party, Nepal, merged to form People's Socialist Party, Nepal.

On 18 November 2020, in a dramatic development, a faction within the Nepal Communist Party led by Prachanda, Madhav Kumar Nepal and Jhalanath Khanal accused Prime Minister Oli of inefficiency and pressured him to give up either the party presidency or the premiership or else face a vote of no-confidence in both party and Parliament. On 20 December 2020, amidst the deepening internal crisis within the Nepal Communist Party, Prime Minister Oli dissolved the Parliament that was promptly approved by President Bidya Devi Bhandari and called for the general elections. On 22 December 2020, Prachanda-Madhav Kumar Nepal faction expelled Prime Minister Oli as the chairman of the Nepal Communist Party and appointed Madhav Kumar Nepal as the chairman of the party. In counteraction, two days later, the Oli-led faction of Nepal Communist Party expelled Prachanda as the chairman and suspended his party membership on the basis of disciplinary charges. Hearing the matter, on 25 January 2021, the Election Commission of Nepal declined to recognize neither Oli's faction nor Prachanda-Madhav Kumar Nepal's faction as the legitimate holder of Nepal Communist Party's registration.

On 23 February 2021, Nepal's Supreme Court overturned Prime Minister Oli's decision to dissolve the House citing Articles 85, 76 (1), 76 (7)—failure to provide sufficient grounds to dissolve the House. The Apex Court also ordered a summoning of a meeting of the Parliament within thirteen days. On 8 March 2021, the Supreme Court nullified the unification of the Nepal Communist Party stating that the name of the party was already allotted in the past to a party led by Rishi Kattel, and thus by extension, the merger was void ab initio. After this ruling, the Nepal Communist Party was no longer legally recognized, and also the CPN (UML) and the CPN (Maoist Centre) were revived to their pre-merger state. Subsequently, on 10 May 2021, Prime Minister Oli lost a vote of confidence in Parliament. Within the next three days, Oli was reappointed as prime minister with the Opposition failing to prove their majority.

On 22 May 2021, President Bhandari dissolved the Parliament again on the recommendation of Prime Minister Oli and called for elections. The move was in response to CPN (Maoist Centre) along with Madhav Kumar Nepal and Jhala Nath Khanal's decision to support the Nepali Congress-led alliance. On 12 July 2021, Nepal's Supreme Court overturned Prime Minister Oli's decision to dissolve the House and issued an order to appoint Sher Bahadur Deuba as prime minister within twenty-eight hours

citing Article 76 (5) of the Constitution. On 13 July 2021, Sher
Bahadur Deuba was appointed prime minister for the fifth time.
On 25 August 2021, Madhav Kumar Nepal and Jhala
Nath Khanal along with other politicians left the CPN (UML)
and formed a new party called the Communist Party of Nepal
(Unified Socialist).

On 24 July 2022, Baburam Bhattarai left the People's Socialist
Party, Nepal, and formed the Nepal Socialist Party. Nepal's
general elections of 2022 were held and the Nepali Congress
emerged as the single largest party with eighty-nine seats; CPN
(UML) secured seventy-eight seats while CPN (Maoist Centre)
got thirty-two seats. In an unusual coalition formation, on 26
December 2022, Prachanda emerged victorious despite having no
significant numbers on his own and became prime minister for
the third time with backing by CPN (UML), Rastriya Swatantra
Party, Rastriya Prajatantra Party, etc. The coalition didn't last
long. On 10 January 2023, Prime Minister Prachanda won the
vote of confidence in Parliament with the formidable support of
Nepali Congress. Overshadowed by political instability, Nepal's
presidential election of 2023 was an important test for a new
coalition of Nepali Congress and CPN (Maoist Centre). On an
expected line, Nepali Congress leader Ram Chandra Poudel was
elected as the president on 9 March 2023 with the vote of 214
lawmakers of Parliament and 352 provincial Assembly members.

Despite daunting challenges to Nepal's democracy, governance
and stability, and seemingly intractable bilateral irritants, the
prime ministers of Nepal and India had shown that a pragmatic
approach and mutual sensitivity can re-energize bilateral relations.
Nepali prime minister Prachanda's first bilateral visit to India (31
May–3 June 2023) since assuming office in the current term was
notable in this sense. Driven by challenges presented by the post-
Covid-19 world, current realities as well as huge opportunities,

India and Nepal were able to review the entire spectrum of the bilateral agenda covering political, economic, trade, energy, security and developmental cooperation.

Nepal's democracy has come a long way. Notwithstanding the challenges, it is firmly rooted and succeeds well in making Nepal's society aspirational and forward looking.

Nepali author Manjushree Thapa recounts some of the finer elements of the gains out of Nepal's democracy in her book *Forget Kathmandu*:

> Of course democracy brought in much change after 1990. Under a democratic polity that allowed uncensored discourse, intellectual inquiry began in earnest. Nepalis began to contest old national myths and to replace them with new truths—or at least with pertinent questions. The private media boomed after 1990, and books began to be published at an unprecedented rate. Every day there were scores of talks, seminars and debates in Kathmandu. The city's tea shops, restaurants and bars were abuzz with punditry. Nepal's society was in a state of intellectual ferment.[*]

* * *

Even as excitement over the Foreign Secretary of India Harsh Vardhan Shringla's Kathmandu visit (26 November 2020) built up, the *Kathmandu Post*, the leading English language daily in Nepal, ran a headline on 21 November 2020 that read: 'Not to be left behind, China also sending top official to Nepal after visits from India.' The story reported on an unconfirmed (at the time)

---

[*] Manjushree Thapa, *Forget Kathmandu: An Elegy for Democracy* (Aleph Book Company, 2013).

visit to Nepal by senior Chinese ministers in the near future. The headline and the story were representative of the broader narrative on Nepal, where everything is cast in terms of the competing interests of India and China and to a lesser extent, the US. China's state councillor and defence minister Wei Fenghe did visit, arriving in Kathmandu on 29 November for a day-long visit just two days after Shringla departed Nepal, and heading to Pakistan and Bangladesh thereafter.

Every domestic political development in Nepal, including a bitter internal power feud within the core power circle in Kathmandu, is routinely dissected for any hint of foreign influence—real, perceived or outright illusionary. Development projects supported by India, China and often the US are assessed in terms of geopolitical interests: an airport funded by one versus a railway by another, counterbalanced by transmission lines from the third. The misunderstood context of Nepal's development paradigm, the absence of consensus among the major political players and the centralization of power in a federal framework help fuel this discourse. Nepali politicians across all parties routinely exploit the geopolitical narrative to shift focus from their own failings. For instance, as the feud within the erstwhile Nepal Communist Party was just surfacing, the then prime minister of Nepal K.P. Sharma Oli publicly accused external forces of plotting to oust him in a charge that implicated top leaders within his own party. For both the ruling and Opposition parties, mixing domestic political fault lines with foreign affairs has strengthened the possibility of making Nepal a 'geostrategic hotspot' in South Asia.

The resulting composite view of this narrative is of Nepal as a playground for competing foreign interests in an increasingly volatile geopolitical arena. Beneath this narrative, however, are some thirty million Nepalis in flesh and blood, attempting to direct the course of their collective destiny. Nepali aspirations are unbounded and are struggling to be realized within a young but fragile democratic republic. A post-conflict national conscience is yet to come to terms with a tormented history. Pervasive and corrosive corruption has stifled hope. Millions of Nepalis have no choice but to toil in distant foreign places to eke a living. Underneath all this, the fire of change that could undermine Nepal's recent democratic gains burns dangerously.

The Nepali conscience remains haunted by a bloody decade-long conflict that toppled the monarchy and ushered in a new federal democratic republic. In 2006, Nepal concluded a Comprehensive Peace Agreement that ended the conflict started with Maoist insurgency. A process for transitional justice that would investigate the conflict-era human rights abuses was part of the deal. But it took nine years to establish the Commission of Investigation on Enforced Disappeared Persons and the Truth and Reconciliation Commission. Of the approximately 2500 complaints of disappearance and 63,000 cases in the truth commission, only a miniscule fraction has been investigated. Leadership of the commissions comes via political appointments. There is no end in sight for the transitional justice process.

A new Constitution that ushered in a federal democratic republic with a highly devolved power structure was a direct result of the conflict. The peace agreement was its implicit foundation. The Constitution and subsequent elections offered hope and unleashed Nepali aspirations across the country. While the formal structures of government are in place, the supporting institutions and spirit of the Constitution have failed to germinate in an acerbic environment where there is a peace agreement, but no resolution. Without truth and reconciliation for victims of the conflict, Nepal remains at war with itself. Without truth and reconciliation, Nepal's new Constitution remains a fragile achievement.

Nepali aspirations have been stifled by a surge in corruption that pervades almost every aspect of society. In a report[*], Transparency International found that 58 per cent of Nepalis thought that corruption had increased exponentially in Nepal, the highest increase among the sixteen Asian countries that had been surveyed. In public perception, corruption is not only rampant across public procurement, but has also seeped into service delivery at the lowest levels of government. There is an overwhelming sense that this pervasive corruption is politically sanctioned and protected. Several movements led by civil society have attempted to fight back but failed to generate adequate support. A sense of public resignation has begun to creep in, eroding public confidence in government and institutions.

The Covid-19 pandemic exposed Nepal's economic vulnerability with a major fall in remittance income, resulting in harshly impacting its largest foreign exchange earner. There was always a darker social cost to the remittance economy. Images of body bags arriving with the bodies of overseas workers routinely echo through the national consciousness. Every day, thousands of Nepalis shuffle through the border exits, headed to overseas work destinations with an air of resignation—it may be dangerous or risky abroad, but at least there is a living to be made. Populist political rhetoric plays upon this national consciousness with all parties promising to create jobs and opportunities at home. To those Nepalis abroad and those managing out a living at home, Nepal's young federal democratic republic has yet to deliver on the aspirations it set loose.

---

[*] Citizens' Views and Experiences of Corruption, Global Corruption Barometer 2020, https://www.transparency.org/en/gcb/asia/asia-2020.

Far below geopolitics in Nepal, the heartbeat of a Nepali tells a different story: of the erosion of public trust from pervasive corruption; unfulfilled aspirations from the lack of economic opportunities; the failure to achieve truth and reconciliation for the victims of the conflict. All of these are fertile grounds for dissenting groups that are seeking reversal on some element of the Constitution. There is the pro-monarchy, pro-Hindu group that seeks a return of the monarchy and the Hindu State. Maoist splinter groups, though some have been outlawed, are seeking an overthrow of the entire system. There were traces of secessionist movements across Madhesh, though the largest such movement was brought into the mainstream several years ago. Where these forces will end up is unclear. But these fires are simmering in pockets across Nepal, feeding off the discontent that is building up. It may not take much for the fires to flare up and engulf the whole country if the aspirations of people are not understood and supported curing the chronic developmental deficits in the country.

The failure of the political leadership is not all nefarious. It is also a reflection of the individual capacities of men and women stretched to the limit as they deal with many elements of their country's history colliding and exploding simultaneously. Nepal's chaotic, dishevelled foreign policy is in part an expression of these many undercurrents. Buffeted by these deep internal challenges, its political leadership appears overwhelmed by the demands of an increasingly complex geopolitical region. Nepal appears uncertain how to play its hand and balance its interest. India, China and the world perhaps expect too much from Nepal that is still struggling to come to terms with its own inner complications. For thirty million Nepalis, this is the very best opportunity for Nepal and for themselves that they have ever had, to truly build a new, peaceful, inclusive and prosperous nation. The present generation must ensure that this is not squandered away. India too will have to rise to the occasion, provide it with the space and support it needs to consolidate the gains of the young democracy. It must seek to broaden the touch points between Nepal and India, reaching out not only to the government but also civil society and encourage the flow of business across borders. It must speak to all the people of Nepal, as much as it speaks to the political leadership, and lead the world in responding to Nepal the yearnings of its people. This is what centuries of a shared history with Nepal now requires of India.

* * *

Remembering B.P. Koirala

No account of Nepal's long and painful search for democracy can be complete without understanding the life and times of B.P. Koirala.

Born in 1914, Bishweshwar Prasad Koirala, or B.P. Koirala (BPK), was an internationalist and statesman with whom Nepal's quest for liberal democracy began during the atrocious Rana rule. He was a maverick and never followed any existing half-baked political trend for the purpose of shaping Nepal's democracy. He embraced broader world views and kept striving to make Nepal a liberal parliamentary democracy. The monarchy was not a just ruling system for him; he maintained his struggle to replace it with a democracy and succeeded to an extent in making a reasonable transition. Once the Panchayati pattern was abolished, things didn't take shape ideally. The other old ranks of those earlier democratic movements lost the much required vigour to carry forward desirable democratic pursuits.

Amidst a very challenging scenario, the first General Convention of the Nepali Congress was held in Bhawanipur, Kolkata, India, on 25–26 January 1947. Tanka Prasad Acharya was the president and B.P. Koirala was the acting president at the time. The second general convention of the Nepali Congress was held in Banaras, India, on 2–3 February 1948, and B.P. Koirala was elected president. Matrika Prasad Koirala was the president of the third general convention held in Darbhanga, India, from 1–3 March 1949. Matrika Prasad Koirala was re-elected as the chairperson of the fourth general convention held in Kolkata, India, on 8–9 April 1950. After the fifth general convention of the Nepali Congress was held in Janakpur, BPK was re-elected president. Subarna Shamsher Rana was the president of the Sixth General Convention held in Birgunj from 23–27 January 1956 and BPK was president of the Special General Convention held in Biratnagar on 23–24 May 1957. BPK was elected president at the seventh general convention held in Kathmandu from 7–13 May 1960. With the foundation of Nepali Congress and institutionalization of political struggle, Nepal's tryst with democracy started.

B.P. Koirala's own words, which he had written in his autobiography, *Atmabrittanta,* bring out an essential reflection on early difficult phase of transition from absolute monarchy to one with limited democracy:

> With the World War over, a new situation arose in the region. Many Nepalis had been jailed in the context of the 1942 movement against British India, for example, Dharnidhar Sinha, Surya Bikram Gyawali and many others from Darjeeling. In Banaras, too, many Nepalis had been taken, including Surya Prasad Upadhaya, Dilli Raman Regmi and myself. Everyone knew Juddha Shumsher Rana was a harsh and bull-headed ruler incapable of understanding the changed situation. Padma

Shumsher Rana, on the other hand, was a more flexible man. Even earlier, his views had favoured a benevolent policy. I was happy when Padma Shumsher Rana became prime minister. I even wrote to him when he assumed the office, suggesting that he begin the process towards democracy by allowing people to engage in politics. All this while I was still in Bombay undergoing cancer treatment. Returning to Patna, I was sure that the British were leaving, but it was not clear how they would go and what they would leave behind. We may have to engage in another fight, perhaps one according to Mahatma Gandhi's beliefs and under his leadership.*

B.P. Koirala grew up in colonized India and shared great concern for its pathetic political status under British rule. He was a voracious reader of progressive texts and a writer of high literary sensibility. He was strongly leaning towards socialist ideas during his university days in Banaras Hindu University (BHU). He was taken up with the fine spirit of Left ideology but the personal appeal of Mahatma Gandhi and the Indian National Congress's people-centric policies during the independence movement drew him closer. Banaras was then a major centre of socialists in the Congress. There, he came in close contact with Acharya Narendra Dev, Ram Manohar Lohia and Jayaprakash Narayan. He was sent to Indian jails on many occasions for actively speaking in favour of India's independence from British rule. He had sensed the vitality of circumstance that could make the Ranas weaker. For this, he fought against the British. His approach broadly favoured the betterment of the entire South Asian region. Later, as a young law practitioner, he worked for labourers in north Bihar

---

* B.P. Koirala, *Atmabrittanta: Late Life Recollections (1914–1982)* (Jagdamba Prakashan & Himal Books, Kathmandu, 2001).

and again spent time in jail. In those days, Indian jails were filled with high moralists. So, he was on good terms with the leading figures of Indian politics—Jawaharlal Nehru and Rajendra Prasad (respectively later became India's first prime minister and president), among them.

Along with his fellow activists from Nepal and India, B.P. Koirala fought for India's independence and unsurprisingly, his ideological grooming shaped during those phases and that of late created an ideological position for the Nepali Congress to establish democracy in Nepal. About early political struggle and collaborative approach for launching a pro-democracy campaign in Nepal, he writes in his autobiography:

> On 4 October 1946, I released a statement stating that since the World War was over, it was time for freedom. Nepalis must join a broad-based democratic organization to take advantage of the situation. In addition, the statement urged all those who agreed to get in touch. That was printed in *The Searchlight* as a letter to the editor, and other papers also carried short notices. I had discussed the matter with my socialist friends Jayaprakash Narayan, Ram Manohar Lohia, and others. I felt that the Indian Congress Committee and socialist leaders would support the democratic movement we were about to start, for the movement led in India by Mahatma Gandhi did have an international aspect, one which supported the freedom struggle of people everywhere. For that reason, and also because I had extensive contacts with them, I felt that they would be supportive. There was an overwhelming response to my call. I received letters and people came to visit, some of them secretly from Nepal.

India's former ambassador to Nepal and a close relative of Jayaprakash Narayan, Bimal Prasad (with Sujata Prasad) wrote in

The Dream of Revolution with giving emphasis on B.P. Koirala's importance as a public figure in India:

> The arrest of Achyut Patwardhan was followed by the arrest of Lohia and other socialists on 25 May 1949, for demonstrating in front of the Nepal embassy, demanding the release of Nepalese leader B.P. Koirala. Jayaprakash issued a strongly worded press statement against the arrest the next day: 'Free India is being slowly converted into a vast prison . . . citizens in a free country possess the fundamental right to assemble peacefully and the right cannot be taken by the simple device of declaring such assemblies as unlawful. There are more restrictions on the liberties of citizens in Free India today under Congress rule than under the worst of British despots. This must cause deep anxiety to all freedom lovers in this country and perhaps the day is not distant when they all must join together irrespective of party creeds to save this country from fascism.' Through the rumble of history and politics, Jayaprakash's life oscillated constantly between the quotidian and the monumental—and that's what makes it so special. He campaigned for a building grant from the education ministry for the Nritya Kala Mandir in Patna, wrote to the chief engineer of the public works department, to complete work on a bridge before the monsoon, and appealed for the proper care of B.P. Koirala, ailing in prison in Nepal, all with equal intensity.*

Back home during the last years of Ranas' rule, B.P. Koirala succeeded though in establishing a very weak democratic system, which ended up working as the monarchy's puppet. His first

---

* Bimal Prasad and Sujata Prasad, *The Dream of a Revolution: A Biography of Jayaprakash Narayan* (Vintage Books, 2021).

ministerial stint as home minister brought him embarrassment from various quarters, following the shooting of a few protestors by security officers in Kathmandu. The struggle became more difficult once King Mahendra succeeded to the throne in 1955. Mahendra was firm in his resolve to destroy democratic changes but B.P. Koirala was not easily defeatable. By 1959, the King was forced to call a general election. This was unprecedented. The Nepali Congress won the election and B.P. Koirala became prime minister. But the King was wary of B.P. Koirala's growing popularity at home and in the world, especially in India. By the end of 1960, a coup took place (planned by the King) and B.P. Koirala was sent to jail under the pressure of landed aristocrats. He was destined to struggle, but surprisingly, his brother Matrika Prasad Koirala sided with the monarchy and served as Nepal's ambassador to the US. During those testing times, B.P. Koirala's personal fate was at stake, but he was well connected in India and in other parts of the world. King Mahendra knew the limit of his acts, but the hardship stayed as the 'rule of game' against B.P. Koirala and other dissenting figures.

In his latter days in exile and spearheading the flame of real democracy in Nepal, B.P. Koirala appeared as independent as he was always, irrespective of all pressure. He was a tough administrator, an able diplomat and a leader who could handle adversity with courage and clear conviction. His unflinching determination for democracy did not waver with his ailing health, and hostility from King Mahendra. Despite the odds, he maintained his persona and the decency of the democratic movement. His diplomatic instinct was unquestionable. He proved on many occasions that stable leadership can rescue a nation from internal loopholes at crucial international junctures. B.P. Koirala was a respected name in India during his lifetime, and is, even today. It was a major misfortune for Nepal that he couldn't cope with his failing health and died prematurely in 1982, eight years before the country attained the remarkable landmark of a constitutional monarchy. His younger brother, Girija Prasad Koirala, who emerged as a strong centrist and served the country many times, lacked B.P. Koirala's integrity altogether. During Girija Prasad Koirala's time, the hope for real democracy was strengthened, albeit it proved short-lived.

The first generation of the Nepali revolutionary leaders were greatly inspired by India's independence movement and Indian leaders like Mahatma Gandhi, Jawaharlal Nehru, Jayaprakash Narayan and Ram Manohar Lohia. They supported the struggle to end imperialism and tyranny in all forms. Inspired by B.P. Koirala, Krishna Prasad Bhattarai or Kishunji came in touch with him as a student of Banaras Hindu University and worked in unison for founding the Nepali Congress—and thus ushering in democracy in Nepal. In 1942, he was taken into custody for three weeks because of his participation in the Quit India Movement. For establishing the Nepali Congress and democracy in Nepal, Krishna Prasad Bhattarai is rightly remembered as one of the pioneers, and someone only next to B.P. Koirala in terms of decisive contributions in favour of Nepal's democracy.

* * *

Manjushree Thapa's *Forget Kathmandu* chronicles the transition of Nepal's democracy with a real peach:

> Of course, democracy brought in much change after 1990. Under a democratic polity that allowed uncensored discourse, intellectual enquiry began in earnest. Nepalis began to contest with pertinent questions. The private media boomed after 1990, and books began to be published at an unprecedented rate. Every day there were scores of talks, seminars and debars

in Kathmandu. The city's tea shops, restaurants and bars were abuzz with punditry. Nepal's society was in a state of intellectual ferment.*

She adds:

Krishna Prasad Bhattarai of the Nepali Congress served as the Prime Minister of the first interim government, which oversaw the drafting of the Constitution. He also established the Malik Commission to identify those responsible for the excesses against the People's Movement and recommended action against them. In the first Parliamentary elections of 1991, the Nepali Congress won with a majority of votes. But when Girija Prasad Koirala became the Prime Minister, he buried the Malik Commission's report effectively extending protection to Panchayat-era hardliners. He had discovered, apparently, that the Nepali Congress could not survive without the patronage of these politicians, who still held sway in the rural areas and in Kathmandu's inner circle. The CPN (UML) had also come to the same conclusion. By the end of a year, both parties had welcomed as members several Panchayat politicians, allowing them to outrage long-time party cadres.

Man Mohan Adhikari became the prime minister of Nepal in November 1994, the first communist prime minister in the world to win a democratic election. He was heading a minority government with no surety of completing the term in office. His party was in as much disarray as the Nepali Congress. Its charismatic General Secretary Madan Bhandari had been steering the party away from CPN (UML) policies towards more democratic leftist ones when

---

* Manjushree Thapa, *Forget Kathmandu: An Elegy for Democracy* (Aleph Book Company, 2013).

he died mysteriously in December 1993 in a car crash that had left everyone whispering of political assassination. The then serving Girija Prasad Koirala's government had written off the crash as an accident but many thought that Madan Bhandari had been killed for being, in the communists' words, a 'capitalist roader'. At Madan Bhandari's death, the CPN (UML) was caught in suspension as an awkward communist but market-friendly party, a socialist-or-even-liberal-in-ideology party, that, however, could not rise losing its grassroots supporters by eschewing real policies altogether. The party's neo-Marxist reformism was clashing against its own Marxist-Leninist (and even Stalinist and Maoist) past.

As the prime minister, Man Mohan Adhikari tried to reconcile these reformist and revolutionary urges. In its nine months in power, his minority government made one irreversible change to Nepal's governance: It instituted 'Afno Gaun Afai Banau (Let's Develop our Villages Ourselves)'—a programme that gave Village Development Committees (VDCs) funds for the first time, to oversee grassroots governance. The communist-held VDCs could now show up the Nepali Congress-held District Development Committees (DDCs) by constructing roads, bridges and telephones for themselves. In another more obvious populist move, the CPN (UML) also allocated Rs 100 per month stipends to the elderly, hoping to counter the popular myth that the party killed anyone who was economically unproductive. Manjushree Thapa's *Forget Kathmandu* focuses on those fateful years and connects the important dots of political developments in Nepal of the 1990s and the next decade.

In 1990, when the democratic movement gained strong momentum and Nepal finally set to enter in a painfully long spell of transition from the monarchy to a fledgling and aspirational democracy, it had the advantage of having at its helm some of the surviving leaders from the first generation of early democratic struggle. They kept idealism intact from their days of struggle to establish democracy, under a popular feudal rule. They were the same set of people who struggled for India's independence movement against the cunning British colonial rule. They are no longer around—and their counterparts in India, too, were not born to be immortal. In their absence, the void is permanent at Nepal's domestic front or in harmonizing the cooperation with India. Not without serious lapses, Nepal turned out to be a hub of despair. It experimented with a Constitution, which proved to be a 'partitioning document', breaching people's trust in the 'idea of nation'—and in their own existence. While the country kept its freefalling spree, the political ranks were hell bent on practising the distorted versions of 'nationalism' among their fiefdoms, who lost over 8000 brethren and sizable materialistic hope from the cruellest earthquake in the fateful year of 2015 and much before over 17,000 people were killed in a decade-long Maoist insurgency in the country. The earth is still not at peace in this part of the world, as here helms a political system that negates 'reason'—and works under influence of 'abstract dogma' that once provisioned six deputy prime ministers under one prime minister!

In the next phase of 2001–08, the gain of Maoists reached fulcrum. They rose to power with their aggressive socio-economic agenda. The Maoists in Nepal have many successes to count but the failures too are many and can outnumber them. Among those easily visible failures, one is their following the footprint of old political parties like Nepali Congress and democratic Left parties. In actual, the Maoists were endowed with an edge to aggressively pursue the programmes for socio-economic empowerment of the nation. Not much happened in concrete terms unlike expected, and Nepal is still moving without having a sizable middle-class population. Political beliefs and actions are driven by whims rather than carefully judged thinking, and most often than not, politics triumphs economics in Nepal.

Ujjwal Thapa, who died young but before that, tried making an alternative stream of politics in Nepal wrote in his book *Why Nepal?*:

> Faithful implementation of any policy of a nation is dependent on the ethical delivery of politics by its leaders. The North-South doctrine shall evolve according to the challenges of the future but will remain focused on building a prosperous Nepal and an equally prosperous neighbourhood. We envision all foreign relations of Nepal in the next four decades to go through a 'one-door' policy which all political forces, bureaucracy and planners follow through.*

The end goal of any political force who works to stay relevant in twenty-first-century Nepal should be to build a peaceful, prosperous Nepal within our lifetime. And the only ones capable of ensuring that are those with twenty-first-century relevant leaders.

Nepal's search for democracy is yet not over. As a young democracy, it can count on a few important achievements; however, the shortfalls are far too many, overshadowing them. While Nepal's democracy has matured over the years, it has yet not guaranteed a solution for the country's ailing developmental framework. In accomplishing it, Nepal's real search for democracy will complete.

* * *

While reading journalist Sanjay Upadhya's book *Backfire in Nepal*, one can ascertain the seriousness of the political fault lines in Nepal. From the angle this book is written, it reconfirms how the decision-making processes in Nepal has been made

---

* Ujwal Thapa, *Why Nepal? A Journey of Experiments, Reflections and Provocations* (Yatra Publishing House, Kathmandu, 2022).

subservient to the confused trilateralism instead of getting shaped independently.* Due to the obsession with the positioning of India and China, realpolitik is compelling mass aspirations to get lost in transition. Who should be blamed for this?

It is true that the official establishment in India has its own share of misunderstanding Nepal's political transition that finally paved the way for China to go many steps further from not so tough competition, though the bigger concern remains over the Nepali political classes' comfortable posture towards such unwelcoming dynamics. It is the new age politics without accountability that mars promising developmental possibilities for Nepal. The institutional processes are misunderstood, and the political culture has still not developed where the successes or failures of decisions can be acknowledged as purely internal exercises. China's excessive interest in Nepal is unnatural since there is such a transparent urge towards expansionism, and it gets traction as Nepal's political class is not counting as much it should on people and their aspirations. When it comes to India, it is organically linked to Nepal. Be it close State cooperation or unique sociocultural ties on the people's front, there is a past which necessitates having an engaging present and future. It is unlikely that China can still claim to be a natural ally like India is to Nepal. A closer look at its promises and deliveries is enough to disenchant any Nepali. However, in the official establishment of Kathmandu, the Darwinian survivalist spirit defeats truth and logic.

Has India lost the plot to China in Nepal? Going deep into it, one finds it deeply pitiful the way public discourses are being built on it. Logically, what should be discussed is the precariousness of Nepal as a young democracy with a weak accountability system in place. Even with republicanism, secularism and federalism,

---

* Sanjay Upadhya, *Backfire in Nepal: How India Lost the Plot to China* (Vitasta, 2021).

political beliefs and actions continue to be driven by whims rather than carefully judged thinking. In a bid to make the people believe that existential challenges are not as pressing as keeping India and China in the middle of a crisis from Kathmandu's streets to Parliament, the political leadership in Nepal is doing a big disservice to the country and the people. More than India, the people of Nepal have been defeated in the political quagmire. China's geo-strategic orientation in Nepal clearly found traction with the inability of the top Nepali leaders to differentiate between the matters of home and the world, and thus not opening the turf to an avoidable geostrategic rivalry in the homeland.

Without sufficient homework, it will surely not be desirable for Nepal to be in the big powers' league and gain exposure to bruised egos. Amidst an unprecedented crisis with the coronavirus, prolonged lockdown and severely contracted economy, the Oli government's move to create hurdles against free movement near the border points and unusual suspension of flights to India were unsavoury acts when economic rebounding was utmost important in post-pandemic times. When the people on either side couldn't do without each other, it was unfortunate how the government offered insensitivity when handholding was most needed.

A country with immense possibilities, Nepal, and its people, should get an enabling framework for good governance and robust economy. In Kathmandu's political theatre, democracy is a misunderstood system where it is continuously confused with favourable electoral figures and no agenda. It would be a mistake to see factionalism merely literally. It is a virtue and escape route for self-serving politicians. With the promises made in the middle of the last decade, Nepal was supposed to be on a path of peace and progress. The ground reality is strikingly different with a case in the recent past when a transitional government headed by Oli was involved with an armed outfit headed by Netra Bikram Chand and also gave signals for a closer association with the royalists. A juxtaposition of these two images is well-sufficient to know how the people's aspirations are being hammered down, and with it, hope is also turning elusive in transition.

The intellectual community in Nepal must voice and write more about the lost opportunities, wasted sacrifices, demolished institutions and cynical political moves to overshadow all these under the garb of playing the India and China cards.

* * *

Journalist Prashant Jha's book *Battles of the New Republic* chronicles Nepal's political transition and underlines a few crucial patterns that have overwhelmed it during the intervening phases:

> In the past decade, Nepal has undergone arguably one of the boldest political transformations in South Asia. Identity-based politics has brought long-marginalized social groups into the mainstream and upended the bulwark of Nepali nationalism—the Hindu monarchy. Yet, the process of change has repeatedly broken down, and Nepal's fragile polity, under stress from various forces, has continuously fragmented— the first Constituent Assembly failed to draft a Constitution; the Maoists, who sparked the transformation with an armed insurrection, and once represented hope, have been so co-opted into the very political culture they once challenged; never-ending political negotiations have chronically paralysed the governance initiatives needed to address Nepal's problems; and India, the country's powerful neighbour, has played an overwhelming role in national politics, choosing to intervene or stay away at crucial junctures.*

---

* Prashant Jha, *Battles of the New Republic: A Contemporary History of Nepal* (Aleph Book Company, 2014).

Like many other democracies across the world, Nepal's democracy too has been affected with an extreme rise in majoritarian sentiments. Nepal cannot afford to enter another round of political instability; this should be a realization deep within all the movers and shakers of Nepali politics.

What can be an inside account of Nepal? It is all about the power, who did what and what was given in reciprocation. As Nepal is not stopping to surprise even its keen observers, out of necessity, it is highly recommended for them to read the journalist (former chief editor, *Kantipur*) Sudheer Sharma's book *The Nepal Nexus.** In long-form though, it's a sort of a prescription on what all ails the country but keeps it moving with complex background and foreground. He looks back on Nepal's painful political transition and gives an inside account of the 'Maoists, the Durbar and New Delhi', calling it the 'Nepal Nexus'.

At the outset, his insightful contribution throws light on Nepal's democracy, statecraft and its eccentric ways of functioning. The CPN (UML) came to centrestage and benefitted before losing their way to fractures within the party and falling prey to the grand design of 'communist unification' propounded by Oli and his camp. The Durbar ceased to function with the royal massacre and inconclusive follow-up on that; what remained in the form of succession ended too early and on a disappointing note. The third important component, the capital of the friendly neighbour, New Delhi, continues to remain in the public imagination but that's mostly to satisfy the instant gratification of political classes who otherwise could be held accountable for pursuing corruption and incompetence that led to endless miseries for the masses of the homeland.

---

* Sudheer Sharma, *The Nepal Nexus: An Inside Account of the Maoists, the Durbar and New Delhi* (Penguin Viking, 2019).

Since Sudheer Sharma had artfully tried covering 'Nepal's Nexus' that was more about the past than present, it is wishful that the next print run of his book enables him to write about much needed 'Nepal's New Nexus'. No matter what happens tomorrow, Nepal's neighbourhood policy in the recent past sent the message loud and clear. It is not about just exercising the choices or making the balances between India and China; it is to manipulate the troubled equation between two countries with nuclear capabilities and very large economies. In the process, the danger lies where Nepal could emerge as a flashpoint of geo-economic tussle between India and China.

Sadly, in the absence of consultation and rumination, the official Nepal is faring poorly by entering a vicious spiral of mistakes. It needs to be known that it is not the 'Indian virus' that is deadlier than the 'Chinese virus'; what is deadlier is leading the country to a risk zone rather towards normalcy after the global breakdown. The bid for a new nexus has flashed out the brighter possibilities and put a question mark on the Communist unification in Nepal that was never believed to be on ideological lines. The enforced camaraderie ended in no time.

'Standing on the bloodshed by tens of thousands of patriots, we are not willing to bow down before any foreign master,' possibly without knowing it would become fateful, Sudheer Sharma has meaningfully quoted Prachanda from the latter's public announcement of his resignation from the prime ministership in his first term. In the changed times, and as he is now the serving prime minister of Nepal, one wonders whether he would like to recall this. He will struggle to turn attention away from the upturns in geo-strategic scenario that clearly are not in favour of Nepal, China is not altruistic with its Belt and Road Initiative (BRI) and other offerings with merely pull-effects and no positive gains to Nepal. Its imperial intention is easy to be understood as an 'open secret'. Nepal will do better without negating the conventional wisdom and rather approaching for an absolute non-alignment in international affairs.

As the political course of action is still uncertain and the economy is facing a major contraction, Nepal should look within and carefully. Instead of keeping the petty political considerations and urge to overstay at the helm, the political classes must think to revive the level of discourses and make them development centric. An unscientific and irrational position on the matter of national interests, if prolonged, will be troublesome. If the 'nexus' serves the purpose of a lexicon, it should not be relied on beyond the trifling texts!

The electoral verdict in Nepal's recent elections (2022) was a credible one. It reflected a clear emergence of voter preference for more responsive governance and impatience with traditional political power games ignoring aspirations of the youth and disadvantaged. The verdict also reconfirmed the successful taking root of democracy in the Himalayan country whose transition from a Hindu monarchy to a secular republic happened after great struggle, sacrifices and ideological adjustments across the political spectrum. Among major accomplishments was the peaceful mainstreaming of the Maoist movement into the democratic structure, integration of guerrillas into the Nepal Army, transfer of power, adoption of a Constitution and emergence of a federal structure, although admittedly accompanied by shortcomings and controversy. On the negative side, however, the hung Parliament that the final results had created is a sure recipe for instability and frequent changes of government in the coming years, which could easily translate into inability to deal with the many daunting challenges confronting the country and continuing unpredictability in the graph of India–Nepal cooperation. This unexpected development will undoubtedly be a source of satisfaction for China, which had earlier rather conspicuously but unsuccessfully attempted to prod the Left wing in the political spectrum to reunite (to promote its own interests and to the detriment of India's).

Contrary to widespread expectations that Sher Bahadur Deuba and the Nepali Congress, along with an alliance which included the Maoists led by Prachanda, would form the new government as they commanded the largest number of seats in the new Parliament, it was Prachanda who was sworn in as prime minister as he decided to revive his earlier alliance with former Prime Minister Oli, who heads the Communist Party of Nepal, CPN (UML). India can however take this development in its stride. It is used to dealing with political instability in Nepal, frequent changes of government, and even with reputedly anti-India or pro-China leaders heading them. Its focus for many years has been on non-partisan support for inclusive economic development, interdependence, communication links, people-to-people contacts and building on the compulsive logic of economic complementarities especially in hydropower where Nepal has huge but as yet largely unexplored potential. The extent of its linkages of history, geography, culture, religion and economy with Nepal facilitate management of its security concerns within tolerable limits.

Moreover, leaders like Prachanda and Oli are seasoned veterans capable of making shrewd judgments in their long-term political interests even when they talk about the new government adopting a policy of 'equi-proximity' with India and China. The truth is that as is evident even in robust democracies (Israel's being the most recent example), ideological consistency has less and less meaning in the politician's search for power. So, too, in the case of Nepal, labels like pro or anti-India need to be taken with increasing amounts of salt. It should also not be forgotten that ultranationalist leaders like Oli and Prachanda have on occasion spoken with courage and conviction to question senseless opposition to India, as Oli did when he aggressively questioned the strident demand from his own party to oppose ratification of the Mahakali Treaty a few years ago.

* * *

Despite having a functional democracy, it is alarming to see that Nepal has no real economic road map in place. Industries are either being shut down or they are stagnating with major demand contraction and liquidity crunch. Meanwhile, politics is being played out without making much common sense. The present state of Nepal's politics allows for such an unusual condominium of parties that make little sense when it comes to resolving the greater political mess in the country. The overblown ambitions of the political class nullify the earlier efforts of democratic experiments. The state of instability witnessed in Nepal at times merits to be seen more as the result of the behavioural recklessness of politicians rather than the consequence of a celebrated prolonged political transition in the country.

Undoubtedly, such pacts and agreements among politicians who are under pressure to survive have pushed governance issues to an all-time low. When the roads were not all rubble and long power cuts were not the norm, things were different. The people of Nepal had hope in the new generation of politicians and their brand of democratic politics. For instance, the Maoists, until recently, were viewed differently as they focused on inland development and did not wish for Nepal to continue as a dumping ground of imported goods. However, their economic vision has been lost mid-way. Since 1996, Nepal has witnessed a series of troubling developments. Primary among them was the outbreak of the highly violent Maoist insurgency and later the royal massacre of 2001 which pushed the nation into an age of uncertainty. King Birendra had acceptability among the masses and political parties as well, and his willingness to lead Nepal to democracy was well known. Had he still been alive, possibly the credibility of the monarchy as an institution would not have been lost so early.

The tendency to walk with their erroneous ideas is not only a hallmark limited to political players in Nepal, but it also equally charms and drives business leaders. On many occasions, Nepali leaders and business captains visiting New Delhi have no will to execute the Memorandums of Understandings (MoUs) signed with the Indian government or the Indian private sector. Until the political class reacts to economic impulses, things in Nepal will be hard to change. The recent advent of a political party like Rastriya Swatantra Party (RSP) led by Rabi Lamichhane is a testimonial to the fact that Nepal's polity is now increasingly driven by aspiration rather the conventional loyalty seen for many decades while Nepal's democracy was in a phase of maturation. It was caught off guard when a new entrant in politics but an established economist, Swarnim Wagle, left the Nepali Congress to join the RSP, underlining the fact that Nepal's politics is heading to a new turf that is going to be competitive and hosting the changing aspirations in Nepal.

Ironically, a balance in Nepal's domestic front is still elusive till it has a clear delinking of politics with its foreign policy and external affairs. Though it is not succeeding, China's bilateral antics in Nepal are totally ambiguous in the way it involves India at loggerheads for making Nepal, its new Pakistan. China is missing no chances to play on the ultra-radical forces in Nepal by channelizing huge disposable resources for the mainland.

For a considerable period, China succeeded in encircling Nepal in its narrow game for substituting India's prominent place as a reliable partner from the latter's territory. In this tug of war, India was clearly challenged by slipping from its very close tie-up with Nepal. In fact, China outpaced India as a major investor in Nepal, besides controlling the nerves of ultra-radical forces. Nepal should never have taken China's hidden game in Nepal so lightly. Over the last one-and-a-half decade, China has made all efforts to proliferate an embedded version of communism inside Nepal. Ideologically, such a brand of radical movement in Nepal is impure and reflects the personal cynicism of its leadership. Next to the ideological line, these leaders have been nurturing their political ambitions by pumping up a 'sovereignty phobia' or 'Indophobia' in Nepal. Maoists are divided entities now, and those who sit outside the power circle, try to carve a niche for them. They hope that the anti-India demonstration will give them the mileage to do so. In the entirety of the existing scene, nothing could be more misleading than a paranoiac march like this. Of late, China's intentions are better judged by Nepal and this has had a positive influence in efforts to cement its bilateral ties with India.

Beyond regional priorities, Nepal has needed to broaden its strategic choices across the globe. Former US president Barack Obama had shown unprecedented interest in Nepal and intent to make Nepal one of its foremost allies in the South Asian region. In reciprocation, the previous government headed by Nepali Congress leader Sher Bahadur Deuba travelled extra miles to finally get the controversial Millennium Challenge Corporation (MCC) aid passed in Nepal. Though Nepal had been selected as one of the twenty focus countries for Obama's $3.5 billion 'Feed the Future' initiative, the current bilateral trade or diplomatic relations between these two countries are standing much below the actual potential. Nepal has never been given due attention by the world's prominent leaders; it is time to check those unfortunate practices that are hindering the chances of Nepal's prolific rise on the global platform. Under the new strategic environment, Nepal could be a natural ally for the USA in fighting terror and also a significant trade partner with unwavering support from India, the world's largest democracy. Principally, too, democrats have a lot to share with the swiftly democratizing Nepal, which has ushered democracy in a great way and importantly by ending the firmly established system of monarchy. Nepal's ongoing political transition hardly leaves any big hurdle for the wide-ranging cooperation at a global level.

Nepal has a lot to deliver with its untapped natural and human resources; a serious rethink from neighbouring giants and powerful nations, like India and the USA, respectively, could bring desirable outcomes. Here, the political leadership of Nepal has to play a pivotal role as to how they will move collectively on the bigger issues of foreign policy and trade negotiation, setting aside the 'underdog' tone that stopped Nepal from stepping in a normal course of development.

* * *

Since 1990, Nepal's democracy has been grappling with consistent flip-flops and political maneuverings. It has already lost over two decades in coming out completely from the shadow of royal institutions. Nepal's tryst with democracy hasn't always been painful—the country witnessed full-scale transformation into a democracy within a short span of time, compared with other South Asian democracies. The first-generation democratic leadership of the country deserves closer evaluation, as they had a clear grasp over their goals and intentions. Sadly, the scenario that exists now is dramatically different. Nepal has failed to capitalize on many chances to strengthen its democracy and broaden it for public welfare.

The eventful 1990s were spent initially in a tug-of-war between the King and the political forces, and later between the Maoists and everyone else. The new century/millennium began with an unfortunate royal massacre, which not only ended the monarchy's natural continuity but also greatly affected the natural progression of democracy. Since 2001, what has dominated the major political discourse in Nepal should have been avoided— intense factionalism, directionless ideological formations and fragmentations, unprecedented rise in regionalism and an excessive focus on the federalization of the republic. Demands were mostly routed through demonstrations, discarding basic civic and moral sense.

Since the end of the monarchy, Nepal's politics has turned more inward looking. There are breathless twists and turns hatched by political parties, whose working patterns are radically different from one another. Such is the friction among them that the attainment of any goal collectively or even individually has almost become impossible. After the bloodless coup in February 2005, Baburam Bhattarai, a senior leader from the Maoists' camp, came forward against the obstinate ideological hardline pursued by the likes of Pushpa Kamal Dahal, popularly known as 'Prachanda', called for the democratic means of struggle—that was a tipping point in Nepal's democratic transition in a decisive phase. Unfortunately, things were not similarly idealistic and flexible in the long run. Consequently, an unusual assertiveness defined the characteristic of Nepal's elite politicians being on a roll with power but without a strong urge to deliver on promises. This is hardly surprising as every major political change in Nepal (even in the past) has created a new class of elite with shrewd aspirations. That's why the project of democratic revolution has not met with the success that it deserved in Nepal since 1950. Chronic political deadlock is denting the credibility of mainstream political forces in Nepal. There is the need for an immediate consensus among the country's political parties to acknowledge the progress that democratic movements have made since 1990, when the county first tasted democracy, although on a restricted scale.

At this crucial juncture, the reckoning should be that Nepal fared well under a central command. It is a small country where territorial divisions are not as important as its emancipation as an economy and democracy. India and China can be good examples for Nepal, given how far these countries have travelled from medieval monarchies into modern states. The trust in the existing parliamentary model needs to be unshakable. Sans faith in the present system, it will be impossible for political parties to offer a better alternative to the Nepali people, who are more interested in a dignified life than in endless political maneuverings.

For long, Nepali leaders have not looked at political developments beyond the 'surrealist order', which allows unconscious choices to be expressive. This is an existential downplaying and must not be continued. The Nepali people's faith in democracy should reflect in its institutions and institutional culture. Political leaders have to be sensitive to this or they will end up undermining democracy and finally their own utility in public space. Time, as the supreme force, will decide whether democracy in Nepal is a lame duck or a winner.

* * *

The Maoist Phenomenon: Rise, Mainstreaming and Decline

The Maoist phenomenon was an inevitable consequence of a combination of brakes on a natural evolution of democracy to a mature and responsive one: the paucity of leaders with courage and vision, the games that the Palace played, unending destructive intra-party feuds, ultranationalist prejudices against India, and India's preoccupation bordering on obsession about China. It was also an irresistible magnet for the huge number of people who had felt marginalized and discriminated against for centuries. Violence and threats against innocent people also helped them to gain adherents, as did their ultranationalist anti-India rhetoric and their tall promises of radical socio-economic-political reform. The unwillingness of the Palace to unleash the RNA against them due largely to its calculation that discrediting democracy was to its advantage, and the somewhat lax supervision of its cross-border activities from jungle hideouts in India for several years, also helped.

Their overtures to the Palace, to political leaders, to India flowed from acceptance of the fact that they could not win by military force; the international community and especially India would come down with force to destroy them because of the threat from global terrorism, and the tempting prospect of becoming part of the power structure if they gave up their most radical demands.

They saw their golden opportunity when Gyanendra became King and decided to take on the Maoists as well as the political parties while crossing India's red lines on China. India too sensed an opportunity to get Nepal's Maoists off its back, deal a mortal blow to the institution of monarchy against which there had always been a bias, and bring a semblance of peace and stability to Nepal. The Maoists opted to get mainstreamed under peace arrangements brokered by India, and soon after their surprise victory in the first elections, exposed themselves as simply another party hungry for power at any cost, abandoning their radical programmes and promises of ending discrimination and poverty. India also exposed itself by its blatant interventionism and pressure tactics when things were not going according to its plans, thereby ensuring that anti-Indianism would have a life of its own with or without a monarchy.

India played an important role in bringing the Maoists and mainstream political parties together, with King Gyanendra then playing an unintended helpful role through his impatience with both, and a series of misjudgements.

The Maoists, who had during the last few months of King Birendra's life tried to forge an understanding with the monarchy to isolate and disempower the political parties, changed their strategy once Gyanendra took control. It suited their political arithmetic better. In the words of former Foreign Minister Ram Sharan Mahat, the Maoists had always considered 'the monarchy as the historical bulwark of all class, caste, gender, national and regional and religious oppression'.

'Nepal is a country of indigenous people, the Janjatis, Madheshis (Terai people) and Dalits who form nearly 70 per cent of the population and are excluded from power. A republican Nepal could produce a very different polity,' was the Maoist calculation as assessed by sociologist Krishna Bhattachan.

Interestingly, other political parties, including the traditionally pro-India Nepali Congress, have taken ultranationalist positions on sensitive issues such as the boundary dispute. Pro and anti-India labels have less and less meaning. Nepalese across the political spectrum seem united on irritants where Nepal is seeking India's adjustment and India is in a non-compromise mood, such as the 1950 Treaty, Kalapani, or the Expert Group Report. India is less of a domestic issue in elections, and development assistance is being implemented smoothly. There is much more honest heart-searching among Nepal's intellectuals about deficiencies on the home front without rectifying of which Nepal is in real danger of becoming a failed State.

The democracy scorecard has several positives too. Nepal can be justly proud of the fact that the Maoist insurgency ended peacefully, albeit after ten long years of suffering in which thousands of people died and atrocities were committed by all sides; that the Maoists gave up their arms or accepted the control of the Nepali Army after joining it; that they departed from their core ideologies of radical changes, accepted multiparty democracy, and have obeyed voter verdicts even when they were on the losing side; and of late have shown a welcome trend towards pragmatic policies focusing on development priorities rather than ultranationalist posturing.

The democratic transition is still enduring in Nepal. This is painful if taken into consideration the honest revelations. The administrative edifices of the nation have suffered immensely in the wake of promises made and broken in over the last two and half decades—by the mainline political parties and comparatively new entrants, Maoists.

There is introspection on the country's recent past, as well as on present disappointments, in equal proportion—to have in sight the lack of political accountability and tenets of participatory democracy. Still the quest to firmly ground democracy is notionally very much alive. This shows a spread of typical South Asian style of democratic experimentation, with an underlying characteristic of not bridging the crucial gaps. Under this, completion of whole democratic processes stays a far cry, more often than not.

More than any other phenomenon, the homegrown (and internationally supported) Maoists have influenced the current of Nepal's modern history. The next big phenomenon was of course the abrupt end of royal rule. Journalist and a keen watcher of Nepal's Maoist movement Aditya Adhikari's ground-breaking book *The Bullet and the Ballot Box* presents a vivid picture of radical movements and their impacts on contemporary Nepal. Aditya Adhikari has touched in detail the nuances that made it possible to reach to the level of privilege the Maoists have been enjoying—irrespective of odds, in their internal and external vision.*

The book offers rich details with the author's own diary, anecdotal accounts and interviews carried out with the top Maoist leaders and common cadres. It offers a balanced overview of the trend that made Maoists in Nepal a force to reckon with in a very brief period of their struggle and action for overwhelming the political establishment and processes in Nepal:

> With their firm commitment to revolution, the Maoists were thus swimming against a powerful tide. They not only rejected the parliamentary system, but also denounced—despite Nepal's heavy dependence on foreign countries—'imperialist' and 'expansionist' powers such as the United States and India. It was generally thought that no Nepalese government could survive without Indian support. A political group that was openly hostile towards India was not expected to go far. Both Nepali and foreign observers saw the Maoists as an irrelevant and fiction-ridden group obsessed with an obsolete ideology.
>
> After a decade-long armed struggle, the Maoists finally signed a peace agreement with the mainstream parties that were opposed to the King's usurpation of power. Together they led a historic uprising that brought down the monarchy and paved the path for elections to a Constituent Assembly, one of the rebels' key demands. The Maoists won around 40 per cent of seats in the Constituent Assembly. Other parties trailed far behind. The Maoists joined the government, and their political agenda came to dominate Nepal's public debate.

---

* Aditya Adhikari, *The Bullet and the Ballot Box: The Story of Nepal's Maoist Revolution* (Aleph Book Company, 2014).

However, it is widely known how the Maoists initially rebelled and with a grander ambition that aimed for 'total state control'. Once mainstreamed into a very fragile and unpredictable multiparty system of Nepal, the Maoists were compelled to accept the terms required to survive in a competitive polity. This possibly helped their astounding growth as a political force. Noticeably, the Maoists in Nepal proved to be the only experiment in the post-Cold War era that gained State power through Mao's strategy of a people's war. Adhikari's observations on the factors that made it possible are worthy to be mentioned here:

> By the late 1980 the Panchayat had lost whatever reforming zeal it once possessed. Confronted by various challenges to its authority, most notably the student movement and the referendum of 1980, the regime had grown primarily anxious to perpetuate itself and the privileges of its elites. It maintained a secret police and deployed groups of violent youth to identify and crush subversive activity. But the system was inefficient and had lost legitimacy, leaving plenty of space for banned political parties to spread their networks among the urban population.
>
> The democratic uprising that swept across the globe after the fall of the Berlin wall strongly influenced political leaders in Nepal. Around this time, India had imposed a trade blockade on Nepal, causing much resentment among the Nepali population. Taking advantage of the public mood, the banned parties came together to instigate a mass uprising against monarchical autocracy. The movement was led by the Nepali Congress, the party that had been struggling for parliamentary democracy for over four decades. Some of the more influential communist parties (CPN-ML) joined the movement, forming an alliance called the United Left Front (ULF). At the other end of the Communist spectrum was the United National

People's Movement (UNPM), an alliance of radical Maoist parties including Mashal. The UNPM was an unwanted interloper in the movement, and the Nepali Congress and the members of the ULF did their best to ignore it. Compensating for what they lacked in popular support by voluble rhetoric and violent street action, this alliance had made clear from the outset that they were not merely demanding a parliamentary democracy—a system them continued to define, in keeping with the traditional moralist view, as the dictatorship of the bourgeoisie. They attempted to buttress the crumbling bastion of Marxism-Leninism-Maoism against the current of the times, rejecting the idea that the movements of popular resistance in Eastern Europe represented a moral victory of liberal democracy over communalism.

The Maoists clearly didn't get any prominence with the mass uprising that took place in the months of February and March 1990 for democracy. Thousands of people were on the streets of Kathmandu and finally King Birendra came forward on 9 April 1990 with offerings of lifting the ban on political parties and removing the word 'party-less' from the Panchayat system in the Constitution. As expected, the lead forces of the movement Nepali Congress and CPN (ML) accepted the new terms. The arrangement was a sort of compromise from both sides as the movement was getting violent, to the extent where it was difficult to control. Remarkably, the Panchayat system was dissolved and an interim government was formed under the leadership of Krishna Prasad Bhattarai of Nepali Congress. This came like a watershed moment in Nepali politics. Sooner than expected, a Constitutional Recommendations Commission was established and its members nominated by the interim prime minister represented the Nepali Congress, the ULF and the Palace. While the Constitution-making process was in offing, the ignored group UNPM (coordinated by Baburam Bhattarai) continued demand for elections to a Constituent Assembly. This was an idea that was perpetually rejected by the Nepali Congress, to avoid risking another round of tussle with the Palace.

On 8 November 1990, King Birendra promulgated the new Constitution that established a parliamentary democracy with regular elections, political freedom, a bicameral legislature and the separation of powers. Under the newly introduced system, the executive authority was jointly vested in the King and the elected council of ministers, but with a provision of the former exercising the authority on latter's recommendation. For the first time, even though symbolically, the King of Nepal was supposed to follow the true spirit of democracy in which even his authority was kept under a limit. As anticipated, the radical Maoist group UNPM that included Prachanda's Mashal and Mohan Bikram Singh's Masal and a communist faction of ULF (Nirmal Lama's Fourth Convention), held the view that the Nepali Congress and its allies had once again betrayed the Nepali people by aligning with the monarchy to prevent the making of the Constituent Assembly. The Maoists and allies refused to recognize the Constitution's legitimacy but such resistance could not succeed with their inherently weak position and under the jubilation of the success received with the experiments of the Nepali Congress in 1990 that finally helped democracy take a firm root in Nepal. The Maoists though came back into the public imagination by 1996 with an armed insurgency that lasted for a decade and changed the political landscape of Nepal forever.

How did the Maoists find their wings in Nepal? The movement represented the long-suppressed voices of the masses and found traction of support based on fighting against the persistence of rural oppression, especially so in the hinterlands and isolated corners. A 1999 novel by Khagendra Sangroula *Junkiriko Sangeet* (The

Music of Fireflies) throws light on the success factors of Maoists in Nepal, notable among them is their propensity to fight against the semi-feudal forces and caste and class oppression of the poor. Before violence characterized the Maoists' actions and a series of mistakes at the organizational level, they received strong support from a large section of the population that was on the periphery and never benefited from the monarchy and its local representatives except for a chronic disadvantageous existence with no hope for the future. In some manner, the arrival and success of Maoists on Nepal's political turf was in response to Kathmandu's elites; for them, socio-economic emancipation was never a part of the rule.

One of the key architects of the Maoist insurgency who later became finance minister and prime minister of Nepal was Baburam Bhattarai. He was known to be an academically sharp mind who never stood second in his academic life and wrote his PhD dissertation at Jawaharlal Nehru University in the 1980s on *The Nature of Underdevelopment and Regional Structure of Nepal: A Marxist Analysis*. When the monarchy was still blooming in Nepal and democracy was subservient to the Palace, he and many other radicalized youth of Nepal were devoting time on reading the country's history to reshape its future.

The rise of lead cadres like Prachanda, Baburam Bhattarai, Mohan Vaidya (now estranged from the mainstream Maoist camp and running a highly reactionary fraction group) and others were in sync with the need of the new time—so, the focus shifted from bullet to ballot. This brought a decisive turnout of acceptability for same Maoists who were not seen through friendly eyes just a few years back. The democratic upheavals had made space for a mature polity in Nepal's breeding ground for democracy, but the real effects failed to reach to the last mile, alas!

As of now, the Maoists are keeping a formidable position for themselves. Nevertheless, these radicals in the revisionist fold are inflicted with intra-party feuds and devious directional leaning. Thus, the country is still running through the high experimentations of constructive democratization rather than getting a stable system at work.

* * *

The China Factor

The new post-monarchy dispensation only hastened the expansion of Chinese influence and removed possibilities of ending long festering irritants like the border dispute in the Kalapani area—a unanimous multiparty parliamentary vote endorsed a new map of Nepal incorporating border areas which it had not claimed earlier.

India has made its Nepal ties a function of Nepal–China relations. Yet the fact is that Chinese influence in Nepal will continue to expand. It is only natural that the people of Nepal, particularly the younger generation, yearn to take advantage of all kinds of economic opportunities and benefits that China has to offer. Nepal's importance to China was initially because of its desire for security on the question of Tibetan refugees. It did not seem to mind India's preponderant influence over Nepal.

Today China has additional reasons to assert itself: one is to reduce India to size to the extent possible, the other to ensure that its Middle Kingdom credentials are enhanced. But India can draw comfort from the increased wariness of Nepal about Chinese intentions because of its overtly intrusive interest in the former's internal affairs, and the long-term price of too close a Chinese embrace.

The official website of the Nepal embassy in Beijing is very categorical in exemplifying its crucially important trade ties with Nepal and contradicting it with the cases of falling trade with China and growing trade deficit:

Nepal has been pursuing open and market-oriented trade policy. The country is a member of WTO, SAFTA, BIMSTEC and MIGA. The Trade Policy 2015 aims to create a conducive environment for promotion of trade in order to make it competitive at international level. The Government of Nepal has incorporated trade agenda as a main strategy in its development plan. The country is making every effort to increase exports and minimize the trade deficit. Currently the Nepal Trade Integration Strategy (NTIS) 2016 is in implementation in order to increase trade competitiveness. Nepal and China have been doing trade since ancient times. The border points that are open between the two countries are Kodari-Nyalam, Rasuwa-Keyrong, Yari (Humla)-Purang, Olangchung Gola-Riwu, Kimathanka Riwu, and Nechung (Mustang)-Lizi. However, border trade takes place through forty old different passes. The border inhabitants of the two countries may, within an area of 30 kilometres from the border, carry on the traditional trade on barter basis. Kodari-Nyalam and Rasuwa-Kerong are the two points of international trade via land route. Currently, the land routes have permitted quota of vehicles from China to Nepal owing to the outbreak of the Covid-19 pandemic. At present, China is the second largest trading partner. Though the volume of bilateral trade is small, the trade deficit against Nepal is widening. Nepal has duty-free access for 7787 items in China. The Government of Nepal is encouraging businessmen to increase exports to China. Along with bilateral trade agreements, there is also an intergovernmental trade and economic committee at Vice Ministers' level for enhancing trade and economic activities between the two countries. There is also a separate trade facilitation mechanism between Nepal and Tibet Autonomous Region (TAR) of China. Nepal and TAR of China also hold

Nepal-China's Tibet Economic and Trade Fair every two years in Kathmandu and Lhasa alternatively.

On 14 March 2023, a Reuters report amplified the glaring disadvantages Nepal is facing while going extra miles in engaging with China both politically and economically:

> Nepal's Prime Minister Pushpa Kamal Dahal asked China to provide 'easy and more generous' market access to products from the Himalayan country to help narrow its wide trade deficit with Beijing. The landlocked Himalayan nation of 30 million people has traditionally looked to India for economic support and trade, but Nepal has increasingly been courted by China with transport, trade and transit deals, to New Delhi's unease. Nepal's imports from China fell to $1.84 billion in 2022 from $2.38 billion a year ago, while exports totalled $5.39 million, down from $8.37 million in the same period, official data showed. Nepal's growing trade deficit with China and the apparent gaps in commitment and actual investment of FDI from China are some of the issues that needed a practical solution, Dahal told a business meeting organized by the Confederation of Nepalese Industries (CNI) and China Council for the Promotion of International Trade (CCPIT) in Kathmandu. China is among the top investors in Nepal's infrastructure. Beijing accounts for 14 per cent of Nepal's international trade while India holds nearly two-thirds of it, trade officials said.

Based on a leaked report of the government of Nepal accusing China of encroaching into Nepal along the two countries' shared border, a BBC story by Michael Bristow (published on 8 February 2022) exposed the first official claim from Nepal of Chinese interference in its territory. The report was commissioned in September 2021 following claims that China has been trespassing in the district of Humla, in the far west of Nepal. Hardly surprising, China's embassy in Kathmandu denies there has been any encroachment. The report is yet not brought in the public domain by the Government of Nepal, and except a few sustained stories in the *Kathmandu Post* by journalist Anil Giri, the news hardly got the prominence it deserved in Nepal's national media. In fact, another English, the *Kathmandu Republica,* ran a story on 25 August 2020 countering a BBC report and many other reports published in India with an unusual headline: 'Nepalis surprised by Indian media's repeated romance with fake Nepal-China border dispute.' And on 23 September 2020, it ran the next one echoing the voice of an official Chinese embassy spokesperson in Kathmandu and with the headline: 'China denies encroaching Nepali territory in Humla; asks Nepal to verify the border points.'

At times, there were public outrage and protests in Kathmandu against Chinese advances but such incidents were usually never properly reported in Nepal's national media. With keeping 'the China factor' in mind, the deafening silence rather than an answer was offered by the official establishment in Kathmandu.

The report's findings were likely to put pressure on the growing links Nepal has with China considering their proximity and common border runs for nearly 1400 km (870 miles) along the Himalayan mountains. It was laid out in a series of treaties signed between the two countries in the early 1960s. Much of it is in remote, hard-to-reach areas. On the ground, the boundary is demarcated by a chain of pillars, set kilometres apart. This sometimes makes it hard to know exactly where the border is located. The Nepal government decided to send a taskforce to Humla after a few reports (including one in BBC) about possible Chinese encroachment. Some claimed China had built a series of buildings on the Nepalese side of the border. The team consisted of representatives from the police and the government. In its report, passed to the BBC, the group found that surveillance activities by Chinese security forces had restricted religious activities on the Nepalese side of the border in a place called Lalungjong. The area has traditionally been a draw for pilgrims because of its proximity to Mount Kailash, just over the border in China, which is a sacred site for both Hindus and Buddhists. The report also concluded that China had been limiting grazing by Nepalese farmers. In the same area, it found China was building a fence around a border pillar and attempting to construct a canal and a road on the Nepalese side of the border.

The tall Himalayas exist to be the natural barrier to China's greater outreach bid with its southern neighbour, Nepal. After Nepal's deadly earthquake in 2015, China was forced to close the Tatopani–Zhangmu land border with Nepal due to heavy damage inflicted in the tragic earthquake. Reportedly, even the Rasuwagadhi–Kerung border remained closed for a long time. After the outbreak of Covid-19 in 2020 when Nepal needed China's support on the trade and commercial fronts the most, the Tatopani–Zhangmu route was completely closed while the Rasuwagadhi–Kerung route was opened only intermittently for the sake of China's advantage only. China imposed an undeclared trade blockade on Nepal and not even once, Nepal could officially contempt such an action during the phases humanity witnessed an unprecedented crisis with Covid-19, a pandemic that too originated from China. What keeps Nepal on such an overtly defensive side? Its answer lies in China's heavy investment on the PR front where it is being projected as a 'healer' while its acts are exactly in the opposite spirit.

China is just not over-pervasive in Nepal with projects and political manipulation, its best edge is with the propaganda machinery that is oriented to damage the finer fabrics of India–Nepal relations beyond the core. The China factor is being played out in Nepal and unfortunately not for a constructive aim of enhancing its economic ties with the northern neighbour but to create a complex web involving India's stake and finally letting a disastrous narrative help the traders of ultra-nationalism for scoring high politically, and ruling the game of late.

The narrative is being manufactured rather than shaped—with an intellectual machinery religiously working to make it happen in favour of Chinese interests in Nepal. In long-form of writing too, the case is not different. Amish Raj Mulmi's unbelievable jubilation of 'Nepal's turn to China and his painstaking efforts in proving the flawed argument how all roads lead north—sweeps over the possibility of a genuine and unbiased account coming on China's misadventures in the South Asian region, their historical progression and Nepal's continuing vulnerability.[*] With sixty-six pages of notes and purposefully featured details without connecting the dots, the book puzzles even a keen watcher of Nepal. The chosen plot is serious and the author's preoccupied romantic notion in dealing with it makes the whole narrative reductionist—and deeply biased in favour of China, an expansionist force in the northern neighbourhood of Nepal. In hindsight, the author was not expected to juxtapose the ground realities with his uncaring assessment and projections—overlooking the fragile polity in the country and regional geo-strategic sensitivities.

The misinterpretation knows no bounds when one reads it towards the end of the book (pp. 209–10):

---

[*] Amish Raj Mulmi, *All Roads Lead North: Nepal's Turn to China* (Context-Westland, 2021).

China is many things at once in Nepal today. It is a superpower, a beneficent aid-giver, a friend in need, an essential provider, a demanding neighbour, an older brother, a competitor, a model of development and a vision of a developed future. China is changing regional and global dynamics in an unprecedented way than Nepal. As China declares itself on the world stage, Nepal wants to tag along for the ride. Relations have never been better than in the contemporary era, but they need to be sustained, nurtured and developed as they evolve. It is in Nepal's interest to do so, and imperative to do it in a way that acknowledges its own aspirations.

Mulmi's prose would have earned praise provided he had written his maiden book as an official spokesperson of the People's Republic of China. As an independent observer, he had all the reasons to cope with any compulsion that made him voice so strongly for China despite its excesses at home and in the world. Just to shun India and downplay the complementarity that India–Nepal relations stand for, he travelled extra miles—and hurriedly and erroneously wrote off India as a sort of 'non-performing asset' (page 213):

Far away, in Delhi, one could imagine a chuckle in the corridors of South Block. Nepal's politics, and its politicians, are a quagmire. Its leaders play each other and its neighbours constantly in the struggle for power. India had long waded into the puddle, played the game and lost. Now, it was China's turn.

Such words are a disservice to Nepal and China as well as India. While presenting Nepal as a welcoming turf for 'tug war', its sovereign status is undermined. India's ties with Nepal hold not much significance, this book suggests—and China is at a loss as it is represented in poor light as the 'next interventionist power' in Nepal. The author acknowledges the significance of 'optics' in international relations; however, he appears unassuming as he selectively drops it as a 'virtue' for judging the political course of action at homeland. Mulmi has not enlightened his readers with loads of preferential sourced materials—besides his travels to places, meeting people and presenting them as the only authentic beholders of truth. More often than not, it seems, Mulmi does not count much on the text, context and people that have not come his way.

The author missed an opportunity to write the first major book about India's share of contributions and mistakes in Nepal as the closest ally integrated through the tenets in social, cultural, economic and diplomatic realms—Nepal's inability to dissect the fallouts of mixing the domestic and international policies—and China's expansionism leveraging the hiccups in bilateral relations between India and Nepal. As a sovereign country and functional democracy, Nepal should claim a greater stake in South Asia. It would be undeserving on anyone's part, if such a chance is denied for just polarizing the discourse—thus leaving behind the aspirations of the mass Nepali.

A clear demarcating line between the official and social historiography is essential for featuring the most pressing issues, concerning masses. The book fails to observe this and sadly offers confrontation rather the peaceful co-existence, its well-deserved due (pp. 218–19):

Kathmandu's determination to stand up to what it calls Indian 'bullying' has been partially driven by the weight of a newly resurgent China behind it. And China will only become stronger hereon, and Delhi's ability and influence within the Kathmandu establishment will continue to weaken if it does not swiftly recognize and address the foundational shortcomings in the bilateral relationship.

Negating the actual observations of King Tribhuvan and King Mahendra on the significance of accepting the neighbourhood in its shape and spirit can't be said pragmatic at this point of time when Nepal's 'tryst with the democracy' is still fogged with self-inflicted challenges like endemic corruption and lack of responsibility bearing in public life. Be it the political or economic repercussions of China's excesses in Pakistan and Sri Lanka and letting both countries compromise their sovereign status under the guise of 'developmental projects', they found no particular elaboration from Mulmi. This is again very disappointing since he could have done some damage control here by commenting on China's territorial aggression, including near the borders with Nepal. Mulmi's book should get a long shelf life, in the official circle; it should be used widely for reference. His words are comforting for Nepal's northern neighbour; the book should get translated in Mandarin to add up to China's existing archives of propaganda and misnomers. More than the diplomatic cables, this will give moments of fleeting happiness to the muscle-flexing policymakers in China.

The political classes in Nepal will remain indifferent; this way, they will continue to avail their innocence. India will continue to be a friend, both officially and on the people's front. Lest we forget it!

In fact, the prospects of a hostile India–China relationship are not shocking for the developed world. Though, it is extremely harmful for the Asian economies. It should be noted how India's trade terms with China are seeing unprecedented fall for the first time in years; the bilateral trade between the countries in recent years rose sharply despite bilateral tensions over the border dispute. The development came as China's overall foreign trade declined by about 5 per cent as its economy struggled to recover from Covid-19 blues.

As per a Press Trust of India (PTI) report, China's exports to India in the first half of this year totalled $56.53 billion compared to $57.51 billion last year, registering a decline of 0.9 per cent, according to the data released by Chinese customs in July 2023. India's exports to China during the same period totalled $9.49 billion compared to $9.57 billion last year. The trade deficit in the first half of 2023 too declined significantly to $47.04 as compared to $67.08 billion last year. Last year was a bumper year for India–China trade as it touched an all-time high of $135.98 billion despite the continued chill in the bilateral ties over the military stand-off in eastern Ladakh in May 2020. The total India–China trade in 2022 overtook the $125 billion mark a year earlier by registering an 8.4 per cent increase. New Delhi's trade deficit with Beijing crossed for the first time a $100-billion mark despite frosty bilateral relations.

On the other hand, the US is back in its business with China. In the post Covid-19 times, China's understanding should have to give a halt to its exceedingly damaging 'String of Pearls' action and expansionist BRI and approach for a peaceful rise with its entrepreneurial strength. The BRI is a grand design and meant to enhance China's strategic stature in the region. Nepal will seriously suffer if it falls prey to Chinese advances, especially if it does at the cost of weakening its reliable terms with India and without developing its own capabilities. BRI projects are not for development partnership—an early reckoning among the policymakers would have avoided many complications for Nepal. Noticeably, Nepal's limited negotiation capability with China has been highlighted at times, including for Pokhara Airport that was listed as a BRI project. To refute it officially and officially terming it a non-BRI project, the time taken by Kathmandu's ruling classes was too long.

When the strategic culture is on wane and the challenges from the neighbourhood are real, India should reassess its priorities in international relations and re-align them with an outcome-driven approach. China is upbeat about its plans and without caring for responses, India has no option left but to answer China through different means. Now, it seems that the vision for 'Asian Century' was hollowed, and China must take its credit for it. Of late, China's authoritarian compulsions are posing a serious challenge to the peace of the world. When the novel coronavirus (Covid-19) was not known, and the world was moving ahead with an undivided economic vision where China's ideological priorities were shrewdly made to coexist with consumerism, there was a strong clamour for the 'Asian Century'. Globalization was seen as a cure-all enigma. Sadly, it crumbled when China was blamed for producing the deadliest virus, and an aggressive counter by neo-nationalism made the world order look like a set of a ten-pin game.

A much stronger Chinese nationalism at home, global trade integration was lost in transition and fast approaching mass poverty for over a billion people the world over ensured the clanging of alarm bells. The pseudo comfort offered by globalization despite its discontents is waning, and unrest is intensifying not just on the streets but in the desperate decision-making process. This makes the State oppressively overbearing. Under the new framework, there is little chance left for the old ideologies to survive, even in the form of symbolism. Democracies are failing their citizens en masse with their clumsy leaderships that thrive on some kind of authoritarianism. Current international relations are being ruled through domestic political compulsions or misplaced priorities, the case of the India–Nepal stand-off in the recent past is an example.

Also, the deep border disputes and low-scale confrontations between India and China can be seen in this perspective. The message that comes out is loud and clear—it implies a disastrous end of flawed diplomatic and strategic manoeuvrings.

As China's integration with the rest of the world is getting troubled now, it should give more focus to Asia with a sense of reality and possibility. Its doublespeak is unlikely to give it mileage like in the past. As the conflict between the two Asian giants has already reached a flashpoint, the onus is on China to act for peace. Nepal, for reasons best known to its decision-makers, had not read China's intentions in the South Asian region.

It is important to recall the apathy of Asians towards their own history and investigate why it is that the Western model—ridden with crises of idea and direction—is still being conscientiously adhered to in Asia. The weakening of radical political ideologies, and the failure of the surviving leftists to find an alternate route regarding 'intelligent economics', has made the scene viciously saturated. India and Nepal are uniquely dealing with democratic Left ideologies where their participation in the mainstream polity is significant, more so in Nepal. Even now, reckoning about the broken Western model is not commonplace; it no doubt continues as a dominating political and economic force.

Not long ago, the prominence of Asia seemed imminent as it had vast untapped potential. However, diverse governing patterns in different Asian countries stopped their rise on an even plank. Among those countries, Nepal is well-placed with its relatively positive fundamentals and its firm embrace of modernism and democracy. But this nation needs to expand its assets in a more engaged manner, besides eliminating the conditions that allow regressive 'partisans' to thrive disproportionately. B.P. Koirala was a nationalist and yet an internationalist without any predicament. Perhaps the serving Nepali politicians of this time should pause and consider Koirala as a role model. Many other first-generation democratic leaders, including those from the Left background, should be remembered and emulated for their balanced stand on crucial international matters.

In an interview with a Kathmandu-based think tank, the Nepal Institute for International Cooperation and Engagement (NIICE), Noam Chomsky said China doesn't have a socialist system. Nepal's interest lies in being neutral, he added. Indeed, Nepal has a fair chance to broaden its developmental agenda by pursuing enlightened self-interest in its foreign policy. There is a need to discriminate between the national interest and political interest; the former should steer the foreign policy and engagements.

Initially touted as the New Silk Road and, furthermore, the New Maritime Silk Route added and, then, the Trans-Himalayan Economic Corridor (THEC) further added, it was becoming too confusing even to the Chinese what exactly all this meant for them. All this happened pursuant to China's 'Look Westward' policy—announced by President Hu Jintao as he sought a far more balanced regional development of China moving from the eastern seaboard to the western and south-western landmass. It was geo-strategically broadened and deepened by President Xi's 'China Dream'. All this has now been simplified and clarified as One Belt One Road (OBOR) or even more simply, BRI. That may be clear and simple for the Chinese, but it should get clarified further for non-Chinese peoples that 'Belt' refers to overland access to Europe while 'Road' refers to the sea route connecting Asia, Africa and Europe.

Undoubtedly, it is the paramount geo-political, geo-economic and geo-psychological global strategy of China to become the supreme global power. It will have profound gravitational pulls on all counties where the BRI passes through. The globalism that occurred from the 1970s around regionalism will, henceforth, be transformed to inter-regionalism based on sub-regionalism as overland connectivity to Europe, which will lead to the formation of a Eurasian economy maneuvered jointly by Russia and China with Turkey in the sidelines. While all this portends well for China, it is also being questioned how far the Chinese promise of a BRI seeking a win-win for all is likely to be a reality. Indian analysts believe it is a China-centric policy starting and ending in Beijing with only a token say by the bilateral partners.

The *New York Times* carried an extensive coverage of Chinese investments in Namibia only to pronounce it as a manifestation of neo-colonialism with the de facto control of everything in the projects with minimal shares and say to the host nation. In fact, *New York Times* goes on to describe the extensive nefarious parleys by Chinese businesses in the domestic politics of Namibia with funds and other perks. Amidst other findings, it was underscored that it is Chinese businesses that get the profits while for the people of Namibia, all they get is a bigger national debt. Similarly, news emanating from Pakistan on the China–Pakistan Economic Corridor (CPEC) speaks about the lack of transparency, the violation of Pakistan laws and customs by Chinese businesses and workers, and need for clarity on the concept of 'economic corridor' as it appears more a transit transport link with unknown economic benefits to the areas it passes through in Pakistan.

President Xi Jinping speaks of China's diplomatic thrust as one of a 'peaceful rise'. However, given the natural hegemonic tendencies in relations between Big Powers and Small Powers in international politics, it may be best if Chinese strategists took cognizance of the existing realities. All said and done, the concept of connectivity must be visualized holistically—transport, institutions, international law, markets, finance, culture and people-to-people (going beyond government-to-government). Sophisticated economic models must be developed for seeking win-win multidisciplinary scenarios for mutual benefit out of any bilateral projects so that they are sustainable and impact economic growth significantly and Nepal does not fall into a debt trap. To look ahead, there should be a looking back to notice a historical trend that confirms Nepal had prospered, until the advent of the East India Company into the subcontinent, as an economic corridor and a civilizational bridge between adjoining northern India and Tibet. Following the calamitous loss by Nepal in the Anglo–Nepalese (Gurkha) War of 1814–16, it was territorially reduced in size by around 33 per cent and its prevalent national 'geo-psychology' was transformed from an emerging Himalayan Empire aspiring to be an economic and cultural bridgehead between India and China to simply of a 'yam between two boulders'. Subsequently, it sought to look inward and close its doors to the outside world.

In a globalized world where Nepal has a close bearing with the developments in the rest of the world, only a forward-looking approach at policy and action front will yield results in its favour. No ruling regime in Kathmandu should give too much preference to the 'India-China equation' and use it for any temporary purpose and in the process, letting the benefits of pursuing 'enlightened self-interest'. The 'enlightened self-interest' will be the 'national interest' too, and help Nepal's neighbours as well in coming to terms with its actual aspirations in place of notions engulfed with doubts and suspicions.

Surely with a perfect reason, the political thinker Hans Morgenthau did recast the national interest as 'interests in terms of power'—that is, the 'national interest' simply became the acquiring, maintenance and expansion of a State's power. Nepal needs a stronger State and stronger central political characters. Such a bright possibility will complete its real transition that lies within and not beyond the boundary.

The broad geopolitical and economic trends are also suggestive of doors opening to more active Nepali participation in the Indo–Pacific economic agenda, with the Nepalese Parliament approving the $500 million MCC grant from the United States; this could substantially upgrade energy cooperation between India and Nepal, and also India agreeing to the United Kingdom, the European Union and other major investment partners working together in third world countries on development projects. Interestingly, the Nepalese seem to have independently made a reassessment of risks in over-exposure with China, thanks in large measure due to Beijing's missteps, and the style and the substance of Chinese-delivered assistance. There is much greater receptivity and a 'felt need' across the political spectrum and in public discussion of the genuineness of India's friendship aimed at contributing to the welfare of the people of Nepal.

The decision of the Government of India to set up an inter-ministerial standing group under the chairmanship of the foreign secretary, to coordinate sections and ensure more rapid follow-up of project decisions is also a welcome step.

Business leaders in India should be encouraged to be proactive in looking for new opportunities in expanding and diversifying trade and investment ties with Nepal including exploring possibilities in the context of a reset of supply chains in the post Covid-19 situation. There is no doubt that the economic challenges in the post-Covid-19 situation, and the overall churning in the geopolitical environment, have created an opportunity for both countries to devise innovative approaches to long-standing issues and to aim for new horizons in bilateral cooperation. It is vital that Nepal deepen its economic ties with India and facilitate joint ventures that create immense economic opportunities. India's unwavering commitment to peace and prosperity in Nepal and its complementarity in its relations with Nepal will help in creating a healthier economic ecosystem in Nepal. While the economic scenario is troubled—and it is unlikely that Nepal will emerge from it soon—it will be wrong to assume that a condition akin to a breakdown is inevitable in Nepal. Economic adversity has created the space for course correction and Nepal should be encouraged to devise a fresh approach to achieve this through calibrated efforts and enhancing economic partnership with India.

A trilateral front of India–Nepal–China is unlikely as long as China maintains an expansionist intention in the South Asian region and threatens India's geopolitical and economic interests. For Nepal, the China option is not viable either, as its bilateral relations with India will sustain the tides on the strong fundamentals and people to people factor. While China should think of a peaceful rise and contribute its dues to the dreams of an Asian century, India must deliver more, and on time, in Nepal. Nepal, for its part, should do better homework and get into a framework that enables it to act freely without short-term transactional considerations. Its maturity lies in knowing its interest well and not losing the immense goodwill in India. India should always reciprocate. In an uncertain post-pandemic time like this, India and Nepal have a common ground to make a collaborative bilateral narrative and boost regional and sub-regional cooperation as well.

A few key facts about Nepalese disappointment with China in recent times:

— *Trade and Transit Agreement signed with much fanfare in 2016. Several sea and land ports specifically committed by China to reduce Nepal's dependence on India, especially for petroleum products . . . no concrete outcome.*
— *Nepal purchased six civilian aircraft from China in 2012 at an exorbitant cost. One crashed, others grounded due to manufacturing defects.*

— *In 2016, Nepal signed an agreement with China to join its Belt and Road Initiative (BRI) and establish Special Economic Zones near the Chinese border. No concrete outcomes.*

— *1 January 2023, China claims Pokhara International Airport was built by it under BRI. Publicly refuted by Nepal.*

Nepal also knows that it is not the only country which feels cheated by China's false promises. Only recently the Italian defence minister said: 'The decision to join the (new) Silk Road was an improvised and atrocious act that multiplied China's exports to Italy but did not have the same effect on Italian exports to China,' adding that the decision of Italy to join the BRI had been 'an atrocious decision'.

There is no room for Indian complacency, as Chinese intentions are fairly obvious. They go well beyond ensuring that Nepal is not used for anti-China activities in Tibet. A core objective is to dilute India's influence. But beyond a point, as long as it plays its cards intelligently, India can afford to take China's expanding influence in its stride.

Public opinion in Nepal is now very alert to the reality of Chinese intentions, risks of falling into a debt trap, and limitations in terms of Chinese capacities in comparison to India's. China's image itself has taken a huge beating because of the current Covid-19 tsunami. There is however no room for complacency on India's part, and traditional irritants like the 1950 Treaty and the border issue need not be kept festering but should be sorted out in an open and transparent manner. There is no reason why the worldview of the East India Company or British India should be the determinant guide in shaping perceptions or policies, when people on both sides of an open border are impatiently awaiting a better quality of life.

Nepal is a transforming country. India is now a player on the global stage. The world itself is heading towards major transformations, with new challenges, changing priorities and boundless possibilities. The Covid-19 crisis and its long-term fallout is the largest shock to the global socio-economic framework since the Great Depression of the early 1930s. More than a hundred million people have fallen below the poverty line in 2020–21 alone. India and Nepal are uniquely positioned, because of the breadth and depth of ties between them—of history, geography, culture, religion and people-to-people—to jointly rethink economic governance with a view to enhancing human welfare. There are huge challenges but also huge opportunities in expanding and diversifying cooperation to mutual advantage.

* * *

1950 Treaty of Peace and Friendship

The founder of modern Nepal, King Prithvi Narayan Shah, called Nepal a 'yam between two boulders', referring to India and China. For British India, Nepal was a buffer zone between India and China. In the present time and context, by not aligning domestic policies with international affairs, Nepal has a better chance to practise a serious non-alignment policy. Remarkably, Nepal has a long history of sovereignty and independent status. Even nonconformists will not forget that the Gorkha Kingdom appealed to the British Empire for protection from a Chinese attack through Tibet. The first British mission came to Nepal in 1793, followed by the next one in 1802.

The collaboration didn't last long, however, and the Anglo-Nepal War or Gorkha War (1814–16) was fought between the Gorkha Kingdom and the British East India Company. A British victory and the 1816 Sugauli Treaty ended the war. With the treaty, Nepal renounced its territorial claims on the Terai, and parted with its conquests west of the Kali River that reached up to the Sutlej River. Nepal could retain its independence, though it had to be under the supervision of a British resident sent to look after the protectorate. Nepal succeeded in not letting the British resident be a 'controlling agent' of the British East India Company that ruled its immediate neighbour, India.

In the changing times, it will be worthwhile to look back and have deep knowledge about the choices exercised by Nepal on the matters of foreign policy under domestic political compulsions. With hindsight, a saner act will be for Kathmandu's policymakers to do self-introspection rather than blaming their neighbours for all the wrongs they believe that Nepal is grappling with today. Unlike what has been said to be firmly rooted in the collective psyche of Nepalis, the neighbours are not the 'boulders' and Nepal is not a 'yam'. Nepal should not be presented as a conduit for 'bridge diplomacy'. As a country with immense possibilities and aspirations, Nepal should think of carefully judged and open-minded priorities in its foreign affairs. It should give 'the notion of realism' a well-deserved traction. However, this should not be confused as a new system bound to overlook the conventional wisdom that helps in knowing friends and adversaries in difficult times.

As a matter of fact, Nepal can do without seeing India and China in comparison. Nepal, a modern republic, should continue to strengthen its democracy and democratize its institutions. It should get a development strategy with inclusive nature. To bring it into action, a participatory model should be followed. Precisely, for managing its affairs in the world with new vigour and progressive thinking, Nepal has to bring the home in order. Realizing it will be a true diplomatic nicety. Also, it is high time that economic cooperation with India was given its due to ensure a post-pandemic economic rebound. The bilateral engagement has to be proactive. Long-pending matters related to treaties and territories should be dealt with through official mechanisms so they can be tabled and sorted out with a trust-based approach. Such matters should not stop Nepal's top leadership from engaging with India.

The 1950 Treaty came about as insecurity grew in Nepal in proportion to the presence of communist China in Tibet. The beleaguered Rana rulers had few options and hence, secured much-needed traction from India for their survival and as a safeguard against the looming threat of communism. However, that scenario changed in no time and global power politics entered the long spell of the Cold War. India adjusted its diplomatic stance and strengthened ties with communist China. It also recognized Tibet as an Autonomous Region of China in 1954. Nepal, too, followed a similar path without any objection from India. At this point, the treaty was expected to be scrapped and replaced with a new treaty of a broader nature. That, alas, did not happen then, and has not happened since.

King Birendra's stance of making Nepal a zone of peace, maintaining that the country would decide its strategic policies on its own, didn't go down very well with India, which saw the King's actions as an attempt to tamper seriously with the spirit of the 1950 Treaty. Tensions simmered but were short-lived, as India–Nepal relations have always progressed through many dimensions. Time and again, both the countries have displayed 'ambivalence' in their approaches, but maturity has also developed through the ups and downs of diplomacy. From its side, India reconsidered its stand on the two-pillar policy—constitutional monarchy and multiparty system—and recognized political changes and new Nepali sentiments. India's distaste for the absolute monarchy of King Gyanendra and its acceptance of the Maoists as a mainstream political force must be seen as departing radically from any formalist approach that the 1950 Treaty might have led differently.

Since the 2006 popular movement, Nepal has been undergoing an unstable but peaceful democratic transition, which has helped the emergence of new ideological and regional political parties. This development has exerted pivotal impacts on India–Nepal relations. These impacts will need to be factored into a new treaty. Relations between the two democratic nations will not be compromised simply due to the abrogation of the 1950 Treaty. A new treaty should replace the 1950 Treaty, one that will take into account India and Nepal's position as they stand now, not as they were over seven decades ago. The basic spirit of India–Nepal relations must be retained in any such treaty—besides laying greater focus on issue-based cooperation, which would increase productivity all around. The revision of other treaties and dysfunctional MoUs should also be pursued in parallel. Moreover, the asset that is the open border between the two countries must be utilized in a more comprehensive manner to enhance local as well as large-scale trade, while also keeping it secure from terror outfits, which have already made deep footprints in the border regions. Thus, a revision of the 1950 Treaty is desperately needed to take bilateral relations to a new high and secure a threat-free existence for both sides of the border.

It is highly impractical that the Nepal-India Treaty of Peace and Friendship, hurriedly signed by the unpopular and undemocratic Rana Prime Minister Mohan Shumsher and Indian ambassador C.P.N. Singh in 1950, is still being utilized as a framework for defining the terms of its bilateral relations with Nepal. Though an open border regime and many other provisions of this treaty cannot be said to be unequal, after seventy-three years, most issues of India–Nepal relations have outgrown the scope of this document. The treaty has thus become unpopular in some Nepali segments, which is understandable as the closeness of cooperation does not come without ambiguity on sovereignty. The following two articles of the treaty are particularly illuminative of this state of affairs:

Article 6
Each Government undertakes, in token of the neighbourly friendship between India and Nepal, to give to the nationals of the other, in its territory, national treatment with regard to participation in industrial and economic development of such territory and to the grant of concessions and contracts, relating to such development.

Article 7
The Governments of India and Nepal agree to grant, on a reciprocal basis, to the nationals of one country in the territories of the other the same privileges in the matter of residence, ownership of property, participation in trade and commerce, movement and other privileges of a similar nature.

Over the decades, both the countries have seen a radical change in their polity and economy and have accordingly adjusted their policies. But in principle, outdated treaties still have some say in bilateral engagements. Precisely, India–Nepal relations function at varied levels: personal, political, geostrategic, economic, international and socio-psychological. So, person-to-person and back-channel diplomacy are crucial, as they help outline an alternative framework for bilateral relations. Notionally, India's Nepal policy is still heavily influenced by the 1950 Treaty— irrespective of the erosion of many of its elements during the course of implementation. But effectively, Nepal has no such India policy as it has no clear standing on the treaty. Ironically, a section of its political class (especially the Left parties) demands the scrapping of the treaty while out of power, but once in power, they keep it afloat to further ritualistic diplomatic dialogues between power centres. Often, a misunderstanding of history aggravates the power centres' feeble hold on the present and future course, leaving the status quo to persist as a working virtue.

Many multilateral cooperation platforms have eluded smaller nations, contradicting their own rationale for existence. Nepal is no exception to this phenomenon and has badly missed out on chances to carve out a position to deal with major bilateral issues in South Asia and beyond. The country's long democratic transition has made its standing even more precarious. Before 2001, Asia had two distinct royalties: Nepal and Bhutan. With the unnatural ending of the partially feudal legal throne in Nepal, the country ushered in a complex web of political arrangements. Later, the prominent advent of the Maoists and Madhesh-based political parties was in the right spirit of the times, but later developments have shown their inefficiency in dealing with the cores of polity and diplomacy. Living under an unjustified 'big brother syndrome' and making impractical moves have broken down Nepal's conventional edge vis-à-vis its relationship with India.

Nepal's external policy should be directed by its own self-interest instead of excuses. The political establishment in Kathmandu should reckon that the diplomatic engagements of two almost equals—India and China—does not happen on a single front but on many counts. Among them, the most formidable is economic ties. China cannot simply throw off the burden of its past. It has a few allies to date and Nepal should not have irrational expectations from China. In the lexicon of Nepal's political economy, trade should be given extra attention. Trade and diplomacy should ideally be the mainstays of external policy.

There is no reason why Nepal should retract from this fundamental understanding. The hyped plot of breaking conventions has given little positive outcome so far. People's representatives need to come to terms with the fact that the masses are only concerned with leading the country out of the present mess.

In South Asia, Nepal is situated strategically to carry forward its independent stature. Despite the gloom and doom over the last two decades, Nepalis in general have endorsed democracy. This is a sort of accomplishment, as modern ideas and aspirations are routed through such welcome changes. If there is balance on the political home turf, it will be much easier for Nepal to claim its deserved position in the world. There is no tailor-made solution for a firm footing in external matters except for being internally strong while chasing difficult targets externally. Relying less on theoretical paradigms and taking a more practical approach will make foreign policy maneuvering a more informed exercise. As a sovereign State, the boldness of Nepal's action should display its sovereignty. Unlike China or India, it has never earned the ire of cunning colonial motives. This is a reality and not bound to be changed. Thus, it allows Nepalis to take pride in its non-interfering nationalistic pedigree. In the present ideal-deficient time, bilateralism is the order of the day for nations. Hence, Nepal too should define its priorities accordingly. It is time for a course correction in Nepal.

The open India–Nepal border best reflects the strength of ties between these two nations, but their lackluster management reveals the compromised benefits that proper handling could have achieved. With the passage of time, the 1950 India–Nepal Treaty of Peace and Friendship, which broadly defines bilateral strategic and trade relations between the two countries, now needs an overhaul. The 1950 Treaty mandates that 'neither Government shall tolerate any threat to the security of the other by a foreign aggressor' and made mandatory to both sides 'to inform each other of any serious friction or misunderstanding with any neighbouring state likely to cause any breach in friendly relations subsisting between the two Governments.'

Primarily, these accords were meant to strengthen ties between the two countries, give Nepal preferential economic treatment and provide Nepalis in India the same economic and educational opportunities as Indian citizens. Also, it ensured that the India–Nepal border would be open and people from both sides could move freely across the border without passports/visas and live and work in either country. However, by 1978, the trade and transit treaties were separated, owing to demands from Nepal. Unfortunately, in 1988, when these treaties were up for renewal, Nepal's less pragmatic stand to not accommodate India's wishes on the transit treaty forced India to call for a single trade and transit treaty. Nepal maintained its firm position, which led to an unprecedented strain on India–Nepal relations. A kind of Indian economic blockade on Nepal continued till April 1990, which was a painful episode and should be remembered as dubious political moves were made by both sides. The countries hit a new low in bilateral relations after Nepal's arms deal with China in 1988, albeit it was later observed that economic issues were the real determinant. Rajiv Gandhi, then Indian PM, took the matter as a violation of the treaties of 1959 and 1965 but skipped the extraneous clout India was enjoying with these treaties.

In the past, such clauses were uncomfortably seen by Nepal. However, it is also true that King Birendra's actions were focused more on aggressively sensitizing his Indian counterparts than going against those treaties. Thereafter, India linked security with economic relations and took action to review India–Nepal relations. Soon, Nepal had to rethink its position after dwindling economic conditions led to a drastic change in its political system, with the effect that the King was compelled to endorse a parliamentary democracy. As expected, the new government quickly sought to restore normal relations with India. After that, the 'special' security relationship between India and Nepal was re-established during the New Delhi visit of Nepal's newly elected Prime Minister Krishna Prasad Bhattarai in June 1990. Six months later, Prime Minister Girija Prasad Koirala also visited Delhi and the two countries signed new, and separate, trade and transit treaties to provide more economic benefits to Nepal. In April 1995, Prime Minister Man Mohan Adhikari visited New Delhi and negotiated a major review of the 1950 India–Nepal Treaty of Peace and Friendship. These three high-profile political visits from Kathmandu proved beneficial for India–Nepal relations. But 1996 onward, Nepal started losing its usual stream of politics under the effects of an armed insurgency driven by the Maoists. The country ushered in a painful spiral of civil war with conditions becoming much grimmer with the highly suspicious royal massacre of 2001.

Gyanendra, the new King, had neither the acceptance of the masses nor the situation in his favour to deal with a tricky political situation where the democratic movement was getting swiftly radicalized. In further course of time, the Maoists emerged stronger but the country's quest for better economic and diplomatic stakes in South Asia didn't really get the support out of their political action that was expected to be progressive. However, in present circumstances, a new course of action would do much good for the bilateral relations between India and Nepal and for other areas of Nepal's interest. As prevailing strategic challenges are much bigger than in the 1950s and Nepal's biggest quest should be to give its economy continuous momentum, the time has come when the open border must be handled more proactively to redefine trade and diplomatic cooperation between these two countries.

In particular, Nepal's Terai region, which borders the Indian districts of north Bihar and Uttar Pradesh, could be turned into a major source of trade exchanges with India. Here, border management has to be friendlier while being more effective. Notionally, it is true that these two countries share liberal border but sadly, its entrepreneurial benefits have not reached the people living on both sides of the border. Through more progressive border plans, cluster-based trade relationships between India and Nepal could be taken ahead. This will also effectively change the pattern and outlook of bilateral relations at the macro level.

* * *

A Border Dispute with Guaranteed Longevity

On 8 May 2020, the defence minister of India tweeted: 'Delighted to inaugurate the Link Road to Mansarovar Yatra today. The Border Roads Organisation (BRO) achieved road connectivity from Dharchula to Lipulekh (China Border) known as Kailash–Mansarovar Yatra Route. Also flagged off a convoy of vehicles from Pithoragarh to Gunji through video conferencing.'* The announcement and its timing surprised even keen observers of India–Nepal relations. No one thought that a road project in this territory would get inaugurated so urgently and through video conferencing. The announcement immediately put the Nepal government, the people and political players there on high alert. The Oli government's sharp reaction was unexpected—the road was being built for years, so for it to pretend that it was unaware of this development and therefore surprised at its inauguration defied logic.

---

* Sangeeta Ojha, '"Delighted to inaugurate the Link Road to Mansarovar Yatra": Rajnath Singh', *Mint*, 8 May 2020.

In a statement, the Nepalese Ministry of Foreign Affairs expressed regret at India's move. It said, 'As per the Sugauli Treaty (1816), all the territories east of Kali (Mahakali) River, including Limpiyadhura, Kalapani and Lipulekh, belong to Nepal. This was reiterated by the Government of Nepal several times in the past and most recently through a diplomatic note addressed to the Government of India dated 20 November 2019 in response to the new political map issued by the latter.' It cautioned the Indian government against carrying out any activity 'inside the territory of Nepal'. It stated that: 'Nepal had expressed its disagreement in 2015 through separate diplomatic notes addressed to the governments of both India and China when the two sides agreed to include Lipulekh Pass as a bilateral trade route without Nepal's consent in the Joint Statement issued on 15 May 2015 during the official visit of the Prime Minister of India to China.' Nepal said it believed in resolving the pending boundary issues through diplomatic means. It said that Kathmandu had proposed twice the dates for holding the foreign secretary-level meeting between the two countries.

A much-awaited response came to this from the Ministry of External Affairs (MEA), Government of India. Without mentioning any specific date, the MEA assured Nepal that talks would begin after the lockdown was lifted. India's response to Nepal's note said:

> The recently inaugurated road section in Pithoragarh district in the State of Uttarakhand lies completely within the territory of India. The road follows the pre-existing route used by the pilgrims of the Kailash–Mansarovar Yatra. India and Nepal have established mechanisms to deal with all boundary matters. The boundary delineation exercise with Nepal is ongoing. India is committed to resolving outstanding boundary issues through

diplomatic dialogue and in the spirit of our close and friendly bilateral relations with Nepal.*

The strain in ties also reflected the tensions in Nepal's politics. The then prime minister K.P. Sharma Oli stepped out of diplomatic nicety when he termed the 'Indian virus' as more damaging than the 'Chinese virus.'† He also questioned India's faith in 'Satyameva Jayate'. Nepal's foreign minister Pradeep Kumar Gyawali asked why talks on this 'important matter' could not take place under lockdown when the 'inauguration' of the road could take place during the Covid-19 crisis.

India and Nepal enjoy a unique relationship that in fact goes beyond diplomacy and the governments of the day. Both countries are interdependent through shared social, cultural, economic and other civilizational links. Here, the ties are not between the governments alone. Over three million Nepalese live in India and lakhs of Indians live in Nepal. The Gurkha Rifles, known for being the best in warfare, are incomplete without the Nepalese. They fight to keep India secure, so where is the scope for a permanent conflict? The people of Nepal fought for India's independence. B.P. Koirala and many more Nepalese made enormous sacrifices during the freedom struggle. Both countries have open borders and deep ties. Both countries have shared interests on various crucial matters while respecting each other's sovereignty. There is no place for a 'big brother' attitude and the regimes in New Delhi and Kathmandu have to exercise caution and restraint while looking at border disputes. The boundary

---

* Rezaul H. Laskar, 'India rejects Nepal's protest against new road to Lipulekh', *Hindustan Times*, 9 May 2020.
† '"Indian Virus Looks More Lethal Than Chinese, Italian": Nepal PM's Attack', NDTV, 20 May 2020.

controversy on Kalapani, Lipulekh and Limpiyadhura should be seen in retrospect as well as examined based on facts. Nepal's kings and the first-generation democratic leaders of Nepal had a clear view and rarely contested India's position on this matter.

Article 8 of the India–Nepal Friendship Treaty, 1950 states: 'So far as matters dealt with herein are concerned, this Treaty cancels all previous Treaties, agreements and engagements entered into on behalf of India between the British Government and the Government of Nepal.' On the issue of defining the boundary, the Treaty of Sugauli (1816) and the 1960 agreement between India and Nepal on the four Terai districts prevail. The Sugauli Treaty outlines the east of Mahakali River as Nepal's territory, and the west of it as India's territory. The dispute today is with regard to the origin of the Kali River. Nepal claims that the origin is in the higher reaches of this hilly territory which would establish its claim on Kalapani and Lipulekh. The Boundary Committee constituted in the year 2000 did not succeed in resolving the issue. There is a need to renew it to end the periodic cartographic tussle between the two countries.

It is time to repose faith in constructive dialogue with empathy to resolve any matter that disturbs the calm between the two countries. In good and bad times, India and Nepal have to live together. Restoring trust and confidence through constructive dialogue is very much possible and there is no reason that the initiatives will not be taken in this regard and the headlines will not be positive with sustained mutual efforts.

* * *

Army-to-Army Ties: Special but Not Always So

India and Nepal have long-standing and extensive mutually beneficial cooperation in the field of defence and security.

Historically, both armies have shared an excellent and harmonious relationship, and since 1950, India and Nepal have been awarding honorary rank of General to each other's Army Chief. Security agencies of both sides also share close cooperation including exchange of information. Law enforcement agencies hold regular bilateral meetings at various levels to discuss security issues of mutual concern including border management in institutionalized bilateral mechanisms.

The fourteenth round of Bilateral Consultative Group on Security Issues (BCGSI) was held on 28 October 2021 at Bengaluru wherein mutual security concerns, training and capacity building requirements of defence forces of Nepal, exchange of high-level and functional level visits, etc. were discussed. The training focused on Humanitarian Assistance and Disaster Relief (HADR) including medical and aviation support. Both armies stand to benefit mutually from these shared experiences, and this combined training, mutual interaction and sharing of experiences between both the countries further invigorates the continuing historical military and strategic ties, giving further fillip to the bilateral relations and existing strong bonding between both countries.

India has been assisting the Nepali Army in its modernization by supplying equipment and providing training. Assistance during disasters, joint military exercises, adventure activities and bilateral visits are other aspects of India's defence cooperation with Nepal. Several defence personnel from Nepali Army attend training courses in various Indian Army training institutions. The India–Nepal combined battalion-level military training exercise called Surya Kiran is conducted alternately in India and in Nepal with the aim to enhance interoperability in jungle warfare and counter-terrorism operations in mountainous terrain and HADR under UN mandate. The sixteenth edition of Surya Kiran between

India and Nepal was conducted at Nepal Army Battle School, Saljhandi, Nepal, during 16–29 December 2022. Routine exercises like these reassure the commitment of cooperation between army-to-army of two countries.

The Gorkha regiments of the Indian Army are raised partly by recruitment from hill districts of Nepal. Currently, about 32,000 Gorkha soldiers from Nepal are serving in the Indian Army. In addition to the Military Pension Branch in Kathmandu, there are two Pension Paying Offices at Pokhara and Dharan, and twenty-two District Soldier Boards in Nepal, all functioning under the Defence Wing of the Indian embassy in Kathmandu, which arrange the disbursement of pensions and organize welfare programmes for re-training, rehabilitating and assisting ex-Gorkha soldiers and their families.

At the time of Independence in 1947, a Tripartite Agreement between the United Kingdom, India and Nepal was signed concerning the rights of Gorkhas recruited in armed forces of the United Kingdom and India. This agreement did not apply to Gorkhas serving in the Nepalese Army. Under this agreement, four Gorkha regiments of the British Army were to be transferred to the British Army and six regiments were to be transferred to the Indian Army. Pakistan also made a bid for these surplus Gorkha regiments, but they did not press their claim and, of course, Nepal too did not give assent to that claim. Later, post the 1962 conflict, China too claimed and requested Nepal for Gorkha soldiers to serve in its People's Liberation Army (PLA), but Nepal once again did not give assent and kept the tradition alive.

India today has thirty-nine Gorkha battalions serving in seven Gorkha regiments (first, third, fourth, fifth, eighth, ninth and a new regiment raised post 1947, the eleventh). Britain, on the other hand, has amalgamated the four regiments that had joined them, namely the second, sixth, seventh and the tenth, to just two regiments, 1 RGR and 2 RGR. Further, those soldiers transferred to the British Army were immediately deployed to other remaining British colonies, in Malaya and Singapore, where their presence was required to quell the Malayan insurgency and also to Singapore where they replaced a Sikh unit which reverted to the Indian Army upon Independence. Even today, these Gorkha units remain deployed in Brunei and Singapore. In every war fought by the Indian Army post-Independence, the Gorkhas have played a gallant role. They have earned several Param Vir Chakras, the highest award for gallantry.

In 2022, India's new Agnipath scheme created some tensions with Nepal. Where open borders once facilitated the recruitment, mobility, and migration of Gorkhas from Nepal—albeit contingent on their eligibility and capabilities—the features of Agnipath have raised many doubts over the future of the Indian Army's Gorkha regiments. As such, Gorkha recruitment into the Indian Army has significant geopolitical implications, especially since it is believed by many Nepali analysts as something contradicting Nepal's foreign policy of non-alignment. In that sense, India's Agnipath scheme may relieve Nepal, or at least those political parties that view the Gorkha recruitment through its geopolitical significance. Debates on this dimension of the recruitment of Nepali nationals in the Indian Army mainly surface only during stand-offs and scuffles between India and China in the Himalayan region. Still, many parties use the issue for their political gains. For example, Nepal's communist and nationalist parties have often called for halting Gorkha recruitment, but only when they are in opposition. The Maoist rebels had included this as one of their forty demands submitted to the government before launching an armed insurgency in 1996, but it ceased to be a political agenda after they joined mainstream politics in 2006.

Despite opposition from some political parties, Nepali youth from the indigenous hill communities in the western parts of the country are interested in these positions due to the pay, perks and other social security benefits in the Indian Army. Currently, about 1,22,000 Gorkha pensioners in Nepal receive support from the Indian government. But, under the Agnipath scheme, there will be fewer pensioners. Earlier, despite political objections, Nepal was not in a favourable socio-economic position to halt such recruitment.

The concerns on this matter merit to be seen with deep empathy and in favour of keeping India–Nepal defence ties uniquely close for mutual benefits.

* * *

Where Does Madhesh Stand Now?

To know exactly where Madhesh stands as of now, it is imperative to revisit an old treaty of Segowlee (Sugauli) from 1815 that still has a very high influence over the existence of Madheshis besides on India–Nepal relations:

TREATY OF PEACE between the HONOURABLE EAST INDIA COMPANY and MAHARAJAH BIKRAM SHAH, Rajah of Nipal, settled between LIEUTENANT-COLONEL BRADSHAW on the part of the HONOURABLE COMPANY, in virtue of the full powers vested in him by HIS EXCELLENCY the RIGHT HONOURABLE FRANCIS, EARL OF MOIRA, KNIGHT of the MOST NOBLE ORDER of the GARTER, one of HIS MAJESTY'S MOST HONOURABLE PRIVY COUNCIL, appointed by the Court of Directors of the said Honourable Company to direct and control all the affairs in the East Indies, and by SREE GOOROO GUJRAJ MISSER and CHUNDER SEEKUR

OPEDEEA on the part of MAHA RAJAH GIRMAUN JODE BIKRAM SAH BAHADUR, SHUMSHEER JUNG, IN VIRTUE OF THE POWERS TO THAT EFFECT VESTED IN THEM BY THE SAID rajah of Nipal, 2nd December 1815.

Whereas war has arisen between the Honouranble East India Company and the Rajah of Nipal, and whereas the parties are mutually disposed to restore the relations of peace and amity which, previously to the occurrence of the late differences, had long subsisted between the two states, the following terms of peace have been agreed upon:-

ARTICLE 1ST
There shall be perpetual peace and friendship between the Honourable East India Company and Rajah of Nipal.

ARTICLE 2ND
The Rajah of Nipal renounces all claims to the lands which were the subject of discussion between the two States before the war; and acknowledges the right of the Honourable Company to the sovereignty of those lands.

ARTICLE 3RD
THE Rajah of Nipal hereby ceded to the Honourable East India Company in perpetuity all the undermentioned territories, VIZ.

First, - The whole of the low lands between the Rivers Kali and Tapti.

Secondly, - The whole of the low lands (with the exception of Bootwal Khass) lying between the Rapti and the Gunduck.

Thirdly, - The whole of the low lands between the Guynduck and Coosah, in which the authority of the British

Government has been introduced, or is in actual course of introduction.

Fourthly, - All the low lands between the Rivers Mitchee and the Teestah.

Fifthly, - All the territories within the hills eastward of the River Mitchee, including the fort and lands of Nagree and the Pass of Nagarcote, leading from Morung into the hills, together with the territory lying between that Pass and Nagree. The aforesaid territory shall be evacuated by the Gurkha troops forty days from this date.

ARTICLE 4TH

With a view to identify the Chiefs and Barahdars of the State of Nipal, whose interests will suffer by the alienation of the lands ceded by the forgoing Article, the British Government agrees to settle pensions to the aggregate amount of two lakhs of rupees per annum on such Chiefs as may be selected by the Rajah of Nipal, and in the proportions which the Rajah may fix. As soon as the selection is made, Sunnuds shall be granted under the seal and signature of the Governor-General for the pensions respectively.

ARTICLE 5TH

The Rajah of Nipal renounces for himself, his heir, and successors, all claim to or connection with the countries lying to the west of the River Kali, and engages never to have any concern with those countries or the inhabitants thereof.

ARTICLE 6TH

The Rajah of Nipal engages never to molest or disturb the Rajah of Sikkim in the possession of his territories; but agree, if any differences shall arise between the State of Nipal and the

Rajah of Sikkim, or the subjects of either, that such differences shall be referred to the arbitration of the British Government, by whose award the Rajah of Nipal engages to abide.

ARTICLE 7TH
The Rajah of Nipal hereby engages never to take or retain in his service any British subject, nor the subject of any European and American State, without the consent of the British Government.

ARTICLE 8TH
In order to secure and improve the relations of amity and peace hereby established between the two States, it is agreed that accredited Ministers from each shall reside at the Court of the other.

ARTICLE 9TH
This treaty, consisting of nine Articles, shall be ratified by the Rajah of Nipal within fifteen days from this date, and the ratification shall be delivered to Lieut-Colonel Bradshaw, who engages to obtain and deliver to the Rajah the ratification of the Governor-General within twenty days, or sooner, if practicable.

Done at Segowlee, on the 2nd day of December 1815.

PARIS BRADSHAW, Lt-Col., P.A.

Of Nepal's total geographical land area of 147,181 sq km, the Madhesh region occupies only 23 per cent of the area, but it inhabits nearly 51 per cent of the country's 26.5 million population. The country receives nearly 59 per cent of Gross Domestic Product (GDP) and 76 per cent of government's revenue from this region alone. It accounts for 66 per cent of the total cultivable land, 57 per cent of cereal crops production and 74 per cent of total cash crops production. As such, this region is often called the 'green basket' of Nepal.

There is a popular saying in Nepali: *Hariyo Ban Nepalko Dhan* (The green forest, Nepal's wealth). The area of Terai forests accounts for only 10 per cent of the total forests in Nepal. Yet the forests are predominantly high-valued and productive unlike the forests in the hill region which are mostly sparse, low-valued and subsistence-based. During the referendum held in 1979, the Terai forest was largely depleted in the interest of the Panchayat system. Estimates are that forest wood amounting to NPR 100 billion was sold during that period and the amount thus mobilized was paid to the Panchayat loyalists to help Panchayat win in the referendum. The depletion of Terai forest has not yet stopped. Estimates are that forest land in the Terai is depleted each year at the rate of 1.3 per cent. Nearly 97,050 households have illegally occupied 70,256 hectares of Terai forest. In Kailali district alone, 23,095 households have illegally occupied 19,526 hectares of forest land.

Pointing out the historical background of discrimination of Madhesh in Nepal, Hari Bansh Jha writes in his book *Nepal's Madhesh in Turmoil*:

Because of the demographic transition, Nepal has virtually become Madhesh or plain-centric rather than the hill-centric country. It is a significant development of recent years, a new wave of nationalism has emerged in Madhesh. The sense of belongingness to the nation has touched a new height among the Madheshis. They have become active and now they are seeking 'equal status' and 'due share' in each wing of state mechanism. However, the ruling elites of Nepal are yet to make up their mind for sharing the power with over two-thirds of the country's population belonging to the

Madheshi, Tharu, Hill Janjati, Dalit and other disadvantaged groups who have otherwise been excluded from the state mechanism.

Deprivation of Madhesh, however, is not a new phenomenon in Nepal. This process started in 1762 when Makwanpur state was taken over by King Prithvi Narayan Shah of Gurkha. Distrust between Kathmandu and Madhesh started developing over since then. This is one of the reasons why the Madheshi people 'manifested satisfaction at being taken under the protection of the British government' during the war between Nepal and the British East India Company in 1814 when the British took possession of eastern Terai, including Janakpur (J Adam Esq, Secretary to Government). Subsequently, the British East India Company sensed that the Nepalese rulers could take revenge against the Madheshis if the Terai region was returned to Nepal. As such, in clause 7 of the 'Memorandum for the Approval and Acceptance of the Rajah of Nipal' presented to the King of Nepal on December 8, 1816, a commitment was made whereby the Nepalese rulers were categorically asked to refrain from prosecuting and taking revenge against the inhabitants of Terai for taking the side of the British Government during the war between British and Nepal in 2014.

A provision was also made in the Memorandum whereby the people in Terai were allowed to settle in British territory if at all they chose to do so. The Memorandum clearly stated: ' . . . the Rajah of Nipal agrees to refrain from prosecuting any inhabitants of the Terai, after its reverence to his rule, on account of having favoured the cause of the British Government during the war, and should any of those persons, excepting the cultivators of the soil, be desirous of quitting their estates, and of retiring within the Company's territories, he shall not be liable to hindrance (Memorandum for the Approval and Acceptance of the RAJAH OF NIPAL).*

However, against the letter and spirit of the memorandum, Kathmandu started taking revenge against the Madheshis by treating them as aliens in their own territory. Until 1958, the Madheshis had to take a 'passport' to enter Kathmandu as if they were foreigners. The passport used to be obtained at Birgunj, which was checked at Chisapani Garhi en route to Kathmandu. Except during the Shivaratri festival, the Madheshi people were not allowed to enter their own capital, Kathmandu. Even in Kathmandu, they were not allowed to stay anywhere they liked. They could stay only at Tripureshwor, a locality in the southern part of Kathmandu on the bank of the Bagmati River. Such discrimination was made against the Madheshis on linguistic grounds. Those people from the western or eastern parts of the country who spoke Nepali or other hill-based languages/ dialects like the Newari, Magar, Tibetan and Gurung had no such problem. Influenced by the Kathmandu elites against the Madheshis and to convert them into a minority in their homeland, King Mahendra encouraged three million hill people to migrate and settle in Terai. Later on, King Birendra gave continuity to this policy and encouraged further migration of people from the hills to the Terai. All possible efforts were made by the State to weaken the Madheshis during the rule of the two monarchs under the Panchayat system (1960–90).

Of the seventy-seven districts in Nepal, twenty districts including Jhapa, Morang, Sunsari, Saptari, Siraha, Dhanusha, Mahottari, Sarlahi, Rauthat, Bara, Parsa, Chitwan, Nawalparasi,

---

* Dr Hari Bansh Jha, *Nepal's Madhesh in Turmoil* (Highbrow Scribes Publications, 2018).

Rupandehi, Kapilvastu, Dang, Banke, Bardiya, Kailali and Kanchanpur are located in the Terai. In each of the districts, there is a District Development Committee (DDC). The Village Development Committees (VDCs) and municipalities are the smaller units. Each of the VDCs comprise nine wards, while the minimum wards in the municipality are also nine in number.

In another book, *The Economy of Terai Region of Nepal*, Hari Bansh Jha writes:

> Estimates are that the Terai region accounts for 59 per cent of the Gross Domestic Product. It also accounts for 76 per cent of the government's total revenue. Resources generated from the forest areas, national parks, wildlife reserves and conservation from this region is also crucial for the Nepalese economy. Because of its alluvial and fertile soil, the Terai region plays a crucial role in the national economy. It accounts for 66 per cent of the total cultivated land, 57 per cent of the cereal crops production and 74 per cent of the total cash crops production. Therefore, it is called the 'grain basket' of the country.
>
> Furthermore, the Terai region accounts for over two-third of Nepal's total industrial production. The country's major industrial and trade centres in Biratnagar, Duhabi, Birgunj, Bhairahawa, Nepalgunj and the surrounding areas are located in this region. Yet, the industries in the Terai region do not at present absorb adequate manpower as many of them have been closed due to 'bandh', transport strike, labour problem, lack of raw materials and marketing problems. As such, the unemployment problem is severe in this region.[*]

---

[*] Hari Bansh Jha, *The Economy of Terai Region of Nepal: Prospects for Its Sustainable Development* (Centre for Economic and Technical Studies, Kathmandu, Nepal, 2010).

Another aspect of Madhesh's intrinsic issues is the state of Janajatis in Nepal. Janajatis are the indigenous people of Nepal forming 35.6 per cent of Nepal's population and spread over all the seventy-seven districts of the country. The National Foundation for Development of Indigenous Nationalities has identified fifty-nine communities as Janajatis—twenty-four Janajati clusters live in the hill region of Nepal, seventeen in the Himalayan region and eighteen in the Terai region. With themselves, the Janajatis exhibit great diversity of ethnicities, language and culture. They are divided and do not have a unified political front. The Magar is the largest Janajati community constituting 7.24 per cent of Nepal's population followed by the Tharu (6.5 per cent), Newar (5.6 per cent), Tamang (5.5 per cent), Rai (2.8 per cent), Gurung (2.4 per cent) and Limbu (2.4 per cent). With the exception of Newars, most Janajatis are poor and have a low literacy rate and per capita income. Child and bonded labour are not uncommon. Nepal's Janajatis often complain about discrimination, low representation in electoral politics, government jobs and resources.

Based on his research, Hari Bansh Jha's *The Janajati of Nepal* makes an important observation:

> The Janajati people constitute 35.6 percent of Nepal's total population. They live in all the seventy-seven districts of the country, though they are not in the majority in any of the districts. Because of their rich culture, glorious traditions and economic prosperity, they had a higher status in society. They were second to none in the task of nation-building. Yet the state started marginalizing and discriminating with them especially after Prithvi Narayan Shah of Gorkha established his rule in Nepal in the later part of the 18th century. Since then, the degradation of the Janajati people started in the country.

In the Muluki Ain (code of the country) of 1854, the Janajati people were called Matwali (liquor consumer) and they were divided into slavable and non-enslavable categories. Some of them were put in the category of 'untouchables'. In course of the passage of time, certain changes were introduced in the Muluki Ain in 1963, which ensured that all the people of Nepal were equal. Yet, they continue to be socially discriminated, economically exploited and politically excluded in all important state mechanisms. Therefore, their presence in administrative, political and in decision-making bodies is far satisfactory. Because of the growing awareness among the Janajati people in Nepal, they raised their voice to end the age-old discrimination. In the past, the Panchas during the Panchayat system (1960-1990) and the major political parties that ruled the country after the introduction of the multiparty system in 1990 vowed to end state discrimination with them, but that just remained lip service as nothing substantial was done to improve their socio-economic conditions.

The Janajati had pinned a great hope that their demand to end discriminatory practices would be addressed in the new constitution that was promulgated on September 20, 2015. But their hopes were belied. Instead of addressing their issues, the Constitution carved the state boundaries, apart from the electoral constituencies of Parliament, the state assemblies and the local bodies in such a way that they had a very little option left but to remain in minority. As if this was not enough, the Khas-Arya group of Brahmin-Chhetri who are the most privileged group in the society were given a reservation of seats in the electoral bodies as well as in the government services to marginalise the Janajati, Madheshi, Dalit and other disadvantages groups. Therefore, the Janajati issue will continue to remain a burning issue until they are addressed through effective affirmative actions.*

A young democracy, Nepal has confronted far more problems than it really deserved. The painful continuance of agitations in Madhesh for long—with demand for equal citizenry rights and territorial representation—drew not the kind of empathy that was expected from the leadership in Kathmandu, which simply forced Nepal towards the pre-democracy time in the difficult year 2015. Earlier, such a tendency was exemplified in acute form during King Mahendra's rule—and a similar sort of low in India–Nepal relations was thawed and melted back then. It was that 1969 episode of irregular supplies through the Indian routes that caused Nepal's first close trade dealing with China. Although, the then Prime Minister of India, Indira Gandhi, acted promptly to stop aggravating the matter. In 1989, India imposed a declared border blockade for almost 1.5 years—this must be counted as one of the biggest blunders in foreign policy committed by the then Indian prime minister Rajiv Gandhi. His anger was believed to be due to his wife Sonia Gandhi being denied entry into Pashupatinath Temple in Kathmandu—supplemented by Nepal's heavy arms imports from China. As per Rajiv Gandhi, 'Nepal was in India's security zone and was prohibited from purchasing arms without India's approval.'

The common factor in three fateful years (1969, 1989 and 2015) of difficult India–Nepal border movements and bilateral relations at large was that the emerging scenario was taken into consideration. Out of three occasions when the borders constricted and trade and cargo movements entered the complex

---

* Hari Bansh Jha, *The Janajati of Nepal* (A monograph published by Vivekananda International Foundation, New Delhi, 2019).

spiral, 2015 stood out more prominently with the high stake of Madhesh in the schemes of themes. The months-long protests of Madheshi activists at Birgunj coincided with the continuance of dysfunctional or highly restricted border movements, and there was a popular view at that time in Nepal of having India's moral support to the Madheshi movements with not enforcing its official will to end a deadlock. Technically, India didn't impose any blockade in 2015 and there was much that was depending on Nepal's inner political dynamics of that time when to one's chagrin, the genuine demands of Madheshis were overlooked for no reasons by the serving regime in Kathmandu.

Meanwhile, the agitators, especially the elites of Madhesh distracted from their goals and had shown the temptation to stake claim on national authority defying logic as they were expected to end the deadlock first and while securing the demands of Madhesh. Over six months of civil strife finally eased with partial acceptance of the constitutional amendments to meet with the demands related to citizenship and federalism. However, Nepal's socio-economic losses were not possible to ascertain merely in figures. It was clear that Nepal must get its foreign affairs not driven through domestic political compulsions, and for India, 2015 ended with underlining the significance of having a relook on its Nepal policy.

In the recent past, Kathmandu has shown greater accountability to the Madheshi-Janajati, who now have a greater say over political matters and can strongly influence the established political discourse for their long-anticipated rights. With a federal structure and significant devolution of power, Nepal now has a multi-tier power structure but with a continuing supreme eminence of Kathmandu. While this has happened at a cost with execution of the federal model, it is surely not curing the endemic developmental issues and is adding new complications with an added tier of power structure albeit with no practical accountability. The administrative edifices of the nation have suffered immensely in the wake of promises made and broken in the last few decades by the mainline political parties and comparatively new entrants. Through the enormous efforts and endless sacrifices by the common Nepali people and leaders, the country could once make a successful transition and emerge as a democratic republic.

However, the worrying trend of romantically seeing the political processes is yet to be over—and mass Nepalese are bereft of actual democratic rights despite having an essential democratic scripture, called the Constitution, most recently updated in 2015 following mass movements in Madhesh. Another side of the story is equally important but has been left in the lurch. This is about the forgotten Nepalis who are marginalized to the core and have no privilege to shed tears on the flaws in the new Constitution and the political culture that started way back in 2015.

The chauvinistic fondness to negate or lessen the citizenry rights of historically distinct Madheshis—undermining women for their gender and blurring the territorial lines to map seven states under the 'federal canopy'—altogether makes it clear how indifferent Nepal's new Constitution is from the mass aspirations. This interim Constitution made through 'technical mastery'—combining both the 'first post past system' and 'proportional representation'—offered principal progression over the last Constitution (1990). Still what was missed at the height of the crisis was an urge for consultation. This was made worse by showing no urgency to make an outreach to address the concerns of the Madheshi and Tharu communities. Eventually, that led to the two communities to feel genuinely marginalized. It is conspicuous why almost half of Nepal is alienated from the new Constitution even now, which otherwise should have been celebrated as it came after years of struggle and flowing Rs 150 billion of taxpayers' money on the painfully long processes.

George Orwell, the master interpreter of ironies, rightly said: 'Happiness can exist only in acceptance.' This appears to be a prescription today for all those disgruntled souls who have difficulty in accepting that the radicalization of activism instead of struggling for Madhesh causes was a directionless drive to attain a parallel power centre. With the outcomes derived from the new Constitution, Nepal is already headed to a time where the newly formed states host the regional satraps and their wild aspirations—but without entertaining the causes for which the idea of decentralization was brought—in to the political discourse and action. Such a counterproductive trend itself alienates a vast section of people, including Madheshis, Janajatis and women—who otherwise are in the mainstream and rightly deserve to avail of complete equality, justice and fraternity. Janakpur, often cited as the political theatre in post 1990s Nepal, signifies the challenges with the country's functional polity and hindrances in bringing harmony to Pahad-Madhesh discourse. In recent years, the same Janakpur also offered hope to Nepal being an important cultural hub and host of Nepal's rich diversity.

While the lexicon and practices of Nepal's new political grammar are work-in-progress, what is firmly rooted in the meantime is the 'traction of caste' in Madhesh that is radically polarizing and perilous. The working political culture of the new generation of Madheshi leaders is majorly shaped through the radicalized affirmation of caste identity—and not remotely linked with the ideology or causes for which the masses have been undergoing hardship.

The new genre of leadership that emerged with the brush of federalism and identity politics is mostly devoid of the main causes which have created the chasm between Kathmandu and

Madhesh. While the challenges on the ground are humongous, the new traction is hardly reconciling the diverse interests and is thus leaving the new experiment on a path of failure. The lack of basic understanding among the leaderships on democracy and democratic experiments has been harming the prospects of harmony in polity and balance in economy; lately, the lack of good match of politics and economics is serving no good purpose.

The new Constitution created a new culture of activism in Terai, where the people were forced to be part of an uprising—right after their own security forces didn't think twice before shooting over forty-five clueless people in 2015. Similarly, and equally unfortunate, was the manner in which the people resorted to violence against the police—and lost the line of real protest. The amendments had to be made into the Constitution, but for that matter, blocking the trade-transit and making life extremely miserable proved not helpful for the right cause, for which the agitation was initially carried out. The then Prime Minister Sushil Koirala, an ailing and calm person otherwise, proved to be a force that eventually made things worse through a strange set of actions in handling a highly troubled Madhesh of 2015. The year 2015 was disastrous for Nepal, with nature's fury and a man-made crisis.

The Nepali Maoists launched their armed rebellion from the hilly and difficult terrains in 1996—then with feeble ideological ground made and meagre resources, they were not in a position to show their action in an overt manner. The initial five years were highly intense for them, through regular violence and controlling the village economy, much along the lines of Maoism's foundational doctrines. Till 2001, the people were still not for abolishing monarchy from the core—there was a sentimental bond intact for King Birendra, who had shown faith in establishing democracy on the land and admitted that the 'Maoists are our own people and they need to be dealt more through dialogue than the force.' There was a chance of reconciliation.

Statecraft is not doing well in Nepal. We keep hearing it quite often. With no King or the institution of monarchy to blame, the movers and shakers of Nepali politics should think about it. The country's interest lies in downsizing personification, calibrating all-round prospects of development and making the system participatory. In a functional democracy, the statecraft is not supposed to be altruistic till it relies on progressive policy and governance—with an aim to augment the mission of 'greater common goods'. Long ago, the people's war was over in Nepal, with a transitory accomplishment of a goal in a new republic. However, the task is still unfinished as long as people-centric priorities are not driving the political agenda and action.

Despite all the flaws, Nepal should protect its democracy from the actions of political opportunists. It can be said that the only constant in Nepali politics is unpredictability. Nepal's democratic transition has been shaped through the efforts and sacrifices of common citizens and leaders, and the expectation was that the forgotten Nepali would soon get something better than the discriminatory political culture that started way back in 2015 with the new Constitution and selective political maneuverings. The obsession with the positioning of India and China, more so with the abolition of the monarchy, has been a survival game in Nepali politics. The tendency to raise the bogey of the 'hostile neighbourhood' has weakened politics and has diminished the idea of representing constituent interests. It would be helpful to reckon the weak institutional culture as the culmination of an accountability-free political culture and the misunderstood institutional processes—where the successes or failures of decisions are attributed to outsiders—instead of opting for probity in public life and owning the outcomes.

Nepal, now a super-inflationary import economy, is at the cusp of losing its war against the odds confronted during its painful transition to democracy. Anyone who helms Kathmandu should be leader of the whole nation; likewise, all Madheshis should be aware of their citizenry duties, while genuinely striving for the rights they arc entitled to. Deformed ideologies and regionalism are the biggest fissures the Nepali State has today. The ideologues are in safe zones, and they let people fight and struggle for survival—the benefits are being reaped by few. But even in this tough time, people should exude trust in national unity and in making their beautiful country into a strong national economy. Maintaining a 'client state' status will only hurt Nepal's internal affairs. Normalcy is what is required now.

* * *

Conclusion in a Nutshell

'O brave new world that has such people in't!' Miranda said in William Shakespeare's *The Tempest*, on first sighting the shipwrecked courtiers. Today, most of us have a sense of it as the world being in a state of disorder. Everything around us is prominently chaotic. The world was ravaged to a great extent by Covid-19 and the failure of governments and multilateral institutions, and an attempt to see the light at the end of the tunnel may be too simplistic. With the future of humanity threatened and uncertain, the 'new world' has failed to believe in a consensus-based approach to finding a mechanism to decode the global pandemic and creating a common task force to save humanity from suffering an unprecedented crisis. This is the truth and the policymakers in Nepal should take note of it.

Nepal's journey towards democratic transition has been extraordinary and full of surprises. In seven decades of its democratic transition, starting from the intervening years in the late 1940s, Nepal has seen as many as seven Constitutions and since then, none of the elected prime ministers have completed their full term in the office. This is a unique feat achieved by Nepal, a young democracy full of democratic asteroids working against its own interest. Nepal has been gripped with instabilities of all sorts: executive, legislative and constitutional. Its latest Constitution, drafted through the Constituent Assembly—elected twice, and finally promulgated in 2015—has resolved some of the key political issues notionally that stormed the country's political landscape. However, a few crucial issues remain unaddressed, to find a development paradigm to empower the masses with inclusive opportunities, especially for those who were hitherto marginalized.

Contrarily, the issues related to economic emancipation and further transformation are overshadowed with the political infightings that put question marks on the credibility of central political characters ruling the roost in Kathmandu and provinces. Crony capitalism is not just surviving but is thriving in Nepal and a small class of oligarchs are having a major say in politics and businesses. An impure and inefficient system with inherent weaknesses is creating a permanent breeding ground for the masters of capital formation, who are destined to grow but without having any commitment to raising the stature of the country, its people and image in the world.

The next challenge that Nepal is facing and that impacts its democratic politics significantly is a set of external factors. Its geographic positioning between two global superpowers (India and China), landlocked status and over-dependence on the outside world for developmental needs compromise its own voice on crucial matters concerning international politics and policy. Nepal's political transition is entwined with its economic transition; until the latter is dealt with successfully, it is unlikely that Nepal will get its democracy functioning smoothly and with the requisite altruism. Nepal's problems are well-identified and understood but not adequately addressed. At a macro level, striking a balance between national politics and geopolitics and a resolve to attain a reasonable economic bandwidth will help Nepal accomplish true success for its democracy.

Beyond the fast-changing headlines about Nepal's endemic woes on political, economic and humanitarian fronts, there is a need to read between the lines and where the scripts should prompt for a decisive transformation of institutional processes. If Nepal can realize its true potential, there is no reason it will not overcome its developmental disorders. The new aspirations combined with the conventional value system and resolve to make the country a home for all, and not just for a privileged few, will usher Nepal to a bright spot in the world.

At the core of its transformational agenda, welfare of the forgotten Nepalis should occupy a prominent place. It should emerge as the zone of hope, rather than a state of despair with endless human sufferings, natural degradation and ambivalence of political opportunists. Nepal's search for democracy is officially over; now the challenge is to complete its transition smoothly and successfully. This will ensure Nepal its fair place in the world.

SECTION III

Repurposing India–Nepal Relations

K.V. RAJAN AND ATUL K. THAKUR

After several decades of costly trial and error, India and Nepal seem at last to have found a clearer direction in a future relationship, which could signify major strides of inclusive growth for the entire subregion and beyond.

This is because of a combination of factors, which need to be sustained and strengthened.

One is a certain trend in Nepal towards de-politicization of relations with India, a realization that, as General Charles de Gaulle said, the definition of nationalism need not be manifestation of hostility towards another country, but seeing what is in the best interest of one's own people:

'Patriotism is when love of your own people comes first; nationalism, when hate for people other than your own comes first.'

Another is the rapid progress in connectivity projects whether hard (road, rail, air, inland water transport) or soft (people to people, business, cultural exchanges, innovative tourist circuits, education, health, sports).

The third, all important factor—for it promises to be the game changer—is the progress made and planned in harnessing

Nepal's vast hydropower potential for export not only to India but to Bangladesh and eventually other neighbouring countries.

A vision statement on energy cooperation was signed during Prime Minister Sher Bahadur Deuba's India visit in 2022. During PM Prachanda's India visit in May 2023, there was an agreement to import 10,000 MW over ten years. Nepal now sells electricity in both the day-ahead and spot markets reaping high peaking prices—a long standing demand which India had traditionally resisted, arguing that it had 'other sources of power' if Nepal prices became too exorbitant. The 5000 MW Pancheshwar project is now on the front burner. In addition to the 450 MW that it sells, Nepal is seeking approval for another 550 MW.

Indian observers like Ambassador Ranjit Rae acknowledge in his book *Kathmandu Dilemma*:

> [P]rocedures have become somewhat complicated since India refuses to buy power from any Nepalese project that has a Chinese investor or even an EPC contractor. And procedures for importing energy have become very complicated since they scour the financial records of every Nepalese project forensically to ascertain whether there is any Chinese footprint. Since India is the primary buyer for Nepalese electricity, though there is an agreement between Nepal and China for a trans-Himalayan transmission line, there is suspicion in Nepal that India wants to capture the entire generation market in that country.[*]

In addition to the old 132 KV transmission lines, several new 400 KV lines have/are being built. This will make for a more robust trade of energy both ways—in the monsoon season when India

---

[*] Ranjit Rae, *Kathmandu Dilemma: Resetting India–Nepal Ties* (Vintage, 2021).

imports and in the dry season when Nepal imports from India. Prospects for trilateral cooperation with Nepal selling energy directly to Bangladesh through Indian transmission lines have also opened up. There is now an agreement for exports of 50 MW. Hopefully, energy secretaries of the three countries will soon meet to resolve nuts and bolt issues.

In the process, Nepal is happy that one of its other long-standing demands, apart from compensation for peaking power, will also begin to be addressed, with rising power exports to India: a shift in the India–Nepal trade balance.

There are other major positive implications in the progressing regional power trade arrangements based on India–Nepal cooperation. As the *London Economist* notes, integration is also crucial to South Asia's green-energy transition.

India's external affairs minister S. Jaishankar articulated India's priority to its neighbourhood in the following words: 'Foreign policy begins on our borders and understandably, that has seen the greatest transformation. A generous and non-reciprocal approach to immediate neighbours has been backed by vastly improved project delivery. As a result, regionalism in South Asia is making rapid strides, reflected in new road, rail and waterway connectivity, power grids, fuel pipelines and border crossing facilities.'*

These statements are backed by a new pragmatism being displayed by India and Nepal in recent times, for which political leaders as well as the senior bureaucracy in both countries deserve credit. A generous and non-reciprocal approach, addressing complementary strengths with the seriousness they deserve, thinking regional—this is a powerful combination and a promising recipe for rapid economic growth.

---

* 'Nine years of Modi's transformative foreign policy' in May 2023.

Both countries need to strengthen this happy combination with conscious moves to inject sustainable solutions taking into account local needs and capabilities in all development projects, introducing tomorrow's technologies today where possible and advisable, and transferring skills and knowledge so that each project can make a meaningful contribution, to long term improvements in the quality of life especially in poor and rural areas and for the upliftment and empowerment of marginalized communities.

It is noteworthy that at a time when people are shy of using the term 'special relations', Jaishankar referred to India–Nepal ties using precisely that phrase, in a tweet after a meeting with Nepal's foreign minister.

India's G20 vision of 'One Earth, One Family, One Future' will only gain credibility if a beginning can be made with the one country with which it has a unique *roti–beti* relationship, and if the tremendous commonalities accompanied by sheer diversity among and between peoples on both sides of the border are celebrated through tangible projects which also aim at improving human security.

* * *

The breadth and depth of ties between India and Nepal—of history, geography, culture, religion and people-to-people—are probably the most unique between any two neighbouring countries. There are striking complementarities and huge opportunities and advantages in expanding and diversifying cooperation to mutual advantage. Yet, the bilateral relationship has not been able to achieve its true potential and has frequently suffered from misunderstandings and setbacks which often take years to heal. Despite their much-vaunted 'special relationship' (a term rarely used by Nepal in recent times), India–Nepal ties have repeatedly experienced setbacks, some of them with long-term implications.

Nepal itself has undergone several significant transformations since India's independence, many of which India—not coincidentally—has been intimately involved in. What are the real causes of regular anti-Indian eruptions in Nepal, and why is there so much mutual distrust and suspicion despite India's best intentions?

Both at the level of government as well as civil society, Nepal and India urgently need to come to terms with the past, understand comprehensively and objectively the unique challenges and opportunities offered by the present, and to 'repurpose' their relationship if it is to achieve its exceptional potential in the coming years. Undeniably, there is a need to facilitate understanding of how an India with credible aspirations to become a major world player and a transformed Nepal in a transforming world order could revisit their ties to ensure a steady upward trajectory. Both countries owe it to their peoples to free the relationship from political vicissitudes as well as the negative legacies of the past. Concepts of national interest and mutual security need to be relevant to the world of today and tomorrow. Only mutual empathy, as either country strives to overcome its major challenges, can transform the relationship into a truly special one.

The Covid-19 pandemic and several geopolitical occurrences are leaving in their trail huge challenges but also unprecedented opportunities for fresh thinking. In the case of India–Nepal ties, this includes a host of issues, including economic recovery, bilateral, sub-regional and regional cooperation, restructuring supply chains, human as well as conventional security, energy cooperation, development, people-to-people contacts, the untapped potential for technology to accelerate inclusive growth, soft power and empathy as a factor in sustainable friendly ties for maximum advantage to both sides.

While the priorities of bilateral relations are usually well-identified, they do not always steer the official narrative and action. There is a glaring need to come to terms with the changing fundamentals. India and Nepal should know the urgency of stabilizing ties in uncertain times when the global scenario is challenged on both economic and strategic fronts. Hopefully, India will be able to take the unexpected recent developments and prospect of instability in Nepal in its stride, and even find ways to scale up bilateral cooperation.

India is used to dealing with political instability in Nepal, frequent changes of government, some even with reputedly anti-India or pro-China leaders heading them. Its focus for many years has been on non-partisan support for inclusive economic development, interdependence, communication links, people-to-people contacts, and building on the compulsive logic of economic complementarities, especially in hydropower where Nepal has huge but as yet largely unexplored potential. The extent of its links of history, geography, culture, religion and economy with Nepal facilitates management of its security concerns within tolerable limits.

Perhaps the one missing factor in bilateral ties has been mutual empathy: the will of the political class across party lines, bureaucracies and civil society on either side of the border to understand what the world looks like from the other side. Empathy is now more of an urgent necessity than ever before as a factor for sustainable friendly ties. Innovative approaches are clearly needed on both sides. What all Nepalese yearn for is a sense of equality and Indian respect for their identity.

With a prime minister who has visited Nepal more times than any of his predecessors, an external affairs minister who has won huge respect for his clear and consistent approach to foreign policy priorities, and a foreign secretary who was, until recently, India's ambassador to Nepal, India has a range of policy drivers with huge combined understanding and sensitivity as far as relations with Nepal are concerned. This should stand both countries and the region in good stead in the challenging times ahead.

* * *

Crucial Influencers of Bilateral Ties

Water Resources

What can be an alternative paradigm of flood management or water management at large? In the best spirit of friendship, both sides should restart the water dialogue and come out with the requisite policies to safeguard the interests of all affected people across borders. It is high time that two friendly countries come together and assess the factors causing unimaginable losses through floods. Optimization of infrastructure will be decisive in finding an alternative paradigm of flood management; moreover, management of the Himalayan glaciers and the green cover would remain vital. Water cooperation should drive the next big India–Nepal dialogue; despite the challenges, wisdom should prevail to turn the crisis into an opportunity, as water resources are priceless assets for the sake of development and environmental protection. By controlling floods and using the water resources for common developmental uses like hydroelectricity, irrigation and waterways, India–Nepal relations can be further strengthened.

The Terai region in Nepal is endowed with both surface and groundwater. The rivers, ponds and lakes are the major sources of surface water. All the rivers flowing from the Himalayas or the Mahabharata range meet any of the three drains—the Koshi, the Gandaki and the Karnali—up to the coming of the Churiya range, which ultimately flows through the alluvial soil of the Terai, making their destination towards the Ganga in the South in India. Other rivers of the Terai such as the Mechi, Kankai, Kamala, Bagmati, Tinau, Rapti, Babai and Mahakali originate from the Mahabharata range.

In the changing times, India–Nepal water management needs a course correction as well. The two countries need to re-establish water cooperation as a common cause and draw inspiration from the 1950s when the two countries worked together for water management planning and infrastructure creation. Considering his unwavering focus on controlling floods in north Bihar (neighbouring part of Nepal), Bihar's chief minister Nitish Kumar should be credited for bringing disaster management into the popular imagination of Bihar, an Indian state with maximum exposure to Nepal. In his early days as chief minister (2005–10), Kumar made a few noticeable structural changes, with renewed approaches in infrastructure augmentation for dams and reservoirs, detention basins, embankments and channel improvement. Non-structural measures were also adopted in later years such as floodplain management, flood forecasting and warning, flood insurance and financial compensation.

However, despite the efforts made on ground, people continue to suffer with perennial flooding in north Bihar (the Mithilanchal region). Unfortunately, this chronic issue which is making over five crore people of north Bihar in India and Terai in Nepal so vulnerable, does not seem to get the attention it deserves by policymakers on both sides of the border. In 2021, Bihar's Disaster

Management Department released two documents titled *Pre-Flood Preparedness* and *Flood Control Order 2021*. The aim was to help the local administration in terms of preparedness and having in place a relief support system. However, a solution to the issue of chronic flooding lies in revisiting the old plans and arrangements between India and Nepal. This is because flood control in Bihar is just not possible till a dedicated intergovernmental panel is formed through a bilateral mechanism between India and Nepal that in turn can study, assess and offer solutions to this shared crisis. Already facing a humanitarian crisis of sorts following the Covid-19 pandemic, the visible impacts of climate change in Nepal's Terai and north Bihar have been a moment of reckoning. Apart from the flood, now these terrains are also witnessing a rare scenario of flood and drought within the same season.

The fundamentals of flooding need to be well understood by the concerned stakeholders in both India and Nepal. Historically, Bihar has been known to be India's most flood-prone state. The Flood Management Improvement Support Centre (FMISC), Department of Water Resources, Government of Bihar, estimates that 76 per cent of the population in north Bihar faces the recurring threat of flood devastation. About 68,800 sq. km of a total geographical area of 94,163 sq. km, or about 73.06 per cent of the land area, is flood-affected. A large part of north Bihar, adjoining Nepal, is drained by a number of rivers that have their catchments in the steep and geologically nascent Himalayas.

Originating in Nepal, the high discharge and sediment load in rivers like Kosi, Gandak, Burhi Gandak, Bagmati, Kamla Balan, Mahananda and Adhwara Group wreak havoc in the plains of Nepal's Terai and Bihar. The FMISC says:

About 65 per cent of the catchment area of these rivers falls in Nepal/Tibet and only 35 per cent of the catchment area lies in

Bihar. A review by Kale (1997) indicated that the plains of north
Bihar have recorded the highest number of floods during the last
thirty years. In the years 1978, 1987, 1998, 2004 and 2007, Bihar
witnessed high magnitudes of flood. The total area affected by
floods has also increased during these years. The flood of 2004
demonstrates the severity of the flood problem when a vast area
of 2,34,90 sq. km was severely affected by the floods of Bagmati,
Kamla and Adhwara groups of rivers causing loss of about 800
human lives, even when Ganga, the master drain was flowing low.[*]

Unlike the indifference shown by Kathmandu on matters of floods
and water management in recent years, the history of cooperation
between India and Nepal for embankments starting in the 1950s
is worth looking at. When work on the Kosi embankments
started in January 1955, a group of retired Nepali soldiers
came over voluntarily to join hands with Indian volunteers and
start the work. Such a progressive government-citizen interface
could not sustain itself and water cooperation between the two
countries for a common cause waned. Consequently, not much
has happened barring the use of water resources for hydroelectric
generation. For the people of Bihar's districts like Madhubani,
Darbhanga, Sitamarhi, Sheohar, Saharsa, Supaul, Purnea,
Araria, Madhepura, Katihar, Samastipur, Muzaffarpur, Bettiah,
Motihari and Begusarai, the flooding is a part of their lives. In
fact, infrastructural interventions such as building embankments
and re-routing streams have disturbed the conventional pattern of
slow water flow.

---

[*] Santosh Kumar, Arun Sahdeo and Sushma Guleria, *Bihar Floods: 2007
(A Field Report)*, (National Institute of Disaster Management, Ministry
of Home Affairs, Government of India, 2013), https://nidm.gov.in/PDF/
pubs/Bihar%20Flood%202007.pdf.

Earlier, without so many artificial barriers, the flow of water used to aid farming in the region. The Kosi Treaty of 1954, under which the embankments in Nepal were established and maintained, was not futuristic and did not make enough provisions for the maintenance of embankments and the rivers changing their course. The deposition of stones, sand, silt and sediment has led to river beds rising, changing course and causing unimaginable losses. Between the mid-eighteenth and mid-twentieth centuries, the Kosi is said to have shifted over 100 kilometres westward, resulting in large-scale human displacements.

Clearly, there is a need for greater sensitization on climatic imbalances and sustainable development. A major irony: the same flood-affected regions also face the issues of drought and a sinking water table. Notwithstanding Kathmandu's wavered approach on the matters concerning water management with India, it would not be apt to blame Nepal for releasing water from its rivers that cause flooding on the Indian side; and on their part, for believing that India is reaping the benefits from all projects that were taken up in the past. Of late, what is needed is to have a shared concern on the matter and joint action while keeping a ringside view on the situation and a shared approach for a long-term solution to end the perennial problem of flood and drought.

As early as 1937, the transition from the traditional method of flood control to the embankment-based British system was thought out. To control the floodwater at Barahakshetra in Nepal, a high dam was thus planned and finally built after the devastating Kosi flood in 1953. Prime Minister Jawaharlal Nehru visited the flood-affected areas in 1953 and announced a visionary Kosi scheme for the safe resettlement of the affected people. Former Union Cabinet Minister Lalit Narayan Mishra was the first prominent political leader from the Mithila region (Bihar) who relentlessly tried improving infrastructural capabilities with the Kosi Project and other initiatives to control the flooding that affected Nepal's Terai and the bordering districts in Bihar. In the mainstream political and policy establishments, greater attention needs to be given to this annual calamity and its devastating effects on lives and livelihoods. India and Nepal need to be in dialogue to end the crisis of flooding every year. For a policy refresh, with a long-term strategy of water management cooperation between India and Nepal, the matter should be looked into.

To find a sustainable solution to the India–Nepal flood issue, an intergovernmental panel should be formed with representations from the local governments. Many of Bihar's districts frequently face serious challenges because of massive floods. Sometimes, it comes with a double whammy of flood as well as drought. Of late, it is of utmost importance that some of the key aspects of India–Nepal flood management could be seen under the existing arrangements of India's federal system that offers enough room for a closer coordination between the Centre and the state governments A process-driven coordination is the need of the hour between the Centre and the government of Bihar to tackle the menace of flood in Nepal's Terai and north Bihar (majorly the Mithilanchal region).

As part of the long-term measures needed to address the problem of massive and recurrent floods in Bihar, the Joint Project Office (JPO), Biratnagar, was established in Nepal in August 2004 to prepare a Detailed Project Report (DPR) for constructing a high dam on the Nepal side of the Kosi, Kamla and Bagmati rivers. The government of Bihar has raised the matter regularly. The Central Water Commission (CWC), Ministry of Jal Shakti (MoJS), Government of India, convened a special meeting of the Joint Team of Experts (India side) on 10 February 2020 at New Delhi to ascertain the status of the DPR. A group of officers formed by CWC has to work on various aspects of the DPR and propose an action plan for its early completion. The Water Resources Department (WRD), Government of Bihar, has continuously requested the MoJS (most recently through Letter no. 295 dated 2 August 2021) to expedite the progress of the DPR. Despite the best efforts of the government of Bihar, the task remains unaccomplished even after nineteen years. It is essential rather than wishful that Nepal shows the required will for finding a long-term solution with India to end a predictable perennial disaster.

As per the existing India–Nepal agreement on water resources, the state government is authorized to execute flood protection works up to critical stretches inside Nepal territory along the India–Nepal borders. Especially in recent years, all such flood protection works have had to be carried out against increasing local resistance on Nepal's side. Even during the Covid-19 pandemic, WRD, Government of Bihar, intensively engaged both with local Nepalese authorities as well as through appeals to the central government for carrying out flood protection works in 2020. The sustained concerted coordination between the Centre and the government of Bihar and expedited interventions from the Centre with its Nepalese counterpart, Nepal gave conditional permission for manpower and machinery operation in the Nepal area of the Kosi basin. Accordingly, twenty-one out of the twenty-two works could be completed. Also, some progress was made to facilitate smooth movement of manpower, machinery and flood control materials across the Gandak and Kamla rivers situated on the Nepal side for carrying out flood protection work during the flood period of 2020.

Sadly, despite the requisite permission for movement on the Kosi barrage and associated embankments, movement of departmental vehicles and work activities rarely get the due attention of the Kosi Project Authority, Biratnagar, on various pretexts. Since bilateral cooperation remains the fulcrum of water sharing and management between the two countries, Nepalese counterparts must look into the matter and play their part in ensuring a sustainable way forward for the people of both sides.

As per the figures shared by WRD, Government of Bihar, four new flood protection works in the Gandak basin area were proposed before the flood of 2020. A request was made on 22 June 2020 by WRD, Government of Bihar, to the Government of India for entry into Nepal region for the execution of these flood protection works and for maintenance works of the Gandak Barrage Structure located in Valmikinagar. After receiving conditional permission from the Government of Nepal, maintenance work of structure and components of the Gandak Barrage (Valmikinagar), top regulator gates, Right Afflux Bund, and three of the proposed works in the Gandak basin were completed. During execution of the strengthening work proposed on the Right Marginal Bund on Lalbekia River, the local Nepali administration claimed that the said Bund area fell in no man's land. This is notwithstanding the fact that the embankment was built by India thirty years ago and there has never been any dispute regarding its maintenance all these years. Breach closure/protective work of Right Guide Bund of Kamla Weir remains incomplete due to lack of permission. However, any resolution of the impasse is still awaited. This is another important matter to be looked at.

Seeing the operational impasse during flood season 2020, Bihar's chief minister Nitish Kumar visited the Jaynagar Weir site in Madhubani (Bihar), and sensing the seriousness of the situation, instructed WRD to explore converting the weir on the India–Nepal border into an efficiently operated barrage. It is evident through the above that Nepal's attitude towards mutual issues (water sharing, flood control, climate change, etc.) has been short of collaborative recently, unlike in past years.

Water resources are extremely crucial for the developmental needs of Nepal; sadly, the uses have been lacking the scale and economic meaning with many hydroelectrical projects not achieving their goals. In Hari Bansh Jha's *Mahakali Treaty*, one gets a profile of Nepal's rich potential but underachieved status at the water resources front:

> In Nepal, ever since the 1950s the water resources remained not only as an economic issue but also a political one, as well. Sometimes over-politicisation of the issue has also harmed our national interest. It is also due to this reason that there has not been any significant development towards the exploitation of the water resources. Of the total 83,000 mw of hydropower generation potential, Nepal has been able to exploit merely 0.3 per cent so far which is far from satisfactory. The scarcity of power hampered the development of agricultural, industrial, trade and service sectors of the economy. Adequate power at a cheap price could not be made available to the people. As a result, the country remained virtually poor both in absolute and relative terms.
>
> Under Article 9 of the treaty, there is the provision for the formation of a Mahakali River Commission which would be guided by the principles of equality, mutual benefit and no harm to either party. One of the major responsibilities of the Commission would be to provide expert evaluation of the projects and also to coordinate and monitor plans of actions arising out of the implementation of this treaty.*

In the same book, Prof. Lok Raj Baral, the then Royal Nepalese ambassador to India, writes:

---

* Hari Bansh Jha (ed.), *Mahakali Treaty: Implications for Nepal's Development* (Foundation for Economic and Social Change, 1996).

The agreement (Mahakali Treaty, 1996) has created a very good
and optimistic atmosphere for the betterment of the relations
of the two neighbours. Moreover, it will contribute to uplifting
living standards of the people of the two countries. Both sides
have been able to accommodate their interests through a
display of pragmatism and cooperative feelings in resolving the
problems whatever they may be.

The *Kathmandu Post* reported the Mahakali Treaty news very
positively as well:

The 1991 Tanakpur pact with India had been a very vexing
issue for Nepal. Thankfully it has now been resolved with all
of Nepal's major political parties reaching a consensus on the
issue. The Mahakali River deal worked out by the previous
government has also come under the purview of the talks and
the agreement reached on the sharing of the fruits of joint
projects on the Mahakali is bound to have a far-reaching
positive impact.

Nepal's political change in 1990 and urge for enhancing bilateral
water cooperation with India helped the foundational side of the
Mahakali Treaty. On 12 February 1996, the treaty between His
Majesty's Government of Nepal and the Government of India
concerning the integrated development of the Mahakali River
including Sharda Barrage, Tanakpur Barrage and Pancheshwar
Project that was concluded at the highest level between P.V.
Narasimha Rao, Prime Minister of India, and Sher Bahadur Deuba,
Prime Minister of Nepal, was seen as a step towards this direction.

The then Nepal's Water Resources Minister Pashupati S.J.B.
Rana identified the Pancheshwar Project being based on the
principle of equal entitlement. He says:

It is written in Article 5 of the Peace Treaty concluded between the then East India Company and Nepal at Sugauli in 1815: 'The Rajah of Nipal renounces for himself, his heirs, and successors, all claim to or in connection with the countries lying to the west of the River Kali, and engages never to have any concern with those countries or the inhabitants thereof.'

This provision has created an illusion that the Mahakali River belongs entirely to Nepal. Whereas it is stipulated in Article 3 of the Treaty concerning the Return of the New Territory concluded at Kathmandu in 1860, 'The boundary line surveyed by the British commissioners appointed for the purpose extending eastward from the River Kali or Sarda to the foot of the hills north of Bagowra Tal, and marked by pillars, shall henceforth be the boundary between the British province of Oudh and the territories of Maharajah of Nepal.'

According to this article, the territory of Nepal has been fixed towards the east of the Mahakali River. Both these articles make it clear that the Mahakali River has been set as a boundary between Nepal and India.

Following these treaties and after the Mahakali River changed its course in 1913 and in 1918, the border lines in those areas were fixed on the basis of straight lines that join two consecutive points from Bramhadev to Jhilmilya (border pillar no. 1 to 31), and the Chandani and Dodhara areas have thus happened to lie to the west of the Mahakali River. Because a chunk of the land (measuring 2898.5 acres from boundary pillar no. 3 to 8) has already been transferred to India at the time of the construction of the Sarada Barrage as a result of the mutual understanding between Nepal and the then British Government, that part of the Mahakali River now lies entirely in India. It is clear from the documents signed in 1916 that the boundary between Nepal and India north of Border Pillar No.1 is the midstream of Mahakali River.

Prakash Chandra Lohani, Nepal's former foreign affairs minister, writes in *Mahakali Treaty*:

> Nepal is a country sitting in this region as a clean source of energy. We believe that we can raise the economic status of our country through trade in this energy. We want to develop a new model of outlook replacing the past distrust we had. In this regard, there was a positive response from Indian friends. I found them ready to work cooperatively. This change has been brought about by the need of the time. We solved the Tanakpur issue. While concluding the Mahakali Treaty, we stressed on equality and mutual benefits.

Regarding inland waterway connectivity between India and Nepal, discussions are underway for operationalization of four multi-modal routes using inland waterways of India. An MoU was signed between India and Nepal on 1 February 2022 for the construction of a motorable bridge across the Mahakali River connecting Dharchula (India) with Darchula (Nepal), under Indian grant assistance. Cooperation in water resources, primarily concerning the common rivers, is an important area of cooperation. Three-tier bilateral mechanism (with ministerial meetings at the apex) was established in 2008 to discuss issues relating to cooperation in water resources, flood management and inundation. In the area of river training and embankment construction, the government of India has been providing assistance to Nepal for strengthening and extension of embankments along rivers in Nepal. Discussions on flood management and inundation related matters are underway in existing bilateral mechanisms.

Besides the above, there are specialized committees which implement the recommendations of the three-tier mechanism that meet more regularly and report to this three-tier mechanism. These specialized committees are the (i) Joint Team of Experts (JTE) on Saptkosi and Sunkosi projects, (ii) Joint Committee on Inundation and Flood Management (JCIFM) and (iii) Joint Committee on Kosi and Gandak Projects (JCKGP). The fourteenth JCIFM meeting between India and Nepal took place in Kathmandu from 9–13 March 2022.

Water is the most precious natural resource. Its effective management has yet not achieved the desired level, with many unresolved issues at the bilateral water cooperation front. The glimmer of hope is from the increased thrust that has been laid recently on India's resolve to maximize the hydroelectricity import from Nepal and also opening a passage of import of Nepal-produced clean energy to Bangladesh. This one, and renewed attention on water cooperation, shall open up a new chapter.

Trade

India and Nepal share close and friendly relations characterized by age-old historical and cultural linkages, open borders and deep-rooted people-to-people contacts. The multifaceted relations between the two countries have been given a renewed momentum in the last few years through intensified high-level political exchanges, regular meetings of bilateral mechanisms across diverse sectors of cooperation, expanding economic and development partnership, boosting connectivity, cooperative initiatives in water resources and hydropower sectors, defence and security, and most importantly, initiatives to promote people-to-people contacts between our two countries.

India remains Nepal's largest trade partner, with bilateral trade crossing $8 billion in FY 2022–23. India provides transit for almost the entire third country trade of Nepal. India's export to Nepal has grown over eight times in the past ten years while exports from Nepal have almost doubled to $840 million in 2022–23. Despite the difficulties due to the pandemic, India ensured uninterrupted flow of trade and supplies to Nepal. Nepal is India's eleventh largest export destination, up from twenty-eighth position in 2014. In FY 2021–22, it constituted 2.34 per cent of India's exports. In fact, exports from India constitute almost 22 per cent of Nepal's GDP. Nepal's main imports from India are petroleum products, iron and steel, cereals, vehicles and machinery parts. Nepal's major items of exports include soyabean oil, spices, jute fibre and products, synthetic yarn and tea. India and Nepal concluded a MoU for long-term supply of urea and DAP fertilizers from India to Nepal under a G2G arrangement on 28 February 2022. Indian firms are among the largest investors in Nepal, accounting for more than 33 per cent of the total Foreign Direct Investment (FDI) stock in Nepal, worth nearly $500 million.

There are about 150 Indian ventures operating in Nepal engaged in manufacturing, services (banking, insurance, dry port, education and telecom), power sector and tourism industries. India and Nepal have also signed the Double Taxation Avoidance Agreement (DTAA) in November 2011. The bilateral remittance flow is estimated at approximately $3 billion (Nepal to India) and $1 billion.

India and Nepal have robust cooperation in the power sector. Three cross-border transmission lines were completed recently with Government of India assistance: 400 KV Muzaffarpur–Dhalkebar line (2016); 132 KV Kataiya–Kusaha and Raxaul–Parwanipur lines (2017). A total of about 600 MW of power is currently being supplied by India to Nepal through different transmission lines, assisting Nepal to overcome seasonal power shortage in the country. The cooperation in power and energy sectors got another fillip with the notification of the procedure for facilitation of cross-border trade of electricity by the government of India, which enables export/import of electricity with Nepal. The cross-border transmission lines have been augmented and the 106-km-long Koshi corridor double circuit transmission line of 220 KV completed under government of India Lines of Credit to Nepal was handed over to the government of Nepal on 6 October 2021.

The Indian government has granted permission to Nepal Electricity Authority (NEA) in November 2021 to sell its surplus energy under Cross Border Trade of Electricity (CBTE) guidelines issued in February 2021 and in the first phase, 39 MW power including 24 MW produced by NEA-owned Trishuli hydropower and 15 MW Devighat powerhouse, have been permitted for trading in Indian Energy Exchange (IEX). Both these projects were developed with India's assistance. The ninth Joint Steering Committee (JSC) and Joint Working Group (JWG) on Power Sector Cooperation led by secretary (power) between India and Nepal met at Kathmandu on 23–24 February 2022.

An increased thrust on clean energy in India is a big opportunity for Nepal and both countries can benefit immensely from a close partnership for overcoming the transition to green and sustainable energy. A framework of cross-border energy export from Nepal to Bangladesh and through the Indian power grid will have a transformational impact on Nepal's economy. Nepal remains headed for a surplus power of around 5000 MW by 2025. This meets only a small requirement for both India or Bangladesh and can get easily absorbed in India. Furthermore, policies, pricing, administration and other arrangements for cross-border power flow with India have remained established and functional for decades now. In this context, a natural question that runs across is what is the real market for Nepali power?

In its role of facilitator, India is now enabling Nepal to export more clean energy to India as well as to Bangladesh, a new market for Nepal. Nepal does not share any border with Bangladesh. It relies on India not only for its territory but also for its transmission infrastructures for the flow of its power. And this remains severely constrained for India's own usage too. Of late, there is new momentum, as during the recent visit of Nepal's prime minister Pushpa Kamal Dahal 'Prachanda', India came forward in ushering a new dimension of cooperation in the power sector by giving the transmission passage (trilateral power transaction) from Nepal to Bangladesh through India. This is path-breaking if Nepal ensures scale, efficiency and speed in generating and exporting power to both the Indian and Bangladesh markets. A long-drawn plan, this will add significantly to Nepal's overall prosperity. Both sides made their commitment clear towards greater sub-regional cooperation, including in the energy sector, which will lead to increased inter-linkages between the economies for the mutual benefit of all stakeholders.

In continuation of the Joint Vision Statement on Power Sector Cooperation of April 2022, the power sector cooperation was discussed at length for good, covering the development of generation projects, power transmission, infrastructure and power trade. Both prime ministers appreciated the growth in export of up to 452 MW of power from Nepal to India and the progress made in the construction of the 900 MW Arun-3 hydroelectric project in Nepal. A notable development made through the visit is the finalization of an agreement for Long-Term Power Trade wherein it was agreed to strive to increase the quantum of export of power from Nepal to India to 10,000 MW within a timeframe of ten years and towards this end, take all necessary measures to encourage mutually-beneficial investments in Nepal's hydropower generation sector and transmission infrastructure.

The groundbreaking 400 KV Gorakhpur-Butwal transmission line, signing of the MoU for the development of the 480 MW Phukot-Karnali project by National Hydroelectric Power Corporation (NHPC) and Vidhyut Utpadan Company Ltd (VUCL) Ltd, Nepal, and the Project Development Agreement for the development of 669 MW Lower Arun between Satluj Jal Vidyut Nigam (SJVN), the Investment Board of Nepal (IBN), and to fund Bheri Corridor, Nijgadh-Inaruwa and Gandak Nepalgunj transmission lines and associated substations under Indian Line of Credit at an estimated cost of $679.8 million, are other key highlights of Nepal PM Prachanda's India visit in 2023.

In the quest of augmenting its industrial productivity and attaining its actual economic potential, Nepal remains on the path of continued hydropower development and has already acquired a surplus power capacity. As per the Economic Survey of 2021–22 of the Ministry of Finance, Government of Nepal (GoN), the installed capacity of Nepal reached 2205 MW in mid-March 2022. The peak power demand in June 2022 was recorded as 1747.50 MW. As per the Department of Electricity Development of the GoN, Nepal has granted a feasibility licence for 228 projects, with a total capacity of 16,415.40 MW to different companies for performing a feasibility study of project development. Likewise, 217 projects with a total capacity of 8306.50 MW have been granted 'Generation Licences' for actual project development. Nepal's generation capacity is expected to reach 7300 MW by 2025. It will be in a surplus of around 5000 MW.

In all likelihood, Nepal's enhanced power capacity will better equip it to use the surplus power at home and also supply most conveniently to India. For greater reliance on surplus power, domestic use in Nepal should give way to increased use of electrical appliances for household and industrial needs, along with mobility solutions. With a balanced transition to clean energy (here it is hydroelectricity), it will have a long-term benefit in making surplus power truly productive besides lowering the import of petroleum products. As a country gripped by a severe balance of payment and liquidity crisis, Nepal has good reason to explore the potential where it is firmly rooted.

Looking from another perspective, it is essential to note that India remains the biggest market of power for Nepal. It has institutional and infrastructure arrangements already in place with Nepal for cross-border power exchange/trade between the two countries. India is also Nepal's biggest trading partner. Nepal has a huge trade deficit with India. For the first eleven months of the fiscal year 2020–21, the volume of bilateral trade between India and Nepal was Rs 610.49 billion, out of which imports from India to Nepal were Rs 554.12 billion and exports to India from Nepal stood at Rs 56.37 billion. Nepal requires Indian rupees more than any other currency for trade. And for that matter, cross-border power export may prove pivotal in improving the trade balance besides earning the much needed Indian currency.

To positively change the industrial landscape and strengthening Nepal's stake in the India–Nepal bilateral economic ecosystem, there is a glaring need to re-energize the energy partnership between the two countries. The foregone opportunities should be seen as reference for learning instead of irritants, the success stories should continue to inspire partnership, and there should be a resolve to tap the vast potential Nepal has with hydroelectricity.

India needs power not only to sustain its economic growth and future growth developmental aspirations but also to ensure the general welfare of its citizens. As per the World Economic Forum (WEF), India's total energy consumption is expected to more than double by 2040 from what it was in 2020. The installed capacity of 410 GW as of 31 December 2022, though makes India the third-largest producer (and also consumer) of electricity in the world, it is not sufficient to achieve the economic growth that it aspires to through such programmes as 'Make in India', 'Skilling India', 'Digital India' and many more. Sufficiency of power remains paramount for achieving growth.

It is imperative to reckon that India does not just need more energy; it needs clean energy. As India is heading towards an energy transition, Nepal has a big opportunity to increase its bandwidth of supplying clean hydroelectricity through the grids of India's neighbouring states such as Bihar and Uttar Pradesh. To make this happen successfully, Nepal has to keep its pricing strategy truly competitive and that should match or beat the other options India has at the energy front.

At 174.53 GW, India is the fourth largest country in the world in installed renewable energy capacity. With the growing clamour for sustainable development, this is something very important. India has set an ambitious goal of achieving 500 GW of renewable capacity by 2030 and plans to invest Rs 2.44 trillion by 2030. Achieving 500 GW requires stepping up the renewable capacity addition by three times its present value each year till 2030. It is a huge investment. It is a huge investment, also, in the light of the pressing need for investments in other important sectors of economy.

Hydropower provides a clean, reliable, efficient, safe and inexpensive source of power. It can also help to mitigate climate change. It is the power that the world needs not only to meet its deficient energy needs but also for its net zero commitments.

By exporting power to India, Nepal will benefit greatly from bridging the huge trade gap between Nepal and India and enhancing bilateral economic partnership. With such promising prospects, India and Nepal should come forward for an even closer cooperation for hydropower development and catalysing the fundamentals critically important for a transformative outcome. At policy and implementation level, this calls for deeper attention from the stakeholders on both sides. Going forward, initiatives and reciprocations can script a new chapter in India–Nepal relations.

India and Nepal extend visa-free entry in their respective territories to each other's nationals. Nearly eight million Nepalese citizens live, work or visit India every year and around six lakh Indians reside in Nepal. Indians account for about 30 per cent of foreign tourists in Nepal. With a view to strengthen people to people exchanges, sister city agreements have been signed (Kathmandu–Varanasi, Lumbini–Bodhgaya, Janakpur–Ayodhya) and India–Nepal Ramayana Circuit have been launched. The Government of India provides around 3000 scholarships annually to Nepali nationals studying in India and in Nepal at all levels of education in a wide range of disciplines. Under the ITEC programme, professional training is offered annually to about 250 officials from Nepal at various technical institutes in India. From 2007 to 2008, more than 1700 ITEC alumni of Nepal have received training under the ITEC programme.

India's priority in a transforming world is acceleration of regional development in its immediate neighbourhood with Nepal, offering immense possibilities of becoming the most developed country in South Asia, thanks to economic integration with India, and Bangladesh, Sri Lanka and Bhutan becoming other enthusiastic partners in creating a zone of prosperity and well-being for future generations.

Aside from hydropower, India's existing manufacturing capabilities and future plans offer enough room for Nepalese small and medium enterprises (SMEs) to emerge as ancillary units of India's large corporates. Exciting new possibilities are also opening up in the service sector where India is already a global power.

As the world increasingly focuses on a re-set of supply chains, a collective determination to revive regional and subregional economic cooperation in South Asia as a unique integrated region, with India in the driving seat, is an achievable vision.

* * *

The Case for an Alternative Development Paradigm for Nepal

Confronted with the lack of any sign of inclusive development, Nepal's democracy and economy both continue to face a vital question mark. But the big shifts that Nepal has made in the past few decades warrant a serious study. In the post-monarchy phase, Nepal's democracy and realpolitik have shown unique characteristics. But there has long been an absence of a broad analysis from a policy perspective, until now.

Madhukar S.J.B Rana's posthumously published book *An Alternative Development Paradigm for Nepal* (Vajra, 2021; curated and edited by Atul K. Thakur) is just that single document that attempts to explain the country's crucial development profile and fundamentals. In the case of Nepal, it is unlikely that a top-down-driven development paradigm comprising national planning, state enterprises and labour unions will allow inclusion of all. This can only happen when opportunities are created for all by supporting markets garnished by agrarian, economic, financial, administrative and labour reforms—and not through just offering 'Seven Provincial Governments' under the newly introduced federalism. Not least, maximizing a bottom-up development paradigm with maximum scope for local leadership development and culture-specific innovations to achieve Sustainable Development Goals (SDGs) depends much on the locals themselves in tune with their own capacity to deliver.

As early as the 1980s, the idea of 'sustainable growth' emerged as a new growth and development paradigm. For the first time, the basic steering principles of economics necessitated harmony with environmental concerns and lasting growth. For good reasons, the old GDP approach to determining growth—and thus success—was seriously questioned. The 'inclusion theory' was born and it received traction from the new genre of progressive policy practitioners and economists. In the 1990s, Prime Minister Krishna Prasad Bhattarai, a Gandhian statesman, provided a new term to the development paradigm—'pro-poor growth'. This led to some welcome changes in policies and grassroots implementation.

Nepal's development plans thus must consider the structural limitations of its economy and geography. Policymakers must show greater empathy towards the precariousness that Nepali citizens face in the absence of constructive national and sectoral dialogues to strengthen the national economy. With the excessive import of goods and the export of human capital, Nepal is in the midst of a crisis. Unfortunately, the political leadership has not been able to pursue an effective economic development plan. There is thus a glaring need to take up a development agenda that aims to reduce imports and create jobs so that human capital is not exported to foreign lands. Such a metamorphosis will require an alternative development paradigm. Nothing less than a revolutionary resolve is needed to orient Nepal's development planning towards meeting the aspirations of the masses.

Inclusive growth must mean growth with productive employment by creating opportunities for jobs and by investing in the human capital development of oneself and family members for the jobs. Planning must be macro, meso and micro, all harmonized strategically. The macro plan must project the desired structure of the economy for the next twenty-five years and the five-year plan must be focusing on human resource development that addresses the long-term requirements of the economy. To make it happen, it is essential to move judiciously and integrate the manpower supply and demand projections with educational plan that opens up avenues for vocational, apprenticeship, technical and technological options for the variety of occupations in the national economy and in the global markets. Inclusive growth requires that we take in a host of factors and forces like geography, demography, social factors and forces, governance, etc. Hence, it has to be participative to require decisions at all levels and all actors—not just the State guided by Nepal's National Planning Commission (NPC)—with its basic and applied research capacities coupled with rapid turnover of planners with the political changes. What is now needed for Nepal is the framework of an Integrated Sector Programming and National Performance Budget governed by a sound Fiscal Responsibility and Budget Management Act (FRBMA) as exists in India, for example, where outcomes are underscored rather than simply inputs and outputs.

Nepal's development plan has to be framed in the perspective in due cognizance of its economic structure and development constraints. It requires policy planners and business from both public and private sectors to be proactively engaged in national and sector dialogues with each other—to set down targets and outcomes for coordinated policy and designing of sector and multi-sector programmes aligned with the annual performance budgets. Also, the feasible economic growth targets have to be assessed for each five-year period first and foremost in consensus with the political parties—and not be driven by external agents and fanciful notions of the political leadership who are very weak in their understanding of economics and finance. The GDP and sector targets should be set in a realistic manner and accordingly action should take place to secure the best possible outcome. Each target must be supported by a country-wide action plan and programme. This requires developing both import substitution and export promotion strategies in partnership with the private sector to include targeting massive inward FDI to compensate for low gross household savings. This requires a new foreign exchange regime where all commodities are put in a common basket and the foreign exchange rate derived accordingly—and further, the devaluation of the Nepali Rupee (NR) to protect the interests of local agriculture production against the subsidized exports. Subsidies to farmers are a sort of necessity with a national drive on irrigation infrastructure.

Costs have been borne at the household and individual levels with the pain and suffering of international migration and debts incurred for it. However, one can take advantage from the challenges by planning the remittance economy better so as to empower women as heads of households and the girl child with the skills to fill in job vacancies as happened during the First and Second World War that liberated women once and for all in the West. Finally, given all the above parameters and their variables for inclusion, there was really no need for an ethnicity-based inclusive State to render justice to all and the next generations. Yes, Nepal needs an inclusive Constitution to not exclude or discriminate against anyone. Primarily, to ensure the supremacy and the rule of law by having independent institutions to check abuse of political authority and guarantee accountability, transparency, competition and merit in the body politic for public good. It would also have to devolve responsibility to the local government units. Sadly, the newly made provinces have thus far failed to achieve their developmental goals and have ended up adding merely another layer of bureaucratic system at a high cost of public resources.

Nepal's developmental woes are multidimensional and it has the centrality of political instability as a major factor behind the structural weaknesses at economic and developmental fronts. A decade-long Maoist insurgency, transition from monarchy to finally evolving as a full-fledged democracy and countless rounds of political experiments for power made Nepal too vulnerable to sustain its developmental pursuits. With a population of nearly thirty million (July 2010), Nepal is one of the poorest countries in the world. Over 80 per cent of the population in the country is directly or indirectly involved in agricultural activities. As per the preliminary study of the Central Bureau of Statistics, the per capita Gross National Income (GNI) in Nepal was recorded as low as $568 in 2009–210, while the annual rate of economic growth was 3.5 per cent. Nearly 55 per cent of the people in the country fall below the international poverty measure of $1.25 per day. The country is facing drought, acute shortage of food and the highest level of hunger in forty years. According to a report of the Asian Development Bank, Nepal recorded the biggest increase in inequality together with China and Cambodia. About 46 per cent of the people in Nepal are underemployed and unemployed. Each day, over 1300 Nepalese people flee their country to other countries other than India in search of employment.

Many of the problems in Nepal are the outcome of the armed conflict of ten years beginning in 1996. Over 16,000 people were killed due to the conflict, which directly affected the lives of 4,50,000 of their family members. During the conflict, 5800 people were disabled, 71,200 people were internally displaced, 25,000 children were orphaned and 9000 women were widowed. Besides, 1350 persons disappeared. The property of 11,000 people was damaged. Several government offices, schools, bridges and police posts were damaged.*

---

* Ishwar Rauniyar, 'Nepalese "guerilla trail" takes tourists through scenes of civil war', *Guardian*, 5 October 2012, https://www.theguardian.com/world/2012/oct/05/nepalese-guerilla-trail-civil-war.

To know more about the conflict and peace in Nepal, Hari Bansh Jha's *Peacebuilding in Nepal* offers some practical insights:

Human Costs of Conflict: 12980 persons including civilians, security forces and insurgents were killed between 1999 and 2009. In 1999, 400 persons were killed. The figure peaked up to 4500 in 2002. Though the number of casualties somewhat declined in subsequent years, the death figures were still very high until 2005. As many as 1800 people were killed in 2003, 2700 people in 2004 and 1848 people in 2005. The number of people killed declined perceptibly to 480 in 2006, 130 in 2007, 81 in 2008 and 49 in 2009.

Economic Cost of Conflict: During the conflict (1996 to 2006), the strength of the Nepalese national army more than doubled from 46000 to 96000. Along with this, the defence budget had to be tripled from Rs 4 billion to Rs 12 billion a year. Estimates are that additional military expenditures blocked the employment prospects for 60000 primary school teachers and another 60000 pre-school monitors and primary health workers. Besides, a huge amount of money is being spent on 19500 Maoist combatants staying in 7 major and 21 satellite camps in various parts of the country. Nearly two million rupees was spent in 2009-2010 on their salary, ration and management. The government pays a monthly salary of Rs 5000 to each of the combatants over and above a per diem varying between Rs 72 to Rs 110 based on the place in which they are cantoned. Also, the government had to spend additional Rs 570 million for upgrading the infrastructure in and around the camps.

Multi-track Approaches to Peacebuilding:

Track-I: During the Maoist insurgency period, efforts were made with different level of tracks to bring peace to the country.

Under Track-I, three rounds of dialogue took place between the government and the Maoists on August 30, September 13 and November 13 in 2001. This was followed by three rounds of dialogue between the government and the Maoists on April 27, May 9 and August 17 in 2003. During those dialogues, the Maoists wanted to have a round-table conference, an interim government, election of constituent assembly and a republican system.

Track-II: As the negotiation between the government and the Maoists at Track-I level proved futile, various civil society groups including the human rights bodies, NGOs, trade unions, women organizations and professional bodies came forward to facilitate the peace process. Many of them collected information on violations of human rights by the conflicting parties, such as killings, disappearances, abductions, displacements, torture, and recruitment of child soldiers, school closures, conflict transformation and peace rallies. Besides, they also facilitated dialogues and a temporary ceasefire took place due to the appeals made by the civil society organizations, the achievements made under Track-II level were not significant.*

Nepal's economic challenges are real, but suggestions that it is already in deep crisis and may be going the Sri Lanka way are probably premature, unfair and unjustified. The surging trade deficit remains a big concern as it is expected to reach $18 billion this fiscal year. Balance of Payment (BoP) deficit and unsavoury debt liability will pose a very grave risk to the economy already in tailspin. Nepal Rastra Bank (NRB) statistics showing the

---

* Dr Hari Bansh Jha (ed.), *Peacebuilding in Nepal* (Centre for Economic and Technical Studies, 2012).

country's inflation averaged at 7.76 per cent in the current fiscal (FY 2022–23), which is the highest of the last sixty-seven months, which does not reflect well on the state of the economy. Such an inflationary tendency can't be attributed merely to high-rallying global prices of petroleum products, commodities and foods. The Covid-19 pandemic caught the world unaware and disrupted economies unimaginably, thus making economic priorities aligned with domestic compulsions and unprecedented global challenges. It was a moment of reckoning to reshape and reorient Nepal's economic planning with giving optimum attention to boost the domestic production and consumption of goods and export ecosystem. Sadly, it also proved an opportunity foregone!

Be that as it may, India will undoubtedly go the extra mile to help Nepal ensure a speedy and comprehensive recovery. India has not hesitated to be generous in coming to Sri Lanka's aid despite political considerations which might have suggested other approaches. In Nepal's case, it has to give priority to development over playing to political galleries. There is no doubt that the economic challenges in the post-Covid-19 pandemic situation, and the overall churning of the geopolitical environment, has created an opportunity for both countries to devise innovative approaches to long-standing issues and to aim at new horizons for bilateral cooperation.

What Nepal's national economy is facing today is not an acute crisis. However, there is a crisis in the making. Of late, the government is finding it difficult to overlook the unbearable trade deficit but unfortunately with wrongly placed measures like curbing the autonomy of the country's Central Bank NRB and vilifying import per se instead intervening for much needed structural economic reforms. NRB underlines problem areas such as rising inflation, BoP deficit, decreasing remittance inflow, depleting foreign exchange reserves and burgeoning imports beyond the acceptable level. Projection of a looming crisis from NRB has no takers in the finance ministry that is focused on making strange short-term provisions rather finding a way to avert a crisis in making.

The shortfall with pragmatic policy interventions and lack of will to reorient economic planning towards 'self-sufficiency' have suddenly made the structural vulnerability of Nepal's economy ever more glaring as the world is making the transition to a new normal in post-pandemic times. Nepal is clearly in dire need of augmenting its preparedness at the domestic economic front along with a need-based infrastructural haul to give the right momentum to an economy that is overtly politicized and not inspiring the big business ideas to prevail and flourish. Nepal's political economy should get traction of the national consensus to fulfil the aspirations of people and reposition Nepal in the world with its strengthened economic prowess.

In assessing the gravity of turbulence, the most worrying factor is the country's debt to GDP ratio that crossed over 40 per cent at one point of time. This is something to be looked at urgently and with a prudent fiscal management plan. Coming to terms with the urgency at the macroeconomic front, immediate action is imperative to boost the demand and empower the Micro, Small and Medium Enterprises (MSMEs) with soft institutional liquidity support. To emerge from the shocks made of BoP deficit in tune of NR 258.64 billion, decrease in remittance inflow and fall of the country's foreign exchange reserve by 16.3 per cent to NR 1171 billion (in mid-March 2022 from NR 1399.03 billion in mid-July 2021), industry needs handholding from the government and rationalization of taxes. Such a collaborative effort will help in increasing the national economic productivity and contributing in mitigating the systemic risk at the economic front.

In the short run, the government's revenue and expenditure should be assessed for minimizing the establishment cost. Especially so, it is needed for provincial governments where the operational part must be dealt with frugally to not burden the economy beyond a proportion. To not give an adverse response to the usual flow of goods and services, the government should lift the ban on imported goods that have no competent alternatives in the domestic market. Till the time Nepal makes a move to increase the production of domestically consumable goods and end the chronic cartel of businesses embracing competition and innovations, it will be rather helpful if Nepal remains open to successfully complete a mandatory transition of present sort.

Claude W. Bobillier's *Women of the 'Third World'* makes a brief but vital observation on Nepal's chronic developmental distress:

> The development of Nepal as a nation has been frozen or static for decades now and this is lost entirely due to the incompetence, selfishness and stubbornness of corrupt politicians, obviously overwhelmingly males. Massive foreign aid, hordes of tourists and technical advisers have done little to improve the dire situation of Nepal, a country known for its humble and charming people, its soaring snow-covered peaks and unique age-old religious rituals. This sad and deteriorating situation will not change unless the various ethnic groups of Nepal get together, organise themselves, get rid of useless and opportunistic so-called elites and committed serious individuals take over and assume responsibility for the future of the country that deserves much better leaders.[*]

---

[*] Claude W. Bobillier, *Women of the 'Third World': What Can We Learn from Them?* (Vajra Books, Kathmandu, 2019).

There is no magic wand to ensure the economic reforms and avert the crisis. Next door, the world's largest democracy India offers a fine example that braved the severe BoP crisis in 1991 and transformed the economy through a sustained wave of economic reforms without letting political preferences override the significant economic matters since then. Here is an inspiring model. Also next door but very differently, China offers an example on the ruthless uses of expansionist capital that is not altruistic and has already ravaged the economies of Pakistan and Sri Lanka. This makes the case of waking up and dropping the romantic notion of inter-border collaborations sans ascertaining the serious risk factors these pose. At a time when isolation can't steer the growth impulses of the economy, it is vital for Nepal to cope with the shortage of industrial production and pressure of trade imbalance through excessive imports while also remaining open to the world for healthy collaboration.

* * *

Nepal's Economic Downturn and Its Victor Hugo Moments for 'Reforms'

Nepal will not go the Sri Lanka way. If it acts towards making the State much more responsible for inclusive growth and ushering in a wave of progressive economic reforms, it has a chance to come out stronger after the downturn.

'Nothing else in the world . . . not all the armies . . . is so powerful as an idea whose time has come': often cited words of wisdom from French writer Victor Hugo are particularly relevant for Nepal, today, when it surely needs to accept an idea whose time has come and that is the spirit of economic reforms. Not as a corollary, but it would be worthwhile for the policymakers at the

helm in Kathmandu to look back at India of 1991 and the then
Finance Minister Manmohan Singh's much-celebrated reference
of Victor Hugo's quote before changing the course of majorly
State-controlled Indian economy by ushering in an economic
liberalization plan. Going beyond the words of wisdom, what
sacrosanct is to identify the common reasons back then in India
or now in Nepal, are the 'structural flaws' and 'cyclical decline.'

Unimaginable losses which Nepal suffered with Covid-19
can also be attributed to the recessionary tendency in Nepal's
economy that made the decision-makers in both the government
and industry jittery. In all probability, the downturn shall
pass as the economy is on the path of rebounding, despite the
negative growth in the last two quarters. As per a PTI report,
Nepal's economy has, of late, shown signs of improvement after
shock absorption and attained 2.16 per cent growth (source:
National Statistics Office [NSO], Nepal) overcoming the worst.*
However, moving forward, what will be vital are the responses
on the policy front, especially the readiness to reform rather
than stopping it.

Noticeably, Nepal entered an economic recession for the
first time in the last six decades with falling economic output
emanated by demand shock, liquidity crunch, balance of payment
crisis, high inflation and policy paralysis. As far as NSO's latest
projection is concerned, it keeps the GDP growth in tune with
1.9 per cent in 2022–23. In the budget, it was estimated to be 8
per cent. As usual, multilateral institutions too failed in projecting
a figure close by. The NSO estimated it on the basis of economic

---

* 'Nepal's economy slightly improves after entering a brief recession',
Press Trust of India, 2 May 2023, https://old.ptinews.com/news/
international/nepals-economy-slightly-improves-after-entering-a-brief-
recession/562520.html.

fundamentals of the period (July 2022–April 2023) and assumed economic activities would remain normal and the economy would get traction in the final quarter of this fiscal year. While Nepal's economy is in a rebounding phase despite the challenges, NSO's estimate may get wrong if the industrial output and capital spending are not on course as they are expected to be.

Nepal's real developmental dilemma lies in its low propensity to reform while keeping the monopolistic structure in key productive sectors, notwithstanding the promises made by the transition from a monarchy to a functional democracy; its economy is neither handled well by the State nor private enterprises. A sad truth remains that Nepal has the pursuit for getting foreign investments but without opening its economy for fair competition (even if not the perfect one) and ushering market reforms. Another fault line is having its front-running industries showing no signs of recognizing the export potential and recalibrating their capacity to make Nepal a hub of hope rather than despair. Among the policymakers, a realization should be that Nepal has no backup of a command economy to support a few major enterprises, and next, the aspirations of people can't wait for things to get in order with nature's command and control.

To get the system in order, it will be imperative to have a consensus on making a long-term economic vision for Nepal. This will be made possible by giving an alternative development paradigm to Nepal and recognizing the need of a fine balance in having the government and industry work in tandem despite the frequency of changes in political order. To know the evolution and working of a political order, it will be helpful to quote the political scientist Francis Fukuyama who recognized the centrality of three institutions for explaining it: the State, the rule of law and mechanisms of accountability. Kathmandu and provincial elites helming the political might should recognize the merit of 'accountability,' 'home works' and 'rule of law'. They should work for a political economy where the State will act like a facilitator for inclusive economic development. This too is an idea whose time has come.

Going beyond the jargon, there is glaring urgency to identify the bottlenecks in Nepal's economy and act promptly:

Weak infrastructure base with shortcomings in planning and implementation: A few examples are the road projects that have been planned as per whims rather in response to the requirements. Nepal certainly doesn't need eight-lane roads and with a completion phase as long as over a decade. The infrastructure projects have to be sustainable and thus ensuring transparency and efficiency is the need of the hour.

Wasted energy potential: While it was supposed to illuminate the home and the world, with a production capacity of just 2500 MW hydroelectricity and no avenues to sustain its export to India, mainly for offering low cost advantage and cyclical inability to meet the demand at home turf, Nepal is missing to explore the actual benefits. Nepal should brand its hydroelectricity as 'green energy', augment its production and increase consumption at home (with more uses of electric vehicles and other appliances) and keep the export to India unwaveringly. This will be a game changer if the course-correction is made on this front.

Sectoral reforms: The key sectors including telecom, banking and financial services (with focus on making a rational payment arrangement), agriculture and food processing, IT & ITeS, FMCG, and aviation should be opened up for competition where the existing players compete with new entrants and let the end consumers benefit out of it.

Abolishing monopolistic tendency and promoting fair competition: This will be possible with the state's participation in the transformative process of reforms as a facilitator and with a welfarist touch.

Safe and improved mobility/connectivity: On its own and through developmental partnerships, Nepal should particularly make road and air connectivity safe and improved. Its infrastructure should have a welcoming preparedness.

Enhancing tourism potential: Nepal's main source of revenue should be boosted with improved connectivity. Needless to say, the whole world is looking at Nepal as a major tourism destination; it is endowed with natural and civilizational richness and there is no reason tourism should not be treated as a major industrial sector.

Climate change and mitigation: As a country uniquely positioned with the top peaks of Himalayas, huge water reservoirs and an open border with India, Nepal has all the reasons to come forward and play a major role to mitigate climate change. In doing so, it will create a strong basis of sustainability and finally help its economy in many ways possible.

Checking outbound migration and decreasing reliance on remittance: While remittance contributes to about 22 per cent of Nepal's GDP, it comes at the cost of immense human suffering and long-term socio-economic losses. The upward mobility can't be stopped but large masses going to far-flung destinations for the sake of survival can be absorbed with gainful employment in the country if Nepal comes out of self-imposed economic woes.

Improving transparency and removing corruption: Doing it will help in restoring the confidence of the private sector in the country and also help in getting foreign investments.

Recognizing the virtue of 'home work' rather than 'external influence': As a sovereign country and with a firmly established democracy, Nepal should work towards putting things in order at home. Beyond a point, there is no reason to cite 'external influence' as a factor that really harms Nepal's prospects. It should be dealt with much more effectively.

Nepal will not go the Sri Lanka way. If it acts towards making the State much more responsible for inclusive growth and usher in a wave of progressive economic reforms, it has a chance to come out stronger after the downturn. Some of the long-pending actions will transpire the wishful changes ahead for Nepal, and India as a friendly neighbour can certainly partner up for such a metamorphosis.

It will be vital to deepen its economic ties with India and enable joint ventures with the Indian firms to grow in Nepal and further diversify to create immense economic opportunities. Among those crucial provisions to sail with the tide, an ever focused attention given to foster India–Nepal bilateral economic cooperation will be crucial at this stage.

* * *

Beyond Borders: Bilateral, Regional and Sub-Regional Cooperation

India often faces criticism from its immediate neighbourhood that it holds the development projects but does not deliver on time. Even within India, thinktanks, media and foreign policy observers suggest that India speed up development projects in Nepal in the face of growing Chinese influence. However, in the last couple of years, India's image of not completing projects on time has gradually changed with the completion of a few vital projects. Despite the occasional hiccups in bilateral relations, the joint projects are showing welcome signs of professionalism, though many joint projects are still mired in bureaucratic hurdles. While the high-profile political visits have been mostly centered on improving the connectivity between the two countries, in implementation mode, the same spirit was not always replicated.

Noticeably, the Nepalese prime ministers' India visits are known to majorly include issues of pending projects in communiqués. Looking back, the counts of opportunities foregone are too many to be kept on record.

Notwithstanding the poor track of implementation, both countries have made positive exceptions with a few selected projects in the recent past. One of the remarkable projects completed before the stipulated time framework is the cross-border petroleum pipeline. There is a fresh momentum for a few joint stalled projects—the non-operational railway line from Bardibas–Bijalpura–Pipradhi–Janakpur in Nepal to Jaynagar is now fully operational and this has already had a positive impact on mobility and economic activities, giving a new lease of life to the border economy in both formal and informal sectors.

Under Operation Maitri, in the wake of the 2015 earthquake in Nepal, India was the first responder and carried out its largest disaster relief operation abroad. India extended $1 billion to Nepal as part of its long-term assistance for post-earthquake reconstruction in housing, education, health and cultural heritage sectors. The reconstruction projects in education, health, cultural heritage and housing sectors were reviewed by the Joint Project Monitoring Committee on 30 September 2021 in Kathmandu. The government of India had successfully handed over all the 50,000 reconstructed houses in Nepal's Gorkha and Nuwakot districts on 15 November 2021, with assistance of $150 million. Fourteen higher secondary schools have also been completed and inaugurated in recent years. The work on reconstruction of more than 130 hospital/ health centres and twenty-eight cultural heritage sites in Nepal is under various stages of implementation. The Indian government provides substantial financial and technical assistance to Nepal for implementation of large development and infrastructure and connectivity projects, as well as small development projects/high impact community development projects in key areas of education, health, irrigation, rural infrastructure, livelihood development, etc. all across the country.

A series of cross-border connectivity projects like rail links, roads and integrated check posts have been completed or are under implementation with the Indian government's grant assistance. Despite Covid-19 restrictions, work on the ongoing connectivity and developmental projects continued and showed considerable progress.

In February 2021, thirteen Terai road packages were completed with assistance of Rs 400 crore and handed over to the Government of Nepal. Some of the High Impact Community Development Projects (HICDPs) inaugurated in the Covid-19 period include the Fateh Bal Eye Hospital in Nepalgunj, the Rapti Cold Storage Building in Lamahi Bazar and the Rehabilitated Small Hydro Power Plant in Jumla District. India and Nepal have also expanded bilateral cooperation to include new initiatives in the areas of agriculture, railways and inland waterways connectivity. The 'New Partnership in Agriculture' was announced in April 2018, which focuses on collaborative projects in agriculture, education and R&D. India is providing financial and technical assistance for construction of two broad gauge cross-border railway links viz., Jaynagar-Bardibas and Jogbani-Biratnagar. India and Nepal signed a Letter of Exchange (LoE) to the India–Nepal Rail Services Agreement (RSA), which enabled all authorized cargo train operators including private container train operators to carry Nepal's container and other freight. In addition to that, the Indian government handed over the 34.9-km cross-border rail link connecting Jayanagar (in Bihar) to Kurtha (in Nepal; and by July 2023, to Bijalpura) to the Nepalese government and both countries also signed an MoU for conducting Final Location Survey of the proposed broad gauge line between Raxaul and Kathmandu, both during October 2021.

In September 2019, the then prime minister of Nepal K.P. Sharma Oli and Indian prime minister Narendra Modi inaugurated the Motihari–Amlekhgunj petroleum pipeline, the first of its kind in South Asia. The 69-km pipeline is reducing the cost of transportation of fuel from India to Nepal. This project is taken as a game-changing project in Nepal. On 7 April 2018, Oli and Modi had jointly laid the foundation stone for construction of the pipeline. It was to be completed within two years but was done even before the deadline. Now, there will be smooth transport of fuel from India to Nepal and it will not be disrupted because of usual hindrances in bordering areas. Another piece of progress being made in the last couple of years is the completion of seven out of fourteen India-funded roads in the Terai region of Nepal. The third meeting of the Joint Project Monitoring Committee took place in the first week of March 2020; it concluded that these roads will strengthen the Terai road network in Nepal and improve the movement of people and economic activities in the region. There is speedy progress seen in the other remaining projects as well, along with substantial progress in the railway connectivity.

At least six railway projects are proposed and there has been some progress in recent times. These are (i) Jaynagar (India)-Janakpur (Nepal) to Bardibas in Nepal, (ii) Jogbani in India to Biratnagar in Nepal, (iii) Nautanwa in India to Bhairahawa in Nepal, (iv) Rupaidiha in India to Nepalgunj in Nepal, and (v) New Jalpaiguri in India to Kakarbhitta in Nepal, and (vi) Kathmandu-Raxaul. Mainly after the talk of a Chinese railway, the Nepal-India railway line has made good progress because it is feasible in terms of both geography and costs. The Kathmandu–Raxaul railway line has made significant progress in the last one year. The Indian side has already completed the pre-feasibility study of the Kathmandu–

Raxaul railway line and both countries are holding consultations on preparing the Detailed Project Report of the railway line.

Unlike the Nepal–China railway line that is uniquely placed with difficult geography, the construction of the Kathmandu-Raxaul railway line is very much possible as per the earmarked budget and construction plan. Coming to the road network, the two countries are connected as Kathmandu–New Delhi direct bus service is already in place. Similarly, Nepal's other few big cities are directly connected to Delhi through bus services. Several other connectivity projects are also being discussed. For the inland waterways network, Nepal has been keen to work in unison with India. India has already agreed to allow Nepal to use three inland waterways, thus expanding its transit options. Nepal can operate its own vessels on the river Ganga. India has given consent to grant access to the Kolkata–Kalughat, Raxaul; Kolkata–Sahibganj, Biratnagar and Kolkata–Varanasi–Raxaul routes for waterways. India has developed a waterway on the Ganges River which connects Varanasi and the seaport of Haldia, Kolkata. If Nepal gets access to waterways, it will facilitate movement of cargo which it imports from third-party countries to Nepal. Hydropower projects funded by India did not make much progress in the last two decades in Nepal due to various reasons known and unknown to most of us. However, in the last couple of years, there has been some visible progress in hydropower projects. For instance, the Arun-3 hydroelectricity project has gained momentum with financial closure in the first week of February this year. The Arun-3 project was one of the much-talked-about and pending issues since the 1990s.

When it comes to energy cooperation, the two countries have already agreed to go for an energy banking concept and are working to operationalize it. According to this concept, Nepal will export power to India during the summer season which exceeds imports during the dry season. The tasks of construction of integrated check posts have gained momentum in the past couple of years. The Integrated Check-Post (ICP) in Biratnagar was inaugurated in January 2020. The cheapest was furnished with some modern facilities such as electronic weighbridges, fire safety, warehousing facilities including refrigerated cargo, 24/7 monitoring through CCTV and public announcement systems. The post also has the capability of handling around 500 trucks per day. Earlier, in 2018, India handed over the ICP Birgunj to Nepal. Construction was started in April 2011 and it took seven years to complete the construction and bring it into operation. However, constructions of other check posts are not taking much time.

Two countries have already agreed to construct ICPs at four major points along borders. These are: Raxaul (India)–Birgunj (Nepal), Saunali (India)–Bhairahawa (Nepal), Jogbani (India)–Biratnagar (Nepal) and Nepalgunj Road (India)–Nepalgunj (Nepal). Out of the four, two have been completed and the remaining two are being constructed. Additionally, India-funded reconstruction of houses in Nuwakot district is another progress made in this period. It has been four years since the two countries realized that they need to complete the pending projects first instead of signing new projects.

In 2017, during the prime minister of Nepal Pushpa Kamal Dahal's visit to India, a bilateral mechanism was made to identify and address the bottlenecks in existing bilateral projects. The meeting which was attended by the foreign secretary of Nepal and the Indian ambassador in Kathmandu played a vital role in easing the terms of bilateral ties and development partnership between India and Nepal. Similarly, the India–Nepal Joint Commission meeting led by foreign ministers of both countries is also in process to review the state of bilateral projects and issue guidance to authorities to address the bottlenecks. Irrespective of diplomatic highs and lows, India and Nepal should give top priority to speeding up the development projects which can contribute to maintain cordial ties between two countries.

The meetings under the existing bilateral mechanisms should take place on a regular basis; the current pace of work should be continued without any interruptions. Making the initiatives productive has been a key challenge before the policymakers on both sides; now the reckoning should be to calibrate the shifting fundamentals and keep the policies and action in order. Remarkably, India has completed many pending projects in recent times besides maintaining a desirable pace with the ongoing projects in Nepal.

For perceptual change benefitting the economic and strategic fundamentals in the region, the idea of a Trans-Himalayan Economic Corridor (THEC) centred on Nepal should be pursued seriously. It is based on the firm belief that a THEC can profoundly transform the entire south-eastern Himalayan subregion and the Ganges Basin—where most of the world's most poor and deprived people now live—with benefits for all. The south-eastern Himalayan subregion and the Ganges Basin need a big push in infrastructure investments coupled with far more robust annual economic growth rates to meet the challenges posed by its poverty, mass unemployment and massive underemployment of its human capital. Also, risks arise from natural disasters, climate change, global warming, and not least, water, food, health and energy security threats. Amidst the development and security challenges faced by the Himalayan subregion, the emergence of Asia as a world economic fulcrum offers grand opportunities to deal with these challenges.

It will be worthwhile to note that the bilateral ties between India and Nepal have always been supported with treaties which principally appeared beneficial to stakeholders. However, as the implementation mechanism mostly rested with the regimes in New Delhi and Kathmandu—and on their 'fluctuating diplomatic fundamentals'—it could be noticed how at times the best aimed treaties had failed to avoid scenarios such as 'economic/transit hiccups' of the past. The open border between India and Nepal has been the vantage point of the two countries' trust-based relationship. But a closer look at this border regime shows a lack of impetus in transforming this unique arrangement for the enhancement of trade relations between the two countries, thus leading to a failure of the border regions to tap into the potential of trade activities. These shortcomings indicate a flawed approach to border talks between the two countries. There seems to be a clear and sharp disdain for tapping economic opportunities and while delving on this issue, the geographical spread has to go further—to other parts of north Bihar, Uttar Pradesh, West Bengal and Uttarakhand.

The federal structure of India restricts the States' authority and action when it comes to international matters. So, it is imperative that New Delhi and Kathmandu be serious about these issues, which are currently being handled half-heartedly without any vision. It is time for India and Nepal to go beyond formal barriers and translate rhetoric into action. Nepal has emerged as a more confident nation amidst the democratic transition. A large number of Nepalis today no longer see the monarchy as an option. This is a striking development in the country, where, until recently, political authority was seen as inseparable from royalty. Historic political upturns have tested the country in many ways. But amidst many setbacks, Nepal has emerged as a forward-looking modern nation. These developments have a close bearing on Nepal's relations with India.

As India faces the constant threat of terror attacks, safeguarding its open border with Nepal is high on its to-do list. Time and again, Nepal has closely cooperated with Indian security agencies in cracking down on terror outfits, including the Indian Mujahideen network. But there are many problems along the border that must be addressed by both sides. Illegal trade is rampant. This administrative failure could make Nepal a parking lot for terror activities, as India is the most targeted country by both international and home-grown terror outfits in the whole of South Asia. India cannot afford to overlook this aspect, so it has to guard its borders with greater sensitivity. Nepal also has a shared interest here. The border, therefore, should be made a major plank of India–Nepal high-level negotiations. To make trade and diplomacy work fairly, India and Nepal should move beyond tokenism and enter a new phase of cooperation. Nepal should not preclude itself from benefiting from India's economic rise and India should not miss the opportunity to further cooperate with a politically stable Nepal.

The rise of the East is wrongly viewed with scepticism and fear by the West, precisely so, as somewhere it is erroneously made synonymous with the 'rise of China'. This may just be one of the factors of a serious perception gap. However, it is strong enough to not be undermined by the West's strategic and economic thinkers. India's peaceful growth principles are beckoning for all the good reasons. One can wonder whether they can explore the potential of 'the new world order' with the aim of gaining in the post-recovery phases. Sharing a broad mission can be helpful to both India and Nepal, as well as the other friendly countries of South Asia. It will be crucial how these countries view China's aggression in the South Asian region and its adverse implications for regional unity and bilateral relations. Not often discussed, though also not beyond the obvious, a very promising regional association like the South Asian Association for Regional Cooperation (SAARC) could not do as well as expected with China's territorial and market overreach. In comparison, India's posture in the neighbourhood has been conciliatory, and its dominance in the region merits being seen through the same perspectives.

The newly disrupted world is not short on opportunities for the countries that have been hitherto given no due by a niche group of countries. Desperate times call for desperate measures, and as an aspirational country, India's stake is certainly high as the world is reassured of seeing a complete reset. Nepal should see it as an opportunity. There is no single multilateral institution including the UN that can exactly ascertain the level of losses the world has witnessed due to the Covid-19 global pandemic. In fact, the UN's failure in communicating the imminent dangers of unknown biological warfare disguised as a malady and making a concerted effort to constitute an international task force for a global approach to save the world, is too big to be ignored. Today, we are already living in a ravaged world that can't live in harmony if the old institutions find no new way to justify their existence.

At the cusp of a defining change, it is wishful that the South Asian countries come forward for reimagining South Asia and staking a claim in the new world order by supporting the constructive moves for strengthening regional and subregional cooperation. To brave the challenges, some of the inherent weaknesses have to be addressed, especially on the bilateral front. Essentially, for finding a strong basis for regional and sub-regional economic and strategic integration, the bilateral hiccups and unhelpful baggage of the past have to be effectively dealt with. In South Asia, a new chapter of cooperation should be driven by regional unity.

At this point of time, decision-makers in our part of the world would do well to take into consideration the concept of 'enlightened self-interest' as propounded by Alexis de Tocqueville in his work *Democracy in America*. They may or not be altruistic—it is a matter of choice. However, when it comes to pursuing enlightened self-interest, spirit and action have to be forward-looking. Of late, it is important to find virtue in enlightened self-interest for ensuring a greater degree of maturity in public discourse. It is not that all kinds of sentiments should go on the wane, especially the love for the country and the neighbourhood. In the homeland or beyond the border, much can be preserved by simply not making the same mistakes again. It is interdependence that beautifully weaves the true fabric of India–Nepal relations. For re-imagining them, too, one has to understand that we owe each other much more than what is featured in official communications.

Extraordinary times need extraordinary measures. Going forward, political leadership in both India and Nepal should prioritize issues that matter to lives and livelihoods. This is the best time for India–Nepal relations to evolve with greater sensibilities and respect for individual, common and holistic interests. The role of India and Nepal will be that of a catalyst in shaping the narrative of a new regional and sub-regional alignment. The region's self-reliance in economic terms will depend a lot on how these two friendly countries come together—setting aside a few bilateral concerns—and get along with other South Asian countries in putting up a common front to brave the new world emerging with Covid-19. This time in history will be known for a reshaping of the world, which will stay on the course of modernism, but one that will be drastically different from the post-colonial one. The shifted fundamentals will have an impact on the multilateral institutions and advanced economies that enormously dominated the post-World War period.

There is hardly any space for a third party in the unique ties between India and Nepal. The year 2020 proved to be highly forgettable with Covid-19, lockdown and immense losses of lives and livelihoods across the world. This year, China also found allies to encircle India on different fronts. Altogether, such adventurous acts forced India to re-prioritize its choices in the new world order filled with uncertainties. In India's official establishment, there is now a feeling that 'realism' should drive India's strategies and foreign policies, especially in its neighbourhood. In recent years, India's foreign policy has kept a belief in 'optimal relationship' with all the major powers to best advance its goals. Under the same framework, it makes proper sense to advocate for a bolder and non-reciprocal approach to the immediate and extended neighbourhood. In recent times, India has followed that approach in engaging with its immediate neighbours, including Nepal. This is not something of an enigma for policymakers in Kathmandu.

At the highest decision-making level in India, it is believed that the existing era of global upheaval entails greater expectations from India, putting it on the path to becoming a leading power. They should be hailed for making a clear distinction between 'national interest' and 'international responsibilities', and provisioning much needed balancing acts. It is vital to note that India is on the way to reclaiming its prominent place on the world stage and being a civilizational power.

No longer is consistency the sole driving force of India's foreign policy and strategies. Choices have to be exercised in the changing circumstances, hence both constants and changes are supposed to get space in new policy manoeuvrings. China's rise, disproportionate aggression and interventionism in South Asia have been quite instructive for India. India has a way to deal with the changing global scenario. Now it is more flexible in recognizing the greater multi-polarity and unpredictability trends that have increased influence over international affairs. In a new world more receptive to 'transactional terms', there is a litmus test for age-old cross-boundary friendship. Here, if India–Nepal relations are taken into perspective too, the changing norms offer a 'new normal'. If India continues with 'certain constants' beside the inevitable changes, it is for safeguarding the valued terms it has with Nepal. With deep care for its inalienable relations with Nepal and respect for its sovereign status, India remains its most trustworthy neighbour and ally.

India's rise in the world makes Nepal strongly placed in the global order as well. As an integrated market, trade and services are surely going to benefit. It is noteworthy how the process of economic reforms in India that started way back in the early 1990s had a positive impact on Nepal. Economic integration was never so stout and heady for achieving extraordinary outcomes. Now when India is moving in a direction of giving extra traction to 'self-reliance', though without being protectionist, it is again opening the door with bright possibilities for Nepal's businesses to deepen their engagement in India, and further enhance regional and subregional economic cooperation. Sooner than later, India's trade-balancing exercise will have some meaning for China too.

In the South Asian region, India's engagement drives will continue irrespective of strategic challenges curated by China through Pakistan or on its own. India's capabilities are overshadowing the challenges in the region, and it is unlikely that China will get much in the long term from its over-pricey and directionless projects like the BRI and cross-border incursions. However, its expansionism is surely getting an edge with the vulnerabilities of its allies, especially Pakistan. Nepal, with its bright spot in the new world order, should do everything possible to negate China's ploy to use it as a 'strategic hotspot' against India. China is not known to be an altruist power; its ambivalence in the international arena has been seriously puzzling over the decades. In today's time, Nepal needs more strategic minds than the Mandarin experts to know about China's plan in its totality.

Over a long period of time, China has enjoyed its insulation despite showing disregard for 'international responsibilities'. Of late, China stands exposed on the world stage, and it is not possible that its hegemonic advances will not get a counter-response.

In a world badly ravaged by Covid-19, Nepal should do everything possible to revive its industrial prospects and occupy its workforce to attain self-sustainability and control the very high rate of outbound migration. To get greater space in the world order, Nepal has to work extra hard on the domestic front. A balancing approach is wishful thinking, and it is also imperative to avoid acrimonious stances. A progressive developmental narrative in Nepal will enthuse India to give extra focus to the vision of shared prosperity. Working and growing together should drive our bilateral mechanism. India and Nepal will be big beneficiaries if both countries give their due to the trust-based relationship. The 'India Way' is and will be clearly friendly for Nepal. Among those countries, Nepal is well placed with its relatively positive fundamentals and its firm embraces of modernism and democracy. But this nation needs to admire its icons in a more engaged manner, besides eliminating the conditions that allow regressive 'partisans' to thrive disproportionately.

The world is in the process of reset; Covid-19 and a long lockdown have changed the course of history. Western Europe, the United States and the rest of the advanced economies are no longer in a position to continue with their long-surviving trade and investment policies. Geography will be considered differently by these economies now. In transition, the big shift in international business will be disruptive in an unprecedented manner. In such changing times, South Asian countries have a chance to attend to the urgency of having a constrictive framework for regionalism and sub-regionalism. To mitigate the risks imposed by unimaginable disruption, there is a need to revisit the opportunities missed and make a new forward-looking action plan for South Asia. To rejuvenate the economy and sustain the desired level of growth for a fairly long time, there will be a need to revive SAARC and the Bangladesh, Bhutan, India and Nepal (BBIN) initiative. As globalized trade is severely disrupted and it is unlikely that it will see the same kind of buoyancy in the near future, India and Nepal have to come forward and lead the revival plan of these two regional associations in letter and spirit. These two friendly countries, with strong trust in each other, have been pursuing the mission of a united and strong region.

The crisis offers ample opportunities to boost the South Asian spirit and correct the mistakes of bygone times. Particularly for Pakistan, it should be a moment of reckoning to understand the significance of a functionally active SAARC. As the region is facing a sort of humanitarian crisis with total systemic disruption, it has to look within and gain traction for economic and strategic considerations. Any idea of SAARC minus Pakistan can be counter productive. This should be the realization of all member countries. A constructive reciprocation is something that can help Pakistan in its image makeover and let SAARC function to achieve re-imagined goals. The strengthening of regional and subregional economic cooperation in South Asia will be of immediate help in dealing with the pandemic and the broken supply chains and mobility caused by it. SAARC and BBIN members should explore opportunities among themselves. Pursuing meaningful regionalism and sub-regionalism will be the best strategy for member countries willing to strengthen their capacity and sail through the difficult times ahead. In a deeply troubled world, thinking of having a firmed 'home-bound' approach to economic cooperation can be a game changer.

* * *

The Final Words

India and Nepal must return to the core strength of their unique social, cultural, strategic, political, and economic ties. The two countries share deep social, cultural, strategic, political and economic ties that have been forged over many centuries. Unfortunately, ties wither if exposed to the changing fundamentals of time. India–Nepal ties have frayed slowly as the economic bonds between the two countries have failed to keep pace with India's modernization and growth. The opportunities offered by India's prospering economy have become increasingly inaccessible, and thereby irrelevant to ordinary Nepalis. The persistent border dispute between the two countries is an opportunity for them to modernize old ties towards a shared vision of prosperity. India and Nepal must do more than merely resolve boundary issues. They must return to the core strengths of their unique social, cultural, strategic, political and economic bonds and modernize ties to directly connect their people, markets, finance and technology. Such informal ties and the simplicity of those traditional businesses are now under stress. The Indian economy is modernizing, transitioning from the informal into the formal economy. Contracts are being acquired. Complex documentation is needed to move products across borders. Stronger controls are making it difficult to move cash and make payments.

The India–Nepal border that had once never prevented cousins, brothers, sisters, friends and associates from doing business with one another has now become a boundary that separates. For many small and medium Nepali businesses, it is now easier to trade with China. This isn't because China has rendered India uncompetitive. Rather, the rules have made it harder to do business with India. SMEs are being left behind; India–Nepal trading agreements still carry vestiges of old rules. For example, Nepali traders cannot import products from India that are not manufactured in India.

Large businesses that consistently do business find ways to get around this but opportunistic (or spontaneous) trade, which is often small in volume, is significantly hurt by these rules. The end result: opportunistic trade opportunities that are often the basis and spark for longer-term investments are simply put off because the transactions take too much time. The historic complex informal economic network that is the bedrock of India–Nepal trade will not modernize on its own. But these are the ties that will bind—they cannot be left to wither. Decision-makers must recast these ties: modernize and make it relevant again to the people who share in its benefits.

With China now a factor directly or indirectly influencing India–Nepal relations, decision-makers must act swiftly to remove anomalies blocking meaningful economic engagements between India and Nepal. They must allow people across the borders to share in each other's growth just as they did before. For Nepal, this is an era of exciting change. New awakenings and aspirations have taken roots. Like other governments, India has also rushed to engage with Nepal's new government. But India's relationship with Nepal is broader than engagements with governments alone. It works, for instance, directly with many young people and communities across Nepal. Sadly, these Indian development initiatives that seek to connect directly with Nepalis have been sabotaged. Consider the example of scholarships that India provides to Nepali students for higher education in Indian institutions. While technically based on merit, many of the scholarships are awarded on recommendations. The awards fuel a network of patronage but fail to make India's growth accessible to Nepalis in need.

India also works directly with communities and local organizations supporting a wide range of development projects (e.g. building schools, health centres, energy projects, providing ambulances). While such projects provide development benefits to people in the area, the local politician harvests a much richer dividend. India's approach of connecting with the people of Nepal is being undermined by local intermediaries. Development dividends don't flow through so easily. Nepali aspirations have been unshackled. India must recognize this. As an immediate priority, it must realign its geo-political and economic outlook on Nepal to craft a new approach that allows ordinary Nepalis to access the opportunities India's economic growth offers. The diverse but balanced and constructive approaches to India–Nepal relations will contribute to a clearer understanding of the past, better awareness of present trends, road maps for substantive upgrading of ties on a sustainable basis in the years to come, and give much food for thought to practitioners on both sides of the border, while enhancing the understanding and space for constructive contribution on the part of other key actors. Thus, the glaring need is to throw light on the nuances, undercurrents and openings offered in bilateral ties which are often ignored in assessing major developments but which could be extremely relevant if the relationship is to achieve its true potential.

While the India–Nepal relations have historic backing from a series of factors, China's quest to downplay India's special friendly status with Nepal is part of Beijing's greater neo-imperialist plot. Now, both in international relations and domestic politics, Nepal is facing the adverse implications of recently increased political engagement with China. In broad terms, Nepal has suffered a lot by mismanaging its conventional role of a non-aligned and focused nation that tempered its special peaceful standing in South Asia. In his later days, King Birendra shared close relations with China, and so the royal massacre of 2001 shocked the Chinese greatly as well. King Gyanendra, who then occupied the throne in highly suspicious circumstances and without the trust that his predecessors enjoyed from an average Nepali, sought to cement ties with China by offering it space in the South Asian Association for Regional Cooperation in 2005. India had been understandably less than amused by Kathmandu's sudden overtures to China.

India's former ambassador to Nepal Ranjit Rae's *Kathmandu Dilemma* analyses the neo-collective psyche in Nepal that influences India–Nepal relations considerably:

> What's Nepal's own sense of its identity? How is it different from India? Given the asymmetry in size and in population, the fact that Nepal is surrounded on three sides by India, engenders a siege mentality and a desire to break away. The Nepalese also dislike and resent their dependence on India. Therefore, they try and fight geography! Two unique markets that Nepal has claimed for its own national identity are being the birthplace of the Buddha and home to the highest peak in the world, Mount Everest. Unfortunately for Nepal, both these markets are shared, the former in terms of the common Buddhist heritage with India, and the latter with China.*

Notwithstanding the centrality of complementarities in bilateral relations, oftentimes, the official line has taken its own turn in interpreting the not-so-easy situations. While repurposing India–Nepal relations, the prudent move will be to rely more strongly on the trust factor, subsiding apprehensions and complexities. India and Nepal have a credible past as well current practice of engaging with each other—and walking with the changing times. In knowing the new aspirations of both sides, and accordingly creating the background of cooperation, India–Nepal relations will see further heights. In the times to come, hopefully better chapters of India–Nepal bilateral relations will be scripted.

---

* Ranjit Rae, *Kathmandu Dilemma: Resetting India–Nepal Ties* (Vintage, 2021).

Acknowledgements

The accounts and assessments in this joint endeavour are based on countless conversations, consultations and readings—with leaders, scholars, people, some who are with us, others who have left. It would not be possible to name them all, although a few appear in the book. We owe all of them a debt of immense gratitude. They have contributed immeasurably to greater clarity in understanding the past, measuring the present and reimagining the future.

Our deep gratitude for the early endorsements received from Ambassador Satish Chandra, former deputy national security adviser of India and former high commissioner to Pakistan; General (Retd) Vishwa Nath Sharma, PVSM, AVSM, ADC, former Indian Army chief; Prem Prakash, chairman, Asian News International, and author; Prem Shankar Jha, veteran journalist and author; Lok Raj Baral, former ambassador of Nepal to India and author; Akhilesh Upadhyay, former chief editor, *Kathmandu Post*, and senior fellow, Institute for Integrated Development Studies, Kathmandu.

We are grateful to Penguin Random House India (PRHI) for their immediate positive response to the idea of a jointly authoured book, and the strong and consistent personal support from Premanka Goswami (associate publisher and head-strategy,

PRHI). Acknowledgement is also due to the meticulous work of our copyeditor Manali Das and cover designer Sparsh Raj Singh. A warm 'thank you' to the entire PRHI team.

Both India and Nepal are in the throes of tremendous transformation in different ways. The challenges before drivers of policy on both sides, while of course very different, have been many, and often daunting.

It is easy to be wise after the events, easier still to be judgemental about those who could have acted differently for more constructive outcomes. We have tried our best to be as objective as possible, but if the book in one way or another has hurt sentiments on either side of the border, we would like to offer our unreserved apology.

We have tried to respect sensitivities on the Nepalese side in particular. 'Nepal is a privilege, and we should never forget that'— Anglo-Nepali writer Greta Rana's memorable words are in tune with our enduring commitment to reciprocate the warmth and trust we have received from our Nepali friends and well-wishers over the years.

In short, this book is all about the well-being of India–Nepal relations, which we are confident will reach greater heights in the coming years, despite formidable challenges.

We trust that this spirit will come across to readers when they go through the book and find due acceptance and appreciation.

Scan QR code to access the
Penguin Random House India website